THE ITALIAN ANTIMAFIA, AND THE CULTURE OF LEGALITY

Edited by Robin Pickering-Iazzi

This is the first book in English to examine the multimedia battles between the Italian mafia, which relies on internet technologies to expand the power, profit, and myths of its global crime networks, and its grassroots opposition, which comprises a broad spectrum of individuals and community groups. Building on the latest research on the antimafia movement and its place online, Robin Pickering-Iazzi and her group of contributors fill major gaps in the scholarly literature – in both English and Italian – on the sociocultural antimafia activities of Italian citizens. Despite having been largely overlooked until recently, community efforts to combat mafia organizations and corruption have existed for decades. More recently a central component of this civil movement is the innovative employment of web-based technology and forums such as Facebook, Twitter, YouTube, and blogs to create interactive, participatory forms of engagement that facilitate social activism on- and off-line in local and transnational contexts.

The authors employ a variety of critical approaches grounded in media theory. Topics covered include journalism and the antimafia movement, participatory democracy and "slacktivism," digital storytelling and memory, the allure of mafia perpetrators in the digital age, and the relationship between popular music and online community activism. While offering new perspectives on Italy, digital culture, and the antimafia movement, the diverse case studies and analyses enable readers to understand this Italian grassroots cultural revolution, which makes each individual the author of civil transformation promoting social responsibility, justice, freedom, and dignity.

(Toronto Italian Studies)

ROBIN PICKERING-IAZZI is a professor in the Department of French, Italian, and Comparative Literature at the University of Wisconsin-Milwaukee. Her previous works include *The Mafia in Italian Lives and Literature* and *Mafia and Outlaw Stories from Italian Life and Literature*.

The Italian Antimafia, New Media, and the Culture of Legality

EDITED BY ROBIN PICKERING-IAZZI

University of Toronto Press
Toronto Buffalo London

© University of Toronto Press 2017
Toronto Buffalo London
utorontopress.com
Printed in the U.S.A.

Reprinted 2018

ISBN 978-1-4875-0110-5 (cloth)   ISBN 978-1-4875-2078-6 (paper)

♾ Printed on acid-free, 100% post-consumer recycled paper.

Toronto Italian Studies

Library and Archives Canada Cataloguing in Publication

The Italian antimafia, new media, and the culture of legality
/ edited by Robin Pickering-Iazzi.

(Toronto Italian studies)
Includes bibliographical references and index.
ISBN 978-1-4875-0110-5 (cloth).   ISBN 978-1-4875-2078-6 (paper)

1. Mafia–Italy.   2. Organized crime–Italy–Prevention.
3. Organized crime–Technological innovations.   4. Crime
prevention–Technological innovations.   5. Internet–Social
aspects.   I. Pickering-Iazzi, Robin, editor   II. Series: Toronto
Italian studies

HV6452.5.I83 2017   364.1060945   C2016-907213-4

University of Toronto Press acknowledges the financial assistance to its
publishing program of the Canada Council for the Arts and the Ontario
Arts Council, an agency of the Government of Ontario.

 **Canada Council
for the Arts** **Conseil des Arts
du Canada**

 ONTARIO ARTS COUNCIL
CONSEIL DES ARTS DE L'ONTARIO

an Ontario government agency
un organisme du gouvernement de l'Ontario

Funded by the   Financé par le
Government   gouvernement
of Canada   du Canada

To Andrè, quintessential digital native.

Contents

Acknowledgments

I first wish to thank the contributors to the volume, whose extraordinary expertise, rigour, and generous collaboration made the creative process of developing this field of inquiry a delight and the book a reality. The University of Toronto Press has provided valuable support throughout the project, creating a dynamic space that fosters and promotes critical innovation. In particular, the volume has benefited from the intellectual sense and sensibilities demonstrated by Siobhan McMenemy at key points in the volume's elaboration, and by Mark Thompson in the refining stage. I owe special thanks to Anne Laughlin for her exceptional knowledge, eye for detail, and good humour, which sustained me through the various phases of production. In this regard, I greatly appreciate Beth McAuley's copyediting skills, which exemplify sensitivity to language, meaning, and the authors' diverse voices.

I extend my gratitude for the different kinds of institutional assistance that have enabled the research for this project and its completion. I thank Rodney Swain, Dean of Letters and Sciences at the University of Wisconsin-Milwaukee, for his support of my scholarship as a contribution to the UWM mission, and for approval of a sabbatical leave for spring 2016. Jennifer Peshut and Carlotta Generali provided indispensable support during the preparation of the manuscript.

This project has benefited from the vital intellectual exchanges and encouragement gracing my life with colleagues, friends, and family, as well as chance encounters. For these I thank Simonetta Milli Konewko, Michelle Bolduc, Peter Y. Paik, Norma Bouchard, Salvatore Di Piazza, Gioia Panzarella, Catherine O'Rawe, Umberto Lucentini, and Giancarlo Lombardi. Loving thanks for the creative support of Paolo Iazzi, Andrè, Sarah, and the digital natives in the making – Isabel, Peyton,

and Talia. The students in the experimental course on the Italian antimafia, new media, and the culture of legality deserve special mention
for their thoughtful debates about the chapters in this volume and the
new medial connections made with #antimafianewmedia.

THE ITALIAN ANTIMAFIA, NEW MEDIA,
AND THE CULTURE OF LEGALITY

Introduction. Mediating Italian Antimafia Culture: (Cyber)spatialities of Legality

ROBIN PICKERING-IAZZI

No to women breastfeeding their infants, yes to mafia bosses.

Corriere della Sera, 5 January 2009

Taking full advantage of one's own space on Facebook to remember [mafia victims'] sacrifices and their battles against organized crime could be a good opportunity to oppose this new sad phenomenon that is invading the web, apart from the fact the mafia may be carefully orchestrating it.

Fracantonio Genovese, 7 January 2009[1]

In 2009, as Facebook approached its fifth anniversary, a heated controversy exploded over its decision to remove visual images of women breastfeeding their infants, deemed pornographic, yet allow pages idolizing sanguinary Italian mafia bosses to circulate freely in the network territory. Igniting debates about what it termed "strange morals," the British *Times* newspaper charged the global social network with claiming to be "a safe environment for children who browse the Internet, yet not objecting at all to people exalting a killer (Riina) who is serving multiple life sentences" (cited in Roberto Rizzo 2005). In fact, in 2009, the Facebook page devoted to Salvatore Riina, the mafia superboss who was arrested in 1993 and later convicted of over 100 murders, had some 4,640 fans, whose posts on his wall portrayed him in superhero light, and brought new meaning to becoming a friend of friends. Joining in the fray over the embattled social network space produced by mafia and antimafia forces, Italian commentators, politicians, and citizens created diverse positions. Citizen protest groups organized online campaigns and petitions calling for a ban on mafia fan pages. Politicians on the National Antimafia Commission threatened to leave the virtual community and cancel their own Facebook pages if the mafiosi's pages were not removed. In contrast, Rita Borsellino, antimafia activist and member of the European Parliament, argued against censorship on Facebook, to her mind a democratic territory aligned with the ideals of truth, equality, justice, and freedom. She drew a parallel between the spaces of Facebook and Via D'Amelio in Palermo, the site where her brother, antimafia prosecutor Paolo Borsellino, and his bodyguards were slain by orders of Riina, and argued, "We must occupy Facebook so people with bad intentions can't find any space" (Borsellino 2009).

The positions taken, respectively, by Facebook and various Italian antimafia camps on pages dedicated to mafia bosses that make up part of the network geography epitomize critical differences between perspectives on the mafia produced in the United States and Italy, which derive largely from the diverse social, economic, political, and cultural histories of the crime organizations informing them.[2] As a result, there is a tendency among the American populace, and others beyond Italy's borders as well, to take lightly, if not dismiss, mafia criminality in general and the roles of "Facebosses" in particular. Moreover, due in part to this indifference, the importance of Italian antimafia sociocultural interventions crafted through web-based media is likewise overlooked. In order to understand what is at stake and the potential functions of cyberspatial practices of antimafia culture, a brief survey of criminal activities making up today's networked geographies is essential. Indeed, in line with the acute tactics of adaptation exemplified by the history of their criminal forebears that dates to the mid-1800s, what some call the "2.0" mafias have developed new strategies for the current economic, social, and cultural conditions in Italy, capitalizing upon the possibilities Internet technologies put at their fingertips in order to expand their power and profit. Their worldwide crime system, according to the Federal Bureau of Investigation, produces some U.S. $100 billion dollars per year.[3] Members of Cosa Nostra, 'ndrangheta, the camorra, and the Sacra Corona Unita (United Sacred Crown) employ Facebook and Skype for day-to-day communications, which is especially crucial in the case of fugitives in hiding beyond Italy's borders. Internet technologies enable the mafiosi to plan and conduct illegal activities that range from posting threats on the walls of individuals who refuse to pay extortion money and trafficking in humans and weapons, to murder. They also routinely handle transactions for money laundering and investing in legitimate businesses through web-based operations. And Facebook pages have become a boon to the mafia drug trade, replacing brick-and-mortar drug drops. Buyers can now visit a specific page on the social network, use a code and order cocaine, which is delivered directly to their doors. For the purposes of the research gathered in this volume, of particular concern are the ways in which affiliated members of Italian crime clans territorialize cyberspaces through the production of mediated images of the mafia that promote idealized myths, codes of belief and behaviour, and values, which serve to diffuse criminal economic, social, and cultural models. Although some people may view Facebosses and their cyberspatial enterprises as immaterial, as the investigative journalist Lirio Abbate (2012) cautions, "The virtual mafia community is made of real bosses, often hidden behind an alias or sometimes using their real identity, accompanied by photographs and comments [and] the Internet has allowed them to gather an unforeseen reserve of consensus, to which groups dedicated to superbosses attest."[4] Indeed, from its beginnings, the mafia has placed a high premium on its public image, cultivating such myths as honour, loyalty to family and friends, protection of the defenseless, delivering justice on behalf of the poor and oppressed, and courage, which still command the popular imaginary.

The territorial battle lines constituted by tactics producing criminal sociospatial relations in the interrelated material and virtual environs bring into relief some of the reasons why the invention and application of web-based antimafia practices warrant critical attention. In fact, Italian law enforcement has developed cutting-edge tools to combat cybercrime, using Facebook, for instance, to track down mafia fugitives and chart relations between the mafiosi and criminal organizations. More important, the new millennium has seen the flourishing of multiform arts of invention producing artefacts, ideas, practices, sites, and social networks that contest the mafia structures of power organizing its own territories and the weapons of intimidation, omertà, violence, and death employed to secure criminal borders. At the same time, such arts also cultivate a culture of legality. The sites and networks explicitly engaged in fighting all mafia organizations and forms of corruption include, for example, Addiopizzo, Ammazzateci Tutti, the Associazione Antimafie Rita Atria, Libera, and Legalmente m'intendo. Although features of their landscapes vary, such networks solicit travellers through news reports, interviews, videos, discussion forums, comment postings, and opportunities for online and offline volunteer works. These medial forms and enterprises enable engagements with lawful models of identity and the visitors' own inventive expressions and acts composing the cultural formation of legality.

Of hardly negligible significance, the antimafia networks and communities attract thousands of visitors every day. For example, Ammazzateci Tutti registers from 45,000 to 60,000 contacts per day, and Libera Informazione, the online news branch of Libera, has over 10,000 followers on Twitter and Facebook. Exponentially amplifying the media, products, and geographies of antimafia activism are Facebook pages created to give living memory to antimafia activists, postings of photographs, blogs, writings by citizen journalists, songs, and videos produced by film directors as well as non-professionals, and posted on YouTube as well as other sites. While clearly inscribing resistance to mafia organizations and corruption, these kinds of texts make manifest theoretically infinite articulations of the Italian culture of legality, whose scope and meanings reach beyond the rule of law. As former antimafia prosecutor Piero Grasso (2012) explains, the culture of legality denotes "something more than observing laws and rules; it is a system of principles, ideas, and behaviors that must move toward the realization of a person's values, human dignity, human rights, principles of freedom, equality, democracy, truth, and justice as a method of living together in civil society" (294). In the context of the culture of legality, the meanings of the key terms justice, democracy, and freedom are defined by Libera as follows. Justice is understood as the recognition of each person's dignity as indicated by the Universal Declaration of Human Rights. Both democracy and freedom refer to the equality of each person before the law as stipulated in Italy's constitution, regardless of sex, race, and religion, for example, yet also must be understood as freedom from mafia violence, oppression, and culture. (See the Libera home page and the links to the ethical code for donations and volunteer activities.)

With the aim of producing a collective cultural revolution, the members of the antimafia movement take as axiomatic that such civil transformation must begin with each citizen practising the culture of legality. This point is underscored by Paolo Borsellino's ideas on the limits of the law, as recalled by his sister Rita Borsellino (2013). She tells us that Borsellino maintained, "The battle against the mafia cannot consist of just detached acts of repression on the part of law enforcement. It must be a moral cultural movement that involves everyone." The Addiopizzo network explicates the notion of morally engaged cultural transformation that makes manifest the ideals of justice, freedom, and dignity through practices of everyday living in Sicily and global communities. The brainchild of university students, Addiopizzo's online and offline projects specifically target the *pizzo*, the money the mafia extorts through acts and threats of violence in most major Italian cities. According to Addiopizzo (Addiopizzo.org), in 2004 some 80 per cent of the merchants in Palermo paid the pizzo, and experts estimate the mafia profits in Sicily alone to be billions of euros per year. Placing responsibility for this diffuse crime on the mafiosi, business people, and consumers alike, Addiopizzo describes its movement as "open, fluid, dynamic [and] operates from the bottom as a mouthpiece for a 'cultural revolution' against the mafia. It is formed by all of the women and men, boys and girls, merchants and consumers who identify with the sentence 'An entire populace who pays the pizzo is a populace without dignity'" (Addiopizzo.org).

Addiopizzo calls upon merchants to refuse to pay the extortion money, becoming pizzo free and being listed on its website, and consumers to assert their right and responsibility to wield their moral and economic power through purchasing goods and services only from "clean" businesses through the practices of critical consumption (*consumo critico*) and ethical tourism (*Turismoetico*). By so doing, merchants and consumers reclaim their human dignity and create legal, ethical economies. Addiopizzo, like Libera, has an English-language website, and seeks to translate its ethical movement and engage global citizens. As the rich conceptualizations of antimafia practices suggest, the web-mediated verbal, visual, and acoustic texts engaging with the designs of a culture of legality in the fluid processes of its making pose avenues of inquiry into new perspectives on both antimafia cultural production and topics debated today. These include notions of citizenship, social *impegno* (commitment), resistance, ethics, silence and voice, individual and collective memory, and the very functions of mobile technologies in everyday living, which I elaborate below.

Despite the significant roles that web-based media perform in the fight against the mafia and creation of artefacts, behaviours, and collectivities of legality, they have received relatively little attention in studies on Italian antimafia movements and initiatives. Understandably, such media products are absent from the meticulously researched *The Antimafia: Italy's Fight against Organized Crime* by Alison Jamieson and *Storia del movimento antimafia* by Umberto Santino, since their publication in 2000 occurred on the verge of the activists' movement to take their battle online. Yet this field of social engagement also escapes notice in Luca Rinaldi's *Antimafia senza divisa* (2011), which focuses on figures in civil society, and Marina D'Amato's edited volume *La mafia allo specchio: La trasfigurazione mediatica del mafioso* (2013a), a collection of exceptionally informative analyses of representations of the mafia, its members, and to much lesser degree, agents of the law, in diverse Italian media, including print newspapers, film, and television series. However, in the chapter "Da *Scarface* a *Il Padrino*," D'Amato and Attilio Scaglione (2013) venture briefly into the virtual landscapes created in online videogames, commenting on how the interactive possibilities for identification with mafia bosses may work to normalize criminality and diffuse personal wealth, power, and prestige, achieved at any cost, as dominant values. Shifting focus specifically to the antimafia and networking media, Baris Cayli breaks new ground in "Creating Counterpublics against the Italian Mafia: Cultural Conquerors of Web-Based Media" (2013a), which offers a wealth of information about the aims, strategies, and modes of Libera Informazione's online endeavours to combat the mafia and political corruption through the construction of a lawful, engaged counterpublic. In contrast, Paula Salvio scrutinizes the problems posed for antimafia women activists by commemorative martyr discourses in "'Eccentric Subjects': Female Martyrs and the Antimafia Imaginary" (2012), where she examines how gender operates in the Facebook page dedicated to memorializing the late Judge Francesca Morvillo.[5]

Conceived as exploratory chartings of what is largely terra incognita, the studies written for this volume map, explore, and interpret diversified manifestations of antimafia culture of legality that encompass, for instance, digital storytelling and witnessing, rap music, remediations of the popular television series *Crime Novel* (inspired by the best-selling novel and blockbuster film), photography in various modes and sites of diffusion, and the online community Libera Terra, which is a branch of the Libera organization. In the process, the authors put into critical practice acts of mediating between parties within Italy and beyond its national borders, enabling them to know and understand the locations and designs of such artefacts and their roles in the spaces where antimafia realities are performed. They thus contribute to the very culture of legality in question, and, ideally, create avenues for readers to become fellow travellers, and access, reflect upon, perhaps refashion or augment, and recirculate images, thought, music, or stories that give body to its lawful spaces. The term "mediating" in the title of this introduction also bears clearly upon both the texts examined, as products staging encounters through diverse media with antimafia ideals, values, and ways of thinking and acting, and the resultant open-ended process of the online taking place of the culture of legality in which they participate.

By foregrounding the term mediating, I also want to situate this collection in the line of thought developed by Jay David Bolter and Richard Grusin in *Remediation* (2000), whose insights on mediation and remediation in new media challenge tendencies in antimafia studies, and mafiology for that matter, to see Internet-based practices and initiatives as insubstantial. Not sheer semblances of reality, "all mediations," the authors argue, "are themselves real. They are real as artifacts ... in our mediated culture" (55). In like manner, remediations, the importing of pre-existing media into digitally produced spaces, bear directly on the substance of reality in its multiple dimensions. Elucidating this relationship, Bolter and Grusin state, "It is not that media merely reform the appearance of reality. Media hybrids (the affiliations of technical artifacts, rhetorical justifications, and social relationships) are as real as the objects of science" (61). The variety of media, practices of remediation, and different medial experiences thereby created are exemplified by the texts Dana Renga and Amy Boylan examine in their chapters. In "Remediating the Banda della Magliana," Renga scrutinizes the rich territory of hybridized artefacts devoted to telling the infamous criminal band's story, which include creative incorporations of elements from fiction films, the popular television series, documentaries, photographs, and musical scores. Her discussion of the respective conventions and spectatorial relations associated with the original and refashioned texts draws out the implications that new medial aesthetics in digital environs raise for the cultivation of idealized mafia myths and the antimafia culture of legality challenging them. Notably different hybridized registers of reality and social relations form the field of inquiry in Boylan's "Democratizing the Memorial Landscape." She focuses on the varied archival photographs and news articles retrieved and reframed by Casamemoria Vittimemafia (House of Memory for Mafia Victims) in its almost daily postings on its followers' Facebook pages, which enact the memorializations of the lives of girls, boys, women, and men killed by members of all Italian mafias. The case of Casamemoria Vittimemafia illustrates how the practices of remediation create complex social and spatiotemporal relations operating in such sites of production. The reinscription in public collective memory of the images and stories of the individual dead, and otherwise largely forgotten, performs a twofold critique of the material conditions generating geographies of injustice in both the past and present. Such unjust geographies are produced largely by collaborative relations between the mafia and criminal elements in the Italian state and institutions, which fail to protect citizens and provide justice, in the juridical sense of successfully prosecuting mafia crimes and in the ethical sense of giving adequate redress to the dead and their survivors. These enactments of critical consciousness, commemoration, and calls to justice thus reinvent the spaces of collective civil life according to principles and practices of legality, articulating remediation as a process that reforms reality, with the connotations of socially rehabilitating or improving it (Bolter and Grusin 2000, 60–1).

The networked artefacts and sites of the Italian culture of legality examined here are intimately linked with the changing social, economic, and political conditions of their production and, more specifically, practices of resistance in daily living that constitute the long-standing tradition of antimafia movements, which dates back to the 1800s. Such interconnections are made patently clear, for instance, by the staging of antimafia events, performances, demonstrations, art exhibits, and so forth, that social participants frequently capture on smartphone videos or in photographs, upload, and share, putting into motion micronarratives that create cyberspatialities of legality, which can then be accessed, commented upon, refashioned, and recirculated. Intended as one way of thinking about diverse terrains charted herein, my conceptualization of cyberspatiality draws upon both Edward W. Soja's (2010) model of spatiality and the proposition that the configurations of Italian life are engaged in a process of "biomediatic" transformation.[6] According to Soja's thought, human spatiality is a "complex social product, a collectively created and purposeful configuration and socialization of space that defines our contextual habitat, the human and humanized geography in which we all live out our lives" (17–18). In recent years, the spatial network created by computer technologies has become almost seamlessly incorporated into many people's contextual habitat, serving, Mark Nunes (2006) explains, "as an organizing concept for the spaces of everyday life" (xiv). Within the specific borders of Italy, though access problems creating a digital divide persist, human geographies are undergoing transformations driven by the growing use of mobile technologies and Internet-based activities such as YouTube and Facebook, which are reconfiguring the relations between biological, biographic, and virtual dimensions of habitats and the manners whereby they are built and lived.[7] According to the daily newspaper *La Repubblica*, such changes signal a new "biomediatic era" (*era biomediatica*), "in which the virtual transcription and telematic sharing of personal biographies through social networks are fundamental" ("Italiani, il 63% è sul Web, stiamo evolvendo. Censis: 'Entriamo nell'era biomediatica'" 2013). Following this avenue of thought, the invention and socialization of networked spaces structured according to principles of honesty, dignity, equality, and justice, for example, function as integral components of quotidian habitats where Italian agents of such technologies fashion constructions of self, affiliations and collectivities, critical reflections on the past, and ways of envisioning the future. The resultant language and culture of legality inscribed through such medial operations challenge the mafia fashionings of language which, as Salvatore Di Piazza (2010) rigorously demonstrates, perform central functions in identity construction within and beyond the criminal associations.

The Contested Spaces of History, Future Memory, and Civil Society in the Making

What is the meaning of transmitting the memory and history of the battle against the mafia? Memory is entrusting the recollection in order to perpetuate it, because the recollection is essential and necessary to being able to build the future. But memory is actually a way of elaborating what happened. I believe that the knowledge of the past elaborated in the present may truly provide the tools to create a future that is different from what we have lived.

> Rita Borsellino, "La lotta alla mafia non è solo repressione" (2013)

The performative antimafia topographies of such online sites and networks as Città Nuove, Libera, Addiopizzo, Casamemoria Vittimemafia, and Rete 100 Passi (which defines itself as a participatory multimedia network), exhibit a provocative array of distinct features constituting their identities, forms of affiliation, and arts of inventing a culture of legality in daily life. As part of the boundlessly varied and variable enactments of cyberspace, mediations of people and events of bygone times perform structural operations producing richly diachronic spatiotemporal configurations. In these medial spaces, investigations into the making of history in past and present, conducted in service of truth and justice, inform both memory and the practices of bearing responsibility for it through ongoing committed participation in creating civil society. In this model of tightly linked relations between history, memory, and social transformation, online journalism performs fundamental functions that shape the designs of antimafia news sites, social networks like Libera and Ammazzateci Tutti, Facebook pages, and blogs, which import articles, photographs, and videos from the original news sources. As Baris Cayli argues in this volume in "When a Journalist Defies More Than the Mafia," the contemporary ethics and practices distinguishing online antimafia journalism are deeply indebted to the ethical principles of truth, freedom, and justice pioneered by antimafia journalists in the postwar period such as Mauro De Mauro, Mario Francese, and particularly Giuseppe Fava, whose socially engaged investigative reporting of the 1970s and early 1980s resonates online today. Significantly, this resonance is articulated in explicit ways: the very name of the news organization I Siciliani giovani (The young Sicilians) expresses the renewed commitment on the part of a younger generation to put into practice the ideals and values defining Fava's renowned news publication *I Siciliani*, and numerous online antimafia news sites employ Fava's words as part of their visual architecture and identities.

Situated in this lineage, the professional and citizen journalists, sites, and modalities of producing knowledge about antimafia and mafia forces also form an important field of investigation for understanding how media users-consumers participate in the creation of cultural spatialities of legality. They provide different vantage points for thinking about voice, speaking, knowledge, and participatory democracy in what some call a post-scarcity culture.

Viewing the hyperabundant information that continues to expand the dimensions and navigational possibilities of cyberspace may reasonably lead one to assume there is a corresponding excess in acts of speaking about the Italian mafias. Indeed, many critics note the diffuse manner in which web-users upload or view items, comment, post, and share, and how it has become nearly automatic, freely incorporated into hybridized lived geographies. And the sheer number of sites related to the mafia, some 134,000,000 through the Google search engine and 135,000,000 through Google.it as of April 2015, suggests an unfettered flow of information. However, shifting to the microgeographic territories throughout Italy – whose sociospatial conditions of daily living are structured by mafia power tactics, employed by the clans of 'ndrangheta in Lombardy, Emilia, and Calabria, the capital mafia in Rome, the camorra in Campania, and Cosa Nostra in Sicily – the prohibition on breaking the law of silence in sites located in built cities and on the web bears full force. As reported in the newspaper *La Repubblica*, in 2015 some 2,300 Italian journalists had been physically threatened or assaulted, and between thirty and fifty reporters lived under twenty-four-hour police protection.[8] Antimafia journalists Giuseppe Fava, Cosimo Cristina, Mauro De Mauro, and Giuseppe Alfano are among those whose traumatic deaths are recalled on the Day of Memory dedicated to victims of the mafia. It is important to note that journalists who make their investigations into mafia crimes public knowledge online, generally publish under their proper names, choosing not to avail themselves of the anonymity the Internet can afford. They thus become the target of intimidation and death threats. For instance, an incendiary device reduced to charred wreckage the car belonging to Dino Paternostro, the founder of the online newspaper *Città Nuove*; the online news site of Libera Informazione was attacked, and the image of a skull planted on its web page (Cayli 2013a); the antimafia social network Ammazzateci Tutti, whose hypermediated home page features breaking news about the mafia's activities throughout Italy, has been knocked offline by cyberattacks. Such examples illustrate how seriously the mafia takes words and images as weapons that enable the speaker to act as social agent and contest the system of mafia domination and the idealized myths deployed to protect it. Elucidating this idea, former antimafia magistrate Piero Grasso states, "The mafia is concerned about public opinion and how it can be influenced ... [It] tries to capture people's consent and therefore, as in totalitarian regimes, physically eliminates people who try to fight it, even with words" (cited in Marina D'Amato 2013a, 161). Thus, news reports detailing the crime organizations' tactics of intimidation, destruction of property, extortion, drug and human trafficking, illegal dumping of toxic waste, and murder erode romanticized images of mafia "families" as mutual aid societies that provide socio-economic mobility and protection in uncertain times.

Serving as dispersed outposts of legality amidst Facebosses, videos, postings, blogs and fan communities idolizing the mafiosi, web-based antimafia newspapers, magazines, and television broadcasts have proliferated since the late 1990s, and fashion new sites and modes for exercising the right to speak, perform in-depth inquiries into the mafia and political corruption, and remediate antimafia history. They thereby contribute to the cultivation of civil life in lawful society. The production of knowledge about the mafia, the antimafia, their histories, and current initiatives operates in opposition to hierarchies of power constructed by both the mafia state and the Italian state. In the astute analysis "Web Man Walking" (2006), Roberto Salvatore Rossi explains what distinguishes online antimafia journalism from the mainstream national press. The latter, Rossi maintains, tends to run prepackaged news clips that report events playing out on the national stage, and give little, if any attention to reporting crimes that transpire at the local level. Moreover, the national media fail to analyse how criminal undertakings figure in regional, national, and global relations, in essence abandoning the antimafia movement. In contrast, such online news sources as Città Nuove, Catena di San Libero, Terrelibere, and Antimafia duemila have been able, in Rossi's words, "to carve out small but dense web spaces where they confront the most heated topics of Sicilian society ... [and] represent a cultural map on which to chart a course of civil and moral rebirth of engaged antimafia citizenship" (186). Foremost among these controversial topics are glocal mafia crime affairs that demand thorough investigative reporting. Addressing the importance of these bifrontal zones under siege, Dino Paternostro states, "The analysis of the postmodern mafia, engaged in international finance, is incomplete. And the organization carefully continues to interfere in the business deals of small communities, never renouncing any sector of activity, even if only to maintain its control over the territory" (cited in Rossi 2006, 184). From his perspective, the Internet makes such in-depth analyses possible, and offers the advantages of being able to access breaking news in real time, and to freely critique government corruption as well as mafia infiltration in state and financial institutions. The web also creates space for publishing research on past events, figures, and unsolved crimes related to the history of the battles against the mafia, which provides interpretative keys for understanding current events. Furthermore, I would like to suggest that these investigations construct forms of new memory, a point to which I return shortly.

A particularly significant component constituting the cyberspatial relations and functions taking place in online antimafia news sites is the cultivation of visitor participation, which serves to create knowledge communities akin to those conceptualized by Pierre Levy (1997) and to mobilize citizens in diverse ways. The Antimafia duemila, Città Nuove, and even the webtv site for Cortocircuito,[9] incorporate ample spaces for individuals to suggest topics for articles, comment and expand upon investigations, import stories from diverse sites, share their own experiences, or, in some cases, participate in forums and blogs, and post photographs and videos. Although formatted in fairly traditional style, with no blogs or interactive features, the Catena di San Libero is important in this respect, with numerous reader-contributors who, Riccardo

Orioles tells us, "are asked to do their part to expand the content and participate in the gathering of information ... what interests me is that readers demonstrate participatory interest" (cited in Rossi 2006, 189). The ongoing importance of Giuseppe Fava and his example of committed struggles for truth and justice is highlighted at the end of each edition, with Fava's famous words, "What good is living if you don't have the courage to fight?"

The varied forms and modes of online media designed to produce and disseminate factual information about both the mafia organizations and antimafia culture of legality function as strategies of deterritorialization that foster different kinds of knowledge spaces. Following the lines of thought proposed by Levy (1997), the affiliations with what he calls new knowledge communities are mobile, elective, prompted by intellectual and emotional investments, and forever open to change. Most important, such "cosmopedia make available to the collective intellect all of the pertinent knowledge available to it at a given moment ... [and] it also serves as a site of collective discussion, negotiation, and development" (217). Thus, it can reasonably be said that online antimafia news spaces mobilize members through participatory, associative acts of speaking about the mafia and antimafia ways of thinking and being, exchanging information, ideas, life stories, and memories. The members may also expand the communities by downloading and sharing selected items with other people in the world at large, who may elect to join the group. Electing to place oneself in such antimafia communities, as Carla Bagnoli explains in her chapter in this volume, "Structural Modes of Recognition and Virtual Forms of Empowerment," would entail fulfilling normative obligations, rights, and expectations (such as those outlined above), which contribute to the spatial production of freedom, truth, and justice in virtual and land-bound social environs. The very sharing of information about the mafia keeps developments in the criminal underworld in the public eye, a service that is especially critical during the current period of normalization, when the mafia deploys strategies of silence and invisibility in order to conduct its financial and political business unnoticed. Furthermore, such knowledge interactivity may also engage the participants' imagination and hopes, as Paternostro's conception of Città Nuove suggests. He proposes the online site encourages and supports "the creation of 'new cities,' free of the mafia and criminality. A magazine that is able to reflect upon and make others reflect upon events, to delve deep, to imagine a better future" (cited in

Rossi 2006, 184). Appealing to the biomediatic terms of participatory antimafia citizenship committed to building civil society, Città Nuove and Libera Informazione, for example, also employ their news sites to mobilize fellow travellers for offline initiatives.

Antimafia journalism places fundamental importance on disseminating information about how the mafias operate, mobilizing citizens, and remediating contemporary Italian culture of daily living and society, in the sense of reforming it through the values and practices of civil rights and responsibilities, participatory democracy, and social volunteerism. These functions form points of convergence between online antimafia journalism and growing numbers of Italian social networks whose primary terms of self-identification and address to visitors are opposition to all mafia organizations and corruption, and the concurrent production of a culture of legality. Networked communities of this kind provide unique opportunities to speculate about cyberspatialities of legality as lived spaces, as indicated by Nunes's (2006) notion of how the body and practices of everyday living figure in a person's relations to space. He posits, "Not only am I situated *in space*; I *situate space* through my *lived incorporations and articulations of space*" (xx, original italics). Following this trajectory invites reflection upon how such prominent social networks as Libera, Addiopizzo, Ammazzateci Tutti, and the Associazione Antimafie Rita Atria occasion the incorporation of spatialities of legality into the Internet users' biomediatic itineraries of living. For instance, various verbal and visual cyberscape components, such as archives of imported news articles, dossiers, videos, discussion forums, blogs, testimonies, and spaces for comment postings solicit the engagement with lawful modes of thought and practice and, moreover, the invention of expressions and activities composing an exponentially expanding culture of legality. Such interactions have significant sociosymbolic roles in terrains dominated by mafia tactics of physical intimidation and murder executed to instantiate power by isolating and silencing those who rebel. They provide the means for individuals to challenge criminal hierarchies of power by claiming their right to speak out and voice opposition, and to create affiliations with substantial communities of support and activism online, and offline as well. In fact, though the antimafia social networks exhibit distinct home pages, interior architecture, and links, a largely stable feature is a section devoted to volunteer projects, which situate the taking place of civil culture in public piazzas, streets, parks, and often schools.

Remediating Memory, Witnessing, and Popular Culture

We are history and for Libera Terra even more so, history is a search for truth, not a simple celebration of the past but a look toward the future, strong in the knowledge of what has been, because when memory is alive, shared, and recognized it breaks away from anonymity and becomes history. Faces, names, stories, passions. To honor the people who have died means building different conditions for the societies of tomorrow, to pass on the witness through memory and thereby free societies of the criminal lien.

Lucia Lipari, "Diffamazione e diritto all'oblio" (2013)

The ubiquitous acts of online witnessing in everyday living, whose artefacts range from photographs picturing quotidian minutiae to videos capturing in real time horrific events that come to mark the national imaginary, have generated substantial discussion, raising questions about testimony, memory, the relations between personal and collective histories, ethics, and an individual's Right to Be Forgotten. The examinations of previously unexplored enactments of antimafia witnessing conducted in this volume by Amy Boylan, Paula Salvio, and Giovanna Summerfield engage explicitly with these questions. They complicate prevalent paradigms shaping the debates in media studies, and underscore the critical imperative of historical, social, and political contextuality for interpreting how (re)mediated witnessing and commemoration may operate in cyberspatial environs. Indeed, antimafia testimonial discourses conduct diverse critical operations in profoundly contested spaces of knowledge and memory where the Italian state and the mafia endeavour to exert their power, in part through strategic reconstructions of history and memory, or repressing certain figures and events altogether. In what Salvio has termed "the state repression of memory,"[10] such induced mneumonic gaps represent the disavowal of the historic existence of the violent criminal society, its corruption of agents and institutions working under the auspices of the state, and thus also the latter's inability to protect its citizens. Elsewhere, Nando Dalla Chiesa (2007) speaks to the mafia's stake in oblivion, telling us, "The mafia and criminal power vitally need the collectivity to lose its historical memory" (226). From his perspective, the remembering of historic people, politics, values, and democratic ideals shaping civil society, as well as individuals and associations threatening it, can orient ethics and action needed to combat the mafia today. At the same time, the very process of creating bodies of memory warrants close scrutiny in terms of the particular figures selected for remembrance, the manners of representing them, and the ideas and values discursively attached to them. Addressing this problem in her analysis of the architectonic designs and remediated artefacts constituting the House of Memory as countermonument in her chapter "Democratizing the Memorial Landscape," Boylan explains how heroic national discourses cast certain individuals as antimafia martyrs whose highlighted features make them worthy of memory and mourning, and leave other victims to languish in oblivion. In "'A Taste of Justice,'" Salvio charts a similar encoding of select antimafia victims in Libera Terra's production of social networking spaces; postings of photographs, news articles, and images of the Placido Rizzotto Cooperative and products appeal to visitors as calls to remembrance, fostering memories attached to people deemed grievable, while other boldily traces of resistance to the mafia are left to fade.

The dispersed, heterogeneous sites featuring visual, verbal, and acoustic evidence that testify to the people and vicissitudes making up antimafia history invent the conditions for knowledge, memory, mourning, and bearing witness. The remediation of grizzly crime scenes in photographs and video footage, eyewitness testimonies detailing mafia threats and physical injuries sustained, and survivors' pleas for justice clearly create the occasion for confronting the material realities produced by the mafia and state agents who collude with it. They thus combat disavowal while generating conditions for productive engagements, as suggested by Paul Frosh and Amit Pinchevski's (2009) conception of media witnessing and the positioning of audiences. They propose that media witnessing refers "simultaneously to the appearance of witnesses in media reports, the possibility of media themselves bearing witness, and the positioning of the media audiences as witnesses to depicted events" (1). In the case of the witnessing texts discussed in this volume, a vast spectrum of media are imported and refashioned in the remediated products, which also situate viewers as witnesses. As the performative cyberspatialities enact registers of absence and loss they occasion encounters with trauma, soliciting the presence of the viewing witnesses, in terms of intellectual, psychological, emotional, and moral responsiveness. While enabling the work of mourning to begin, scenes of suffering and the void, which mark the present absence of fellow human beings with names, faces, families, and irremediable lives, may foster, as Frosh (2009) suggests, "some of the intense empathetic responses that are assumed to be necessary for moral concern" (66).

Among the diverse modes of witnessing, testimonial videos have become a particularly important genre in participatory antimafia culture. Created and posted on the web by professional and citizen filmmakers, such videos commemorate individuals whose public battles against mafia organizations in service of justice and civil society have been truncated by their assassinations. Even a cursory search on YouTube turns up thousands of testimonial antimafia videos, devoted to the lives and sacrifices of prominent antimafia figures. In April 2015, there were some 21,000 produced in memory of Giovanni Falcone, with certain films registering over 125,000 viewings; over 21,000 celebrate the life's work of Paolo Borsellino; Rita Atria's life story is the inspiration for over 2,000 videos; and over 4,000 short film texts recall to memory the life of antimafia activist Giuseppe Impastato. It is true that these kinds of videos may contribute to the antimafia martyr discourses structuring the power of memory critiqued by Salvio and Boylan in their chapters. Yet Summerfield's chapter "*Per non dimenticare*" constructs a different perspective, focusing on the motivations to make such films and the various roles they may perform in individual and collective identity formation, as she draws upon critical notions of digital storytelling and media witnessing, as well as insights shared with her by the filmmaker and social actors who collaborated on "Per non dimenticare 23 maggio" (Not to forget 23 May). As the title indicates, this audiovisual witnessing text calls to public memory the date of the Capaci bombing in 1992, which claimed the lives of Judge Giovanni Falcone and Judge Francesca Morvillo, and three of their bodyguards. As in this film, the commemorative texts bearing witness to the lives of individuals who battled the mafia and corruption generally exhibit an evocative spectrum of visual elements and materials, including, for instance, footage from news reports and fiction films, interviews, photographs, and musical accompaniments. Interesting in this respect is the film short "Munizza, il cortometraggio per ricordare Peppino Impastato" (Garbage, the film short to remember Peppino Impastato) by Andrea Satta (2013), which also features provocative animated sequences in what is a compelling testimony to Impastato's radical antimafia activism.[11] On YouTube, antimafia social networks, Facebook, and in archives, such proliferating modes of virtual performances of bearing witness amplify the discursive possibilities for witnessing on the part of both the video producers and viewers, who may engage with the imaginative enacting of grief and trauma, and bear the responsibility of the testimony in the future. Providing a useful interpretative key for understanding relations between trauma, performance, and virtual spectators, Roy Brand (2009) proposes that witnessing trauma consists of witnessing nothingness, since trauma acquires "its meaning only in retrospect, by the kinds of memories it will engender and the ways in which these will be interpreted. In other words, performativity implicates the viewer in the production of the meaning of the work" (207). In this light, the specific visual and verbal languages constituting the performativity of commemorative videos can tell us much about memories and meanings that make up virtual antimafia sociospatial relations and form fluid affiliations for creating civil communities.

The spatial and temporal dynamics produced through the selection of visual and verbal evidence, the forms of refabrication and staging of remediating acts of witnessing facilitate spectators' responses to implicit calls for judgment and justice. Andrew Hoskins (2014) asserts that these kinds of web-based processes produce "the past made present," what he calls "new memory," which is "much more easily subject to judgment through the ethical mores of the present" (57). As part of his endeavour to elucidate the productive aspects of forgetting, Hoskins also argues that the digital overlay of the past onto the present creates a never-ending past, which erodes certainties linked to time's passage and what he presents as beneficial forgetfulness, in his view an essential condition for societies to move into the future. However, shifting to the context of antimafia thought and practice, it is precisely the past made present produced through digital media that, according to many activists, provides the psychological and material conditions for reforming Italian civil society. It is also reasonable to say that by eroding the certainties that mafia infiltration of the state and use of physical violence and murder are buried in the past, web-based media can cultivate knowledge about crime organizations' strategies of adaptation, creating an ongoing culture of vigilance and commitment to combatting them. Moreover, new memory constitutes the essential ground for elaborating the past in the present, enabling the construction of the future through bearing witness to the individual lives of mafia victims. In this process each person assumes the responsibility of doing her or his part to invent a culture of legality by means of practices that promote human dignity, moral action, equality, justice, and freedom of speech.

The inventive web-based manners of bearing the responsibility for antimafia testimonies and the reformation of civil life in its various dimensions reconceive notions of citizenship, rights, duties, and justice, which indicate the serious threats that the Right to Be Forgotten poses to the cultural productions of legality. In fact, claiming the right and responsibility to speak out against all crime, professional and citizen journalists, storytellers, filmmakers, photographers, singers, archivists, and commentators craft polyphonic, multiperspectival, and diversified cyberspatialities through ever-changing processes of mediation, remediation, and hypermediation, in some cases rescuing from oblivion victims and denouncing their killers. Such endeavours may be threatened by the Right to Be Forgotten, ostensibly designed to provide global citizens with the right to protect their personal data, which might include posts about indiscretions or even past crimes. Designed by Viviane Reding, European Commissioner for Justice, Fundamental Rights, and Citizenship in 2012, the Right to Be Forgotten guarantees the right for an individual to request that all information making up a person's data life, whether posted by the subject or others, be erased from all search engines and social networks. Although the law makes an exception for newspaper archives and what is deemed still newsworthy for the public, the right to have data removed applies to all news materials that are copied and reposted in social networks, blogs, individual websites, and so forth.

Writing against the dominant tendency to privilege the value of memory, such authors as Hoskins and Norberto Nuno Gomes de Andrade endeavour to elucidate the key roles forgetting plays in the formation of individual and national identities, and suggest the Right to Be Forgotten also protects the right to fashion new identities and new beginnings.[12] At the same time, their insights mark profound conflicts between the rights of potential criminal perpetrators and those of their victims, as well as individual versus collective memory, which have generated heated debates in Italy. Although the Right to Be Forgotten is guaranteed in somewhat different form by the Italian constitution, as the lawyer Lucia Lipari suggests, applying it in the digital age may give the mafiosi a privilege and put a gag order on their victims. In other words, it is tantamount to forcing people suffering mafia crimes to adhere to a law of silence imposed not by the crime organizations, but the law. Such silence, Lipari (2013) argues, threatens history, memory, and new forms of citizenship. She tell us, "The Right to Be Forgotten can not be applied ipso facto. We're moving towards a new right of citizenship whose pillar consists of the pillar of transparency in history as a possibility to know." Significantly, she situates this concept in relation to the massacres committed by members of the mafia and also those in high offices of the state. In this context, history assumes "sacral importance" and memory becomes an "inviolable necessity." And if, as guaranteed by law, certain criminal content is deleted from shared platforms, social networks, and various alternative web-based media, some speculate, the mafiosi can disappear and be more easily transformed into legends. These debates are not merely academic. Renato Vallanzasca, dubbed the handsome René (*il bel René*) and an infamous member of the Comasina gang that committed numerous robberies, kidnappings, and murders in Milan during the 1970s, has asserted the Right to Be Forgotten, and requested information about his history be deleted from search engines.[13] This case may already illustrate how the application of the Right to Be Forgotten enables the unchecked transformation of criminals into legends. Although the application of the right prohibits the free dissemination of information about the gang member's history by citizen journalists, bloggers, and contributors to online encyclopedias, for example, Vallanzasca's Facebook page, generated by his relatives and boasting some 8,000 fans as of April 2015, features the family stories he wishes to tell. Google has received some 90,000 requests for removal of data, of which some 6,000 originate in Italy. The search engine has taken steps to delete articles pertaining to some fifty criminals.[14]

To varying degrees, each of the situated mediations of antimafia cultural products of legality featured in this volume offers particular insights on antimafia and mafia sign warfare conducted in the contested virtual domains of popular culture, a term that warrants rethinking in view of the blurred boundaries between producers and consumers, as well as the biomediatic, or hybridized, geographies many individuals in Italy and beyond now live. Following the trajectory suggested by Michel de Certeau's (1997) conception of walking as a space of enunciation (98) that, through operations fashioned by walkers, articulates stories constituting a culture of everyday life, I propose the movement through cyberspace may be conceived similarly. Thus, the notion of popular culture exemplified by the texts examined in this collection comprises artefacts ranging from the movements of Internet users and the various operations they perform to videos, songs, photographs, and so forth. A pivotal issue arising from the networked spaces that travellers wander and create is how the representations of the mafiosi, agents of the law, and justice may attract them and contribute to perceptions, fantasies, and desires. Antonio La Spina (2013) underscores the critical significance of the relations between media and the criminal imaginary, stating, "Mafia networks are most important in their concrete effectuality ... But they are also important for the way people imagine them, which normally occurs precisely through the media as they perform a role of intermediation between facts and collective perception" (11). La Spina's observations bear upon traditional media as well as the web-based media often employed to remediate them, a point to which I return shortly.

As diverse scholars note, the mafia mystique has substantial purchase on the Italian popular imagination, strengthened in part by representations portraying mafia men as powerful, successful, respected, seductive, and most of all, enigmatic. These attributes, Marina D'Amato (2013b) explains, recur in works of literature, commercial cinema, and, perhaps surprisingly, mainstream print and broadcast news reports (17). Recent work on Italian film and television by Francesca Anello (2013) provides a more detailed picture of the changing mediascape and the respective roles played by the mafiosi and men of the law. Since the early 1990s, of some 100 television mini-series broadcast, sixty-nine of them tell crime stories, and the mafia story in particular undergoes expansion in terms of numbers and genre, with the development of mafia melodrama, women's films, and biography (239). In view of the general fascination with the mafia, it is interesting that Anello documents a preference for antimafia heroes among the small screen viewerships. For the purposes of this discussion, several of the new conventions crafted for such mafia television series are important. The protagonists tend to be a crime fighter or antimafia hero, and they possess character traits that are equally complex as those attributed to the mafiosi. As Anello describes them, these lawful heroes "often lead troubled lives with complicated, difficult, and painful histories that are generally marked by serious emotional losses linked to the mafia. They possess strong personalities, are tenacious, intuitive, courageous, disillusioned, honest, and pervaded by a strong sense of justice and vindication with regard to the mafia" (242–3). In several mini-series, women protagonists represent civil society as they take on the fight against the mafia. What interests me here is how these current conventions, which operate, for example, in the phenomenally popular television movies in the series *Inspector Montalbano* (*Il commissario Montalbano*, 1999–2015), contribute to what can be called a multidimensional antimafia imaginary with terms of appeal that exceed the prevalent image of the antimafia martyr defined by solitude, self-sacrifice, and often traumatic death, eloquently examined by Boylan and Salvio in this volume.[15]

The diversified features of the expanding antimafia imaginary enable speculations about the fantasies, desires, and kinds of affect elicited in the interplay between traditional media and Internet-based operations that mediate and remediate cultural products of legality as tools for combatting the mafia. Through practices of remediation, the modes of reporting on the mafia and antimafia, narrating personal testimonies, and viewing mafia films, for instance, are reformed and invested with something the original production media lacked, thus constructing innovative conditions for different experiences of knowledge, aesthetics, ways of being, and performative participation in the very enactments of the constantly changing digital terrains. In the medial ecology of antimafia engagements, fantasy, desire, and pleasure – a relatively unsounded terrain – figure prominently, potentially fostering the participation of Internet travellers and thus augmenting the sites and modes of diffusing the everyday cultural arts of legality. A case in point is how numerous online antimafia news sites, and the knowledge communities affiliated with them, may produce diverse kinds of pleasure as they fulfil epistemophilic desires and enable consumer-producers to expand the information about mafia activities, corruption, and legality through posting articles, videos, and comments, or engaging in the discussion forums. Such factual-based discourses, like fictional ones, contribute to the ways people imagine crime and the law, and the range of thoughts, emotions, and participation involved in the process. Some scholars, such as Lorenzo Misuraca in "L'antimafia felice" (2015) minimize the significance of virtual explorations of antimafia sites and the traces left by clicking "like" and making a comment, and suggest these actions hardly represent real engagement, a concern given serious scrutiny in this book in the discussion that Paula Salvio (chapter 3) conducts on "slacktivism" and in the arguments that Angela Maiello (chapter 7) develops in support of the cultivation of techno-aesthetic knowledge. Such analysis of the broad spectrum of antimafia operations and how they function is clearly needed. I would also suggest that since the scope of such antimafia organizations as Addiopizzo, Associazione Antimafie Rita Atria, and Libera is to create a global community of citizens who oppose all forms of corruption, illegality, and the mafia, to "like" an article, film, or event represents an act of participation and solidality signified by the traveller's signature on antimafia space, perhaps individualized through a comment or the act of sharing the antimafia artefact with others. Such everyday operations make visible elements of civil identity and practice that create possibilities for engaging with them, and thus also create changes that produce terms of antimafia subjectivity which, as highlighted in Carla Bagnoli's (chapter 1) close reading of Libera's address to visitors at their home page, is the first step in the battle against the mafia. The pleasures derived from such acts of participation as well as experiencing the sense of belonging and empowerment as moral agents by joining antimafia communities such as Libera should not be dismissed. As Bagnoli explains, online collectivities provide the tools for ordinary citizens to work for social changes in order to achieve dignity, freedom, justice, and solidarity, thus bearing a sense of fulfilment and hope.

The kinds of affect invoked by medial content in general and antimafia ones in particular merit considerable critical attention for the ways they may solicit Internet browsers, cause them to linger and reflect, or motivate creative forms of interaction. Types of affect associated with non-pleasure, such as indignation and anger (perhaps incited by acts of injustice, cruelty, and violence) can motivate actions online and offline. Indeed, in 2015, Mark Zuckerberg announced the impending introduction of something along the lines of a "dislike" button on Facebook to enable users to express empathy with sad events, and thus increase engagement in the online community. In February 2016, more varied affective options actually became available. With a click on "like," six images pop up, standing respectively for "like," "love," "haha," "wow," "sad," and "angry." Nonetheless, affects associated with pleasure, such as liking, feeling grateful, optimistic, or fulfilled, appear especially effective at generating participation in the acts of production, diffusion, remediation, and posting of refashioned artefacts, which contribute to manifold medial sites and flows. This point is acutely explained and demonstrated by Angela Maiello in her chapter's analysis of Rocco Hunt's performance of "NuJuornBuon" as an antimafia viral phenomenon, where hope plays a formative role and creates an alternative to the antimafia martyr discourse. Along these lines, we might think of how the social actors and message of the commemorative video "Per non dimenticare 23 maggio" (Not to forget 23 May) convey hope for the future, as Summerfield tells us, and positive affect, thus contributing to the antimafia imaginary in new ways.

Such senses of pleasure, in terms of sensorial experiences, emotions, and meanings, clearly engage consumer-producers in diversified acts of remediating various cultural works of legality. Scenes and music from the *Inspector Montalbano* television series, which adapts Andrea Camilleri's bestselling mystery novels to the small screen, have become popular materials for virtual reinventions featuring the much-adored servant of the state. At the same time, the power of different forms of affect, both positive and negative, to foster interaction with diverse media requires further study, as exemplified by the cases of Giancarlo De Cataldo's *Romanzo criminale* (2002) and Roberto Saviano's *Gomorra* (2006) (*Gomorrah* 2008), which are credited with fashioning innovative storytelling practices associated with the non-fiction novel in order to both inform readers about crime organizations and cultivate ethical changes in citizens for the betterment of society. Both award-winning, gritty novels achieved popular success, inspiring the blockbuster film adaptations *Crime Novel* (2005) by Michele Placido and *Gomorrah* (2008) by Matteo Garrone, which in turn were both remediated into successful television series that have attracted active communities of Internet users who perform a range of operations to download and invent upon fragments, scenes, and music, sometimes with notable virtuosity, and then share the reworked cultural products. Dana Renga's meticulous analysis in her chapter of the respective conventions and spectatorial relations operating in fiction films, documentaries, and hybridized texts narrating the story of the Banda della Magliana brings into relief narrative practices that work to gain viewer sympathies for the criminals who commit sometimes brutal crimes, as well as the new aesthetics produced through remediation and the moral judgments they make possible. Her study can serve as a model for thinking about remediation as a way to improve upon earlier media forms through the active participation of user-consumers engaged in cultural practices of legality, as well as convergence culture.

Critical Itineraries

The studies featured in this volume are arranged according to a conceptual progression. The first two chapters examine elements and relations constituting virtual antimafia spaces, as well as the historical traditions in which they are situated, thus creating contexts for the case studies that analyse such specific sites and texts as Libera Terra, the House of Memory for Mafia Victims, and the commemorative video "Not to Forget 23 May." The last two chapters construct critical avenues of inquiry into the ongoing processes of antimafia remediation and speculations about the viral antimafia and ways of cultivating it through techno-aesthetic education.

The very conceptualization and giving of body to cyberspatialities of legality as the subject of philosophical inquiry are examined in chapter

1 by Carla Bagnoli, whose "Structural Modes of Recognition and Virtual Forms of Empowerment: Towards a New Antimafia Culture" problematizes presentations of cyberspace as emblematic of Marc Augé's model of "non-place." In general, such delineations chart the features shared by cyberspace and nonplaces – highways, supermarkets, airports, and malls – solely in terms of their differences from singular environs anchored by particular historical or social elements. Replicable, anonymous, detached, unrooted, and hypermediated, non-places, Bolter and Grusin (2000) explain, are "defined not by their associations with local history or even with the ground on which they are built, but primarily by the reality of the media they contain" (179). Thus, they conclude, cyberspace is a "shopping mall in the ether" (179), fitting seamlessly into current economic, transportation, and communication networks. Shifting focus to the issue of how Internet users may be situated, if at all, in cyberspace, Nunes (2006) maintains that the virtual world is made up of "nonspaces ... where the social placement of individuals has more to do with access to international flows of material, information, and capital than the specificity of situatedness" (62). In relation to these pivotal positions, Bagnoli takes a different, innovative tack, employing Augé's (2008) concept of "non-place" in order to direct critical attention to the normative aspects of phenomena involved in the process of web space *becoming* a place, which, she contends, are largely the same as those structuring offline communities. Bagnoli's elucidation of the ways in which the selection of relevant others, the individualization of references, and practical identities figure in placing oneself in web communities that are defined through distinctive signs and spatial configurations, enables an understanding of the normative expectations, responsibilities, practices, and liabilities forming them. In the process, Bagnoli deftly draws out the fine distinctions between online and offline articulations of these concepts and the social identities and relations they make possible. She suggests that the dynamic cyberspatial antimafia communities share structural similarities with historical land-bound counterparts, yet, through the process of deterritorialization performed by virtual networking and practical identity formation, they create unique possibilities for the empowerment of moral agents and cultural productions of legality. Her examination of Libera as a sample case presents significant considerations for thinking about such other sites of antimafia communities as Addiopizzo or Ammazzateci Tutti, whose sociospatial relations are constituted through bearing the individual and collective responsibility to resist all mafia organizations

and forms of criminality, while engaging with everyday practices operating for truth, freedom, equality, and justice.

Baris Cayli's "When a Journalist Defies More Than the Mafia: The Legacy of Giuseppe Fava and Italian Antimafia Culture" (chapter 2) constructs an important historical frame for understanding the values and professional practices forming the lived geographies of web-based antimafia journalists, who frequently serve as witnesses providing testimony, knowledge, and future memory in the battle against the mafias. He examines the paradigmatic functions performed by Giuseppe Fava's life's work in shaping the ethics and practices of online journalism as committed social activism. Novelist, playwright, and founder of the monthly magazine *I Siciliani* (1983), Fava worked as an investigative journalist from the 1950s into the early 1980s, when the streets of Palermo became battlegrounds for the second mafia war (1981–3), known as the slaughter (*mattanza*). Rich evidentiary information and acute analysis testify to Fava's skills at conducting inquiries into mafia crimes. Yet the most striking feature of his exposés is perhaps the bold, explicit language he employs to break omertà and reveal the criminal collaboration between Italian politicians, prominent members of the business sector, and mafiosi. For example, during Enzo Biagi's television interview with Fava in 1983, Fava indicted the political elite, telling thousands of viewers, "The mafiosi are in the Parliament, the mafiosi are the ministers, the mafiosi are the bankers, the mafiosi are the leaders of the nation" (Fava 1983a). Soon after, Fava was gunned down in front of the Teatro Verga in Catania. As Cayli argues, Fava's legacy of public resistance in a battle for truth and freedom from the oppression of mafia politics and his traumatic death inform "the dynamics of contested spatialities of legality and antimafia culture in the new media." He supports this proposition by charting the traces of Fava's ethical code of socially committed journalism in the scope and practices of the online news reporting developed by I Siciliani giovani and Libera Informazione. Cayli's analysis invites reflection on the points of continuity, innovation, and difference in the field of antimafia journalism elaborating sociospatial relations online and offline, while also offering a different perspective on the roles of speaking, creating knowledge communities, and memory.

The conceiving, employment, and roles of Italian social networks in the embattled spaces of conflict between antimafia and mafia forces have been largely overlooked in mafia and media studies. Creating

avenues of inquiry in both fields, Paula Salvio's "'A Taste of Justice':
Digital Media and Libera Terra's Antimafia Public Pedagogy of Agrarian Dissent" (chapter 3) explores the public pedagogical projects
articulated by Libera Terra through its morally purposeful networking designs to educate citizens in the cultural formation of legality.
Through the leadership of don Luigi Ciotti, who founded Libera in
1995, with the explicit aim of "engaging civil society in the fight against
the mafias and promoting legality and justice" (http://liberaterra.it/
it/), today Libera is the largest non-profit antimafia organization in
Italy, coordinating the activities of some 1,600 associations and groups.
Situating the Libera Terra project in the context of its historical formation of non-violent agrarian protest, Salvio focuses on the specific
ways in which the organization crafts and utilizes blogs, Facebook,
and other forms of digital media to enjoin travellers to become affiliated with and contribute to the dismantling of mafia controlled spaces
and their reconstruction as civil habitats. Anchored by Jodi Dean's salient work on the psychoanalytic notion of drives and how they may
operate to place us in digital networks of pleasure and production,
Salvio's analysis provides a refined interpretation of the ways diverse
forms of social media elaborated by Libera Terra "capture, invest, and
cultivate political energies in the name of educating society for civility
and legality." In the process, her study puts into question the foundations of paradigms that represent practices of blogging and texting,
among others, solely as distractions from committed organization
and revolt. At the same time, her commentary on the public face of
antimafia activism constructed by Libera Terra poses the problem of
gender, and how the female body is cast onto the margins. In fact, in
the fight against the mafia conducted by the Sicilian peasant leagues
(Fasci siciliani) in the 1890s, and then the pitched battles in the 1940s
and 1950s, the presence of Italian women loomed large. Milena Gammaitoni (2013) cites several examples of female agrarian activism, such
as that in the peasant league of Piana dei Greci in Sicily. Of the 9,000
town inhabitants, some 2,500 men participated in the antimafia league
along with 1,000 women, whose roles have been overlooked. Similarly,
as Salvio's work, along with Boylan's, suggests, the ways in which
gender figures in the production of online antimafia culture warrants
concerted critical attention.[16]

The complexities of antimafia makings of new memory – in terms of
materials, remediating techniques, and artefacts – and their relations
to the right to memory and silence are brought into high definition

by Boylan in her chapter. Her unprecedented cartography maps the spatiotemporal configurations of the Facebook group's House of Memory for Victims of the Mafia and the constitutive features that articulate its mneumonic scope. On the cyberspatial landscape, the artisans constructing the ever-expanding House of Memory "give voice to silence," Aldo Penna explains, and "stave off the oblivion of forgetfulness. The recollection of the victims as memory is the antidote to today's new acts of violence."[17] Building on theoretical underpinnings proposed in Marita Sturken's (1997) and James E. Young's (1999) studies on countermonuments, Boylan provides salient analysis of the ways the Web memorial reinvents strategies for remembering individual mafia victims, many of whom would otherwise remain in oblivion, as intrinsic to the creation of collective memory. Foremost among the tools fashioned to engage Facebook friends in memory work is the calendar of loss, which creates diverse systems for registering the anniversary of each victim's traumatic death at mafia hands and produces, one can say, the digital overlay of the past onto the present through the remediation of news articles and photographs. As Boylan suggests, this calendar of loss reappropriates for civil memory and life mafia systems of calendarization of vendetta's, whereby murders are planned according to dates and anniversaries of sociosymbolic importance in the criminal referential system. In mafia practice, the vendetta instantiates domination, and serves as a warning to those who might challenge it, as demonstrated by the case of Claudio Fava, Giuseppe Fava's son. According to the testimony of a *pentito*, a mafioso who becomes a witness for the state, upon receiving orders to kill the young Fava, he and fellow hit men planned the attack for the anniversary of his father's murder, on 5 January, "to serve as a warning to the men who symbolized the struggle against the mafia" (cited in Siebert 1996, 39). The remembering of anniversaries of victims of the mafia performed through the calendar of loss's remediation strategies also contests heroic national narratives that spotlight specific aspects of particular antimafia activists, such as Judges Giovanni Falcone and Paolo Borsellino, while repressing others, a problem Boylan explores in relation to ongoing national trauma.

Irremediable loss, the labour of mourning, and hope as truths driving the production, posting, viewing, and sharing of witnessing texts form the interpretative field for the timely critical intervention performed by Giovanna Summerfield in her chapter "*Per non dimenticare*: Antimafia Digital Storytelling and Reflections."[18] Born in Catania,

Summerfield is an engaged antimafia activist whose contributions to the culture of legality include teaching courses on the mafia and anti-mafia, and organizing conferences and events designed to combat the criminal organization at the local and transnational levels. In her chapter, she takes readers inside the process of making the witnessing narrative titled "Per non dimenticare 23 maggio" (Not to forget 23 May). Summerfield thus creates the invaluable opportunity to gain understanding about what moves the invention of the antimafia testimony, the roles digital storytelling performs for the video makers and social actors, and the ways this text and similar videos enable mediated distance witnessing. Her study draws upon interviews and discussions with the creators, including the director Giuseppe Musumeci (who was an academic senator of the University of Catania), high school and university students, and individuals associated with the local prison. The significant studies on the psychological, social, and cultural roles performed by putting lives into narrative conducted by Marshall Ganz, Pam Allyn, Jerome Bruner, and Paul Frosh inflect Summerfield's investigation of the diverse ways in which digital storytelling figures in the fluid process of individual and collective identity formation, as well as the mobilization of fellow citizens to oppose all mafia activities and act on behalf of social and cultural change. By becoming speaking social protagonists, the assertion of moral agency and such values as honesty and responsibility overcomes, Summerfield suggests, the forces of isolation, resignation, and apathy, upon which the mafia depends. Furthermore, the creation and posting of this witnessing text, and others like it, preserve the fragile testimonies attesting to the meanings made of loss and the re-elaboration of the past in order to fashion arts of resistance and civil culture, while making them accessible as part of future memory for generations to come. Elucidating the significance of such narratives, Michel de Certeau (1997) maintains they are the memory of life as well as a craft that "establish a link between generations, transmitting to the youngest members fragments of earlier practices and ways of know-how" (131). The performances of witnessing captured on the YouTube video thus make distant witnessing, in spatial and temporal terms, possible, conveying knowledge about lawful ways of thinking and acting for the transformation of biomediatic geographies lived every day.

The contradictory attractions exerted by antimafia and mafia culture forms the overarching problem in Dana Renga's "Remediating the Banda della Magliana: Debating Sympathetic Perpetrators in the

Digital Age" (chapter 6). Focusing on the differentiated redactions of the Magliana gang's exploits in Rome during the 1970s and 1980s, which include fiction films, documentaries, and videos merging fiction and non-fiction materials, Renga investigates complex questions related to the allure of mafia perpetrators among mass audiences. She advances the theory that viewers of hypermediated short films are less disposed to identify and sympathize with the members of the Magliana gang, in contrast to spectators viewing the fiction films. Renga grounds this proposition by scrutinizing the diverse fiction and non-fiction representations of the gang members and their stories in relation to the mechanics of film identification and spectatorship, and devotes particular attention to what she identifies as a process of splitting evidenced in viewer responses to the hybridized videos. The traces of this splitting inscribe contradictory pulls between the lure of the mafia mystique and the sense of ethical consciousness, a key element of the cultural practices of legality. Significantly, through the blogs, user comment tools, and chat rooms associated with the texts devoted to the Magliana gang, consumers, antimafia activists among them, create communal knowledge spaces, sharing their particular information about the fiction or non-fiction materials in question, as they relate to the members historical criminal record of memory, and thus to moral judgments.

The particular ways in which music and song figure in the creation of communities in built or metaphorical cities, the nation, and virtual spaces has garnered increasing critical attention of late, particularly in the frame of networked society and culture. Engaging with these diverse spatial constructions and their potential points of convergence, Angela Maiello's "#NuJuornBuon: Aesthetics of Viral Antimafia" (chapter 7) examines the exemplary case of Italian rapper Rocco Pugliarulo, known by the stage name Rocco Hunt, and his award-winning song "Nu Juorn Buon" (A good day), in order to prompt thinking about the very notion of the viral antimafia, the domains of possibility open to its cultivation of community, and ways to undertake the transformation of online participation into offline cultural practices of legality. Upon winning first place in the New Talents category of the 2014 Sanremo Music Festival, the song "Nu Juorn Buon" performed in Neapolitan dialect by Rocco Hunt, immediately became a viral phenomenon, as millions of viewers accessed, viewed, and shared it, spreading the antimafia words for which both song and rapper came to stand. Indeed, the lyrics conjured the land of fires in

Campania, where earth, inhabitants, and community are ravaged by a "massacre of garbage," toxic wastes dumped in the course of the camorra's lucrative criminal business. In order to interpret how this viral antimafia rap song may operate in new medial structures and modalities, as well as material sociospatial relations, Maiello provides an acute charting of the acoustic city of Naples, and the static created by competing traditions of classic Neapolitan and neomelodic music. Pivotal to her approach are Emilio Garroni's (1986) aesthetic theories of sense, sensation, and meaning, as well as Henry Jenkins's (1992, 2006) works on convergence and participatory culture, and Pietro Montani's (2010, 2014, 2015) insightful ideas on techno-aesthetics.

Maiello fashions historical and critical contexts in which to situate "Nu Juorn Buon" as a product and producer of viral antimafia culture. Particularly important in this regard is how the representation of the camorra and the land, which, as Hunt tells listeners, "is the land of sun," not garbage, deconstructs the contemporary myths of the camorra diffused in certain neomelodic songs. Cautioning against threats posed by the crooned stories of cammoristi that can literally fill the streets of Naples as they flow from the windows of homes, storefronts, cars, and smartphones, Roberto Saviano (2012) highlights the new ethic they convey. It is not universal, he states, but "particular, modeled on the notion of the group. It's wrong to kill, but it's necessary. It's wrong to live the life of crime, but it can be done with honor."[19] Maiello's close reading of the sense and sensibilities fostered in "Nu Juorn Buon" and reworked through participatory operations forming medial flows draws out the implications for practices of antimafia ethics and, by means of techno-aesthetics education, their translation into offline cultures and communities. By so doing, her analysis opens future lines of investigation into the rich field of antimafia music, comprising songs composed in memory of mafia victims such as Rita Atria and Giovanni Falcone, and performances that are captured on videos on YouTube and in diverse archives, where they are accessed, viewed, and shared at will, and may play significant roles in community formation.

These varied critical mediations of the heterogeneous range of antimafia operations, modes, and forms of cultural production that enact cyberspatialities of legality perform timely interventions as they challenge prominent images of Italy, Italian citizens, the antimafia movement, and new digital media as well. Most important, they make visible the individual and collective methods of creating, reinventing, and propagating knowledge about the ideals, ways of living, responsibilities, and rights driving the construction of lawful civil life. The resultant perspective on Italy contrasts sharply with the images of the mafia state that have dominated Italian headlines in print, television, and online news sources since March of 2014, and exposed a succession of monumental cases of illegal business conducted between politicians and the camorra, 'ndrangheta, and the crime network in Rome, dubbed the capital mafia.[20] Significantly, through singular acts of what have become ordinary usage – liking an article or film, posting comments, or reinventing and sharing products of legality – practitioners of antimafia arts of invention make places for resisting criminal structures of power, reforming sociospatial relations and the values, desires, hopes, and actions constituting them.

By charting diverse remediating antimafia places on the itineraries of hybridized geographies numbers of Italians live, these studies also put into question current notions that the antimafia has largely become an institutionalized part of the state, in Attilio Bolzoni's (2015) words, "a feigned antimafia" that is submissive, malleable, and concerned with making a business of the traumatic memory of antimafia activists. The examinations of, for example, online antimafia news organizations, Libera Terra, and ironic remediations of *Gomorra* or *Crime Novel*, as well as the viral antimafia, demonstrate the need to expand the field of inquiry and consider the online places where increasing numbers of citizens participate in civically engaged action based upon specific social issues and elective affiliations, creating points of resistance to mafia networks of power, and perhaps the conformist elements of the antimafia movement as well. In the latter instance, the various artful online operations performed by new media practitioners who appropriate, refashion, repurpose medial contents in service of a culture of legality, as in the cases of "Nu Juorn Buon" and parodies inspired by *Gomorra*, remediate the antimafia movement, improving upon it with the dynamic modes and forms of participation, bound only by imagination, intellect, and the technologies making them possible. The creation and circulation of such artefacts construct portals for developing new perspectives on such critical concepts as media witnessing, visual and acoustic memory spaces, silence and the right to speak out, as well as the drives situating Internet users in networks of pleasure and production, which contribute to the geographies of everyday life today.

NOTES

1 While serving as Regional Secretary of the Democratic Party in Sicily and
   Secretary of the National Antimafia Commission, Genovese provides this
   insight, among others, in Donato (2009).
2 Among the excellent histories of the mafia in Italy and its relations to crime
   organizations in the United States are Alexander Stille's *Excellent Cadavers*
   (1996), John Dickie's *Cosa Nostra* (2004), and Umberto Santino's *Mafia and
   Antimafia: A Brief History* (2015).
3 The Federal Bureau of Investigation's web pages on Italian organized crime
   report that the four mafia organizations total some 25,000 members and
   250,000 affiliates across the globe, with over 3,000 made men and affiliates
   in the United States.
4 For articles examining the Facebook controversy and the infiltration of
   the mafia on the Internet, see Marco Fattorini (2009), Francesco Pellegrino
   Lise (2009), the Editorial, "Il latitante è su Skype" (2012), and Lirio Abbate
   (2012).
5 See also Salvio's "Reconstructing Memory through the Archives" (2014),
   which analyses the fascinating case of Letizia Battaglia's *rielaborazioni*
   (re-elaborations).
6 In *The Mafia in Italian Lives and Literature: Life Sentences and Their Geographies*
   (2015), I explicate the concept of spatialities of legality, which I elaborate in
   the course of analysing the YouTube video *Storie di resistenza quotidiana* and
   the antimafia social network Ammazzateci Tutti.
7 The 2013 Censis reports that Internet usage among the population in Italy
   registers 63.5 per cent, reaching 90.4 per cent among the young. Of Italians
   with Internet access, 69.8 per cent use Facebook and 61 per cent use
   YouTube. Smartphone usage ranks at 66.1 per cent among Italians under
   thirty years old.
8 See the article "Reporter nel mirino," *La Repubblica*, 14 May 2015, 22. The
   problem of mafia intimidation and control over the press has drawn
   national attention in recent days, as illustrated also by Roberto Saviano's
   article, "Il giornalista licenziato su ordine del boss," *La Repubblica*, 14 May
   2015, 23, which exposes the story of Enzo Palmesano, a professional journalist who was fired from the *Corriere di Caserta* upon orders of the camorra
   boss Vincenzo Lubrano, after Palmesano failed to heed signs warning him
   off his investigative reports on the mafia. Bullets were mailed to his home
   and his car was set on fire. See the site RE-LE Inchieste at Repubblica.it for
   information about the Palmesano case and the testimonies of journalists
   who are currently mafia targets.

9 I thank Carla Bagnoli for making me aware of this fascinating example of Italian antimafia webtv. First founded as a newspaper by a group of Italian high school students in 2009, the following year Cortocircuito became a webtv site whose acute broadcasts and interviews related to organized crime in Reggio Emilia have earned it diverse awards. Significantly, the self-representation of Cortocircuito in the Presentazione section of their site opens with an epigraph that invokes the words of Giuseppe Fava, which inscribe their taking of a position and their socially committed ethics of journalism. It states, "Journalism made of truth prevents a lot of corruption, curbs criminal violence, speeds up indispensible public projects, demands effective social services, keeps the forces of the law continually alert, calls for the constant attention of the justice system, and imposes good governing on politicians."

10 See Salvio's "Reconstructing Memory through the Archives: Public Pedagogy, Citizenship and Letizia Battaglia's Photographic Record of Mafia Violence" (2014) and Norma Bouchard's "Fighting *Cosa Nostra* with the Camera's Eye: Letizia Battaglia's Evolving Icons of 'Traumatic Realism'" (2016).

11 I thank Simonetta Milli Konewko for drawing my attention to this important online video.

12 These authors and their fellow contributors to the volume *The Ethics of Memory in a Digital Age* (2014), edited by Alessia Ghezzi, Angela Guimaraes Pereira, and Lucia Vesnic-Alujevic, present insightful perspectives on various facets of memory, forgetting, and the significance of the Right to Be Forgotten. In *L'archivio in rete* (2015), Angela Maiello breaks innovative ground by examining how new technological developments may render obsolete the very devices and systems currently constructing and protecting digital archives of memory.

13 I thank Jake Gertz for drawing the Vallanzasca case to my attention.

14 This data appears in "Il colpo di Vallanzasca" (Bergamonews 2014) and Greta Sclaunich's "Diritto all'oblio, tra i link oscurati anche quello su Vallanzasca" (2008). In 2010 Michele Placido's film *Vallanzasca – Gli angeli del male* was released amidst heated controversy about the seemingly idealized portrayal of the criminals. The film was inspired by Vallanzasca's autobiography, *Il fiore del male: Bandito a Milano* (2009), co-written with Carlo Bonini.

15 It goes beyond the scope of this study to draw out the complexities of the antimafia imaginary, whose configurations are contingent upon changing historical, social, and cultural contexts dating back to the 1800s, as well as the various media that constitute it. Several anthologies and volumes of

literary criticism examine the many fictional and non-fictional works that represent the mafia, antimafia figures, and movements formed to battle the criminal organizations in diverse regions of Italy. These include *La letteratura sulla mafia* (1988) by Elena Brancati and Carlo Muscetta, *Tutti a cena da don Mariano: Letteratura e mafia nella Sicilia della nuova Italia* (1995) by Massimo Onofri, and my *The Mafia in Italian Lives and Literature: Life Sentences and Their Geographies* (2015). Dana Renga's *Mafia Movies: A Reader* and *Unfinished Business* (2013) is indispensable for understanding the scope and development of fiction and non-fiction films and television series on the mafia.

16 Important in this regard is the composition of Ammazzateci Tutti's regional coordinators and directors, with 70 per cent being women as of 2012. Furthermore, the numerous blogs, video testimonies, and comment postings on their site, as well as many others, offer diversified textual ground for researching forms of female-gendered activism in relation to such issues as voice, the body, antimafia identity construction, and practices of the culture of legality.

17 Aldo Penna is an antimafia activist and author. His quotation here is taken from the Vittimemafia Facebook page: https://facebook.com/groups/vittimemafia.

18 See also my analysis of the YouTube testimonial video "19 luglio 2009: Ammazzateci Tutti a Palermo 17 anni dopo la strage di Via d'Amelio" (accessible at Ammazzateci Tutti YouTube), which I conduct in *The Mafia in Italian Lives and Literature* (2015).

19 Jason Pine and Francesco Pepe's "Transnational Neomelodica Music and Alternative Economic Cultures" (2013) provides a wealth of information about the tradition of neomelodic performers, their songs, and fans. However, they devote scant attention to the lyrics, and thus tend to take lightly how romanticized images of the camorristi and the oppressive system they produce contribute to the popular imaginary.

20 The stories that broke in spring of 2014 and are ongoing investigations include the MOSE project in Venice, a system of damns designed to protect the city from flooding, which is mired in a system of kickbacks and illicit public contracts involving members of the local government, as well as those of the Italian and European Community Parliaments, and members of the camorra; Milan Expo, designed to showcase Italy as host to some 140 pavilions representing nations around the world, has fostered criminal bipartisan enterprises of far-right Forza Italia politicians and the leftist Democratic Party, undertaken with members of 'ndrangheta, the crime organization hailing from Calabria and beneficiaries of nearly $600 million

worth of construction contracts; in December of 2014, arrest warrants were issued for some hundred members of the political class, business elite, and criminals for purported crimes conducted through the network *mafia capitale*, the capital mafia, led by Massimo Carminati, neofascist terrorist and member of the Magliana gang active in Rome during the 1970s and 1980s. This network, which appears to have ties with Cosa Nostra, made millions of dollars exploiting immigrants and the homeless, in addition to its industry of extortion, embezzlement, money laundering, and drugs.

1 Structural Modes of Recognition and Virtual Forms of Empowerment: Towards a New Antimafia Culture

CARLA BAGNOLI

What is specific to antimafia culture in the digital era? Which structural features, if any, might distinguish the very formation of antimafia online communities from their land-bound counterparts, in terms of the kinds of possibilities, expectations, rights, and responsibilities constituting these respective spatial collectivities? In this frame, what factors bear upon both the decision to place oneself in antimafia web communities and the active engagements with the culture of legality produced by such organizations as Addiopizzo, the Rita Atria Antimafie Association, and Libera? In the following discussion, I address these questions by working through philosophical arguments about how rational agents form their reasons by engaging in their "grounded" and virtual communities of reference. The philosophical conceptualization of this process sheds light on the structure of recognition that works at the base of non-profit organizations such as Libera, which I situate at the vanguard of antimafia networks. Libera was founded on 25 March 1995, and has been endorsed by the Ministry of Social Solidarity for its merits in promoting the culture of legality.[1]

With the aim of providing the theoretical tools to examine cases such as Libera, I first claim that as rational agents we are engaged in practices of mutual accountability. We produce reasons that explain and justify what we do. In producing reasons, we address demands of explanation and justification. In the attempt to make sense of and justify their actions, rational subjects construct reasons in an ideal dialogue with others. In the practice of exchanging reasons, rational subjects address others under different descriptions. To assess the normative force of reasons, it is thus relevant to ask to whom reasons are addressed. In some philosophical accounts, reasons have a local authority insofar as they address others as members of the same community. This is the particularistic view. By contrast, in some other philosophical accounts, reasons are public and universal and address others as equals. This is the universalistic view. I employ this distinction to articulate some issues about how to understand and measure the normative relevance and impact of web communication in the recent development of antimafia culture. The basic claim is that web communication broadens the scope of the relevant others and thus allows for reasons that have appeal independently of territorial belonging. This argument focuses on the practices of "placing oneself in a space" as distinct sources of normativity. My analysis reflects upon the process of "placing oneself in a space," which I take to be normative, that is, productive of normative concerns and reasons. To do so, I deploy the key contrastive concepts of space and place elaborated by Marc Augé.

Second, and in contrast to Augé's approach, I emphasize that the process of change from occupying a space to taking a place is distinctively normative, and comes with special responsibilities. I thus shift focus to the normative dimension of the cluster phenomena that Augé has identified, hence calling attention to the quality of web communication. The result is a different diagnosis of the role of individuals in appropriating and interpreting information. In short, I dispute that the so-called individualization of reference is a genuine phenomenon of web communication. I then provide the philosophical analysis of what I take to be the scope and the actors of web communication. In particular, I provide an account of what it takes to reason together with others, a normative practice that I consider distinctive of agents insofar as they are rational. On the basis of this argument, and by the means provided by the philosophical vocabulary of public reasons, I interpret both the challenges posed by the mafia, and the antimafia responses that are distinctive of the digital era. For my examination of this kind of communication, I analyse elements of Libera's website, which fights the mafia by making a particularly effective use of social networks in building a virtual community of empowerment. Of key importance are the forms of address to visitors and the various modes of engagement Libera creates for inventing cultural products of legality.

Placing Oneself in a Space and Its Normative Relevance

Originally, the mafia was a local phenomenon, confined to particular geographical areas and rooted in a particular territories. With the expansion of the area of illicit dealings, the geographical boundaries of the mafia are not as definite as they once were. Nonetheless, the mafia has not lost its grip on specific geographical territories (see Pickering-Iazzi's introduction to this volume at page 12). Thus, though there is a more general sense in which we talk of mafia culture, without specific reference to territories or illicit commerce, it also still makes sense to refer to specific geographic territories "controlled" by the mafia. Even recognizing the complexity of these phenomena, it is correct to say that the mafia maintains an important relation to its territory of origins, even though its illicit affairs and criminal relations have expanded well beyond traditional geographical boundaries. There are interesting asymmetries between the way in which the mafia gains affiliates locally and the way in which antimafia culture consolidates over time. At least some of these asymmetries have to do with the normative relevance of occupying a territory and, more generally, with the practices of placing oneself in a space. While the war against the mafia is necessarily conducted locally, antimafia culture spreads across boundaries and attracts sympathy and support from people generally interested in good practices and justice. Arguably, the ones who live in territories largely controlled by the mafia may have a direct interest in joining activities of the antimafia movement. In fact, spreading antimafia culture necessarily involves activities that are anchored in territories particularly vulnerable and exposed to the powers of the mafia. Indeed, this is the main objective of activities undertaken to inform, educate, and raise consciousness. On the other hand, people who live in territories traditionally occupied by the mafia are also the ones more exposed and sensitive to the normative pressure of mafia culture and immediately subjected to retaliation. These are the people for whom joining or not joining the mafia may be a genuine daily dilemma, and not an exercise in counterfactual thinking. However, the educative activities that pertain to antimafia culture have resonance also for people and communities that do not live in territories still governed by or recently freed from the mafia, and thus not concretely under any dilemmatic choice. The impact of providing information and raising awareness is likely to reach beyond the population directly within the area of mafia cultural influence.

To appreciate this impact, I employ the conceptual distinction "place vs. space," which will help us to assess the prospects and predicaments of the antimafia movement in the web era. I use the concept of non-place (*non-lieu*) – originally introduced by Michel de Certeau, then refined and made famous by anthropologist Marc Augé – to identify some features of global communication, which help to articulate the normative relevance of the activities under scrutiny. The task is to isolate some phenomena relative to the web space *becoming* a place, as a starting point for identifying the novelties of global communication that might represent opportunities of development for the antimafia movement. There is a very close relation between space organizations and social organizations. This relation takes specific forms whether the space is territorial or non-territorial. The distinction between "space" and "place" assists us in addressing the problem of the normative relevance of belonging to a place. The distinction is not a dichotomy in value. I use these concepts to address the issue of whether and how "web places" ground us in some social structures. The difference in the way territorial and non-territorial spaces are organized produces further differences between the way in which corresponding "places" become *normative sources*, and produce responsibilities and normative expectations of any sort (e.g., associated with obligations, reasons, entitlements, and rights). For instance, in domestic environments the distinction between communal rooms and private rooms defines special kinds of normative relations. Being invited into, prohibited or kept away from, or allowed to enter another person's room are ways to establish particular normative relations of intimacy or distance. Responses to such invitations, prohibitions, and permissions are also acts of normative significance and carry with them distinctive responsibilities.

Groups express their identity through distinctive configurations of public space. Belonging to a place comes with distinctive responsibilities and liabilities (Augé 1995, 57). Where we come from tells something about who we are, our history, allegiances, and relations. As Augé (1995) has forcefully argued, places importantly contribute to forming our identities: "place of birth is constituent of individual identity" (53). "If a place can be defined as relational, historical, and concerned with identity, then a space which cannot be defined as relational or historical, or concerned with identity will be a non-place" (77–8); "place and non-place are rather like opposed polarities: the first is never completely erased, the second never totally completed; they are like palimpsests on which the scrambled game of identity and relations is ceaselessly rewritten" (19). Like Augé, I will consider places as *identifiers*.

Different from occupying a space, sharing a place entails belonging to a community, and thus qualifies for some sort of membership. In the traditional or geographic sense of "place," sharing a place is something associated with normative expectations and emotions of proximity and intimacy. Sharing a place is a fulcrum of activities that are at least partly institutionalized and are socially organized. Spaces become places for symbolic ties and form the grounds and foundations of solid, permanent traditions and relations. Arguably, the web represents an enormous technological change, which has modified the forms of social aggregations and socialization. Placing oneself in the web space is a novel option for socialization and social rooting. Perhaps these novel forms are less permanent and lasting than traditional forms of socialization; perhaps they are less inclined to abide by external constraints and are thus resistant to traditions. I think these are empirical questions that one needs to verify case by case. What concerns me here is to illustrate how new forms of communication in the web space provide antimafia culture with new opportunities of rooting and developing, by redesigning the shape of the relevant communities, personal relations, and social identities.

The Individualization of Reference in Web Communication

Marc Augé has identified global communication through the categories of excess, expansion, or inflation. Web communication expands enormously and very rapidly. A massive quantity of information becomes globally accessible, thus affecting an increasing number of users. This is not a merely quantitative phenomenon, but it is also interestingly associated with other epistemological and normative phenomena. The web produces and makes accessible an abundance of events and objects, which individual users cannot fully master individually, hence there is need for filtering. The epistemic effect is that individuals need selection tools for discriminating the information that is relevant; the normative aspect of this phenomenon is that the tools by which we select information also select knowledge. Hence they significantly affect the distribution and attribution of epistemic authority. The rationale of such distribution and attribution of epistemic authority is neither transparent nor easy to identify.[2]

In traditional forms of communication, data selection is mostly performed by individuals and deliberate screenings, such as selecting information by choosing newspapers, TV channels, advisers, friends, and so forth. This selection is not always fully intentional or thoroughly deliberate, and it is never direct or unmediated. For instance, in some cases, there is an emotional input for the individual screening; in others, the process of screenings may be manipulated or hetero-directed.

If we think of social phenomena such as advertising campaigns, ideology, and persuasion, then there might be serious reasons to doubt that individual choice plays a decisive role in selecting information. Nonetheless, there is room for epistemic agents to choose their sources of information and to address the issue of the epistemic source of information and knowledge. There seems to be a parallel in web communication, insofar as the basic screenings are mechanical filters, which are not necessarily activated by the agent. On the other hand, as Augé remarks, the structure of web communication seems to increment the role of individual preferences. For Augé (1995), excessive information creates also an excess of space (31), that is, the increasing accessibility of space due to global transferring of information. Furthermore, users claim the prerogative to interpret the information by themselves (37). This is the third and most important feature of supermodernity, which Augé marks as the "individualization of references."

Do these features mark a new ontology? Perhaps this question calls upon the anthropologist to rethink her or his methodology, but it can also serve as a guide for the philosopher. My proposal is to provide some help with conceptual analysis, by shifting focus to the normative dimension of the cluster of phenomena that Augé has identified. Rather than focusing on the impact of massive information transferred, I would like to call attention to the quality of web communication. While Augé emphasizes the role of individuals in appropriating and interpreting information, I am not altogether sure that this so-called individualization of reference is a genuine phenomenon of web communication. To be sure, the web prioritizes the information in ways that may respond to the users' profiles, under some descriptions. It may also be true that the very structure of web communication augments the role of individual preferences in selecting the source of information. However, I am not convinced that these factors amount to the individualization of reference in communication. Rather, I would like to suggest that web communication is sparse, opaque, and discretional. These qualities represent distinctive opportunities and predicaments of socializing on the web, but they do not point to the phenomenon of individualization of reference that Augé singles out.

In web communication, identities and personalities are more opaque than in traditional forms of communication. Or, more precisely, the kind of opacity that emerges in web communication is of different sorts than the opacity typical of traditional forms of personal communication, such as opacity of intentions, since web communication is not in presence and, more important, it is shielded and filtered differently, at the discretion of the users. There are technological features that users may decide to activate or not to activate to shield and protect their real identities. In this respect, virtual communication is more protective of some forms of personal autonomy insofar as some information is unavailable or made accessible to a selected community. One may decide, for instance, how to restrict the access to information available on the website, according to circles of associates, friends, acquaintances, or occasional visitors.

While global communication is opaque and discretional, it does not leave interpretation in the hands of individuals. My claim is that the opaque and discretional character of web communication amplifies the possibility of communities whose boundaries are drawn differently and yet perform traditional tasks. I suggest that the so-called traditional tasks are better understood in terms of *constitutive functions*. The primary function is to catalyse and monitor membership, through practices of inclusion and exclusion. It seems to me that the discretional and opaque characteristics of web communication create asymmetries that are relevant for understanding the recent dynamics of antimafia culture. These features importantly affect the scope of our interlocutors. I call this the issue of *relevant others*.

Relevant Others: Why They Matter and How to Select Them

In the project of understanding social interactions, it matters who our interlocutors are. It matters for subjects to define their social and practical identity, and it matters for agents to identify their reasons for action. This is a very basic point that concerns the constitutive structure of reasons. Reasons constitutively or structurally implicate others. If so, then, it is most crucial to consider who the relevant others are.

To make the problem vivid, let me offer a simple example. Anna is a Catholic teacher of biology. With a fair amount of simplification, we can say that she is a member of three groups: she belongs to the group of women, under the first description; to the group of Catholics, under the second description; and to the group of scientists, under the third description. Such identities bring with them commitments to specific values: the value Anna associates with being a woman; the value that she associates with being a scholar; and the value she associates with being a Catholic. The values associated to these distinct identities are not logically inconsistent, and they may be psychologically sustainable, but they may clash in some particular circumstances. Let us imagine, for instance, that Anna struggles to explain biology without making concessions about her Catholic credo. In this case, the relevant community for her should be the scientific community, and for the sake of simplicity we assume that such a community uniformly accepts the same standards of adequacy for explanation. That is to say, when Anna is thinking in terms of the considerations to bring as reasons, she considers scientists as "the relevant others" to whom to address such considerations.

Let us consider a second scenario in which Anna searches for reasons: she is planning for her wedding day. The relevant others that count in her reasoning about this case are the ones included in her Catholic community. This is to say that when she is searching for considerations that count for reasons in dealing with the preparation of her wedding day, such considerations are the ones that would count as reasons relative to her Catholic community. It is tempting to say that these reasons are qualified, insofar as they function as reasons relative to the Catholic community. Their authority is indeed local, grounded in membership in the particular Catholic community. However, their claims range universally over that community. Let me introduce some complications. Suppose that Anna is planning to marry Bertie; they met through a social network, knowing that they each come from a small Italian town. They chose to make this information available to potential acquaintances because they each thought this was a relevant aspect of their personality and an indication of the life they want to lead. Their particular place of origin matters to both of them, and thus they seek out people with the same background. While Anna is a rather traditional Catholic, Bertie is a liberal man reluctant to undertake any prefixed wedding arrangements. As soon as they start planning their real life together, conflicts arise. Bertie exposes Anna to a range of considerations that she had not anticipated. Conflicts become increasingly intense and eventually push Anna and Bertie apart. As a result of this confrontation, Anna is profoundly shaken and starts revisiting her general outlook. This process of reconsideration of her roots and allegiances leads to an attempt to articulate the conflict she has just experienced. To make sense of the conflict, she takes into account reasons that spring from different but equally important sources. The inner conflict surfaces when Anna considers what counts as a reason. At this point, the question arises as to which community is more relevant in the construction of her reasons. On the one hand, there are the traditional recommendations of the church. On the other hand, there are the considerations that Bertie endorses. What is the relevant interlocutor for Anna? Interestingly, this is an open question. To respond to this question, it is not sufficient to appeal to the formal requirement that reasons must be logically universal and that they be applied in all similar cases. It is also necessary to take into account the scope of such a requirement and ask over which domain it ranges.

In previous works I have argued that reference to relevant others is a constitutive constraint on constructing reasons (Bagnoli 2007, 2009, 2011). This philosophical claim is analogous to Augé's (1995) anthropological claim that the "internal other" is the fundamental reference in all systems, "so that it is not possible to mention a position in the system without referring to one or more others" (18–19). It goes without saying that reference to relevant others is not necessarily explicit. In reconstructing the content of reasons we do not typically formulate the question. Who the relevant others are may be implicit all along, even though reference to the relevant others is a constitutive constraint on the construction of reasons. Interestingly, reference to others becomes explicit for external interlocutors when the agent experiences a conflict or she is perplexed and uncertain about what to do. Making the "internal other" explicit is a routine resource we deploy in practical reasoning, in the attempt to figure out genuine allegiances and real concerns. While making the "internal other" explicit is importantly up to the agent, it is by no means something that the agent decides as a sheer act of will.

This is an important qualification when we are talking about "constructing" reasons, because the term may misleadingly suggest that agents merely decide what counts as a reason and, as a consequence, that the force of reasons is conditional and discretional. Instead, the point of talking about the "construction" of reasons is to stress that what counts as a consideration in favour of something is importantly constrained by the ones who are addressed by that consideration. When Anna thinks of the reasons not to go to a church meeting in preparation for her wedding, she tries to figure out the considerations that would justify not going to a church meeting in addressing the demand of justification of relevant others. The reference to relevant others is a constitutive constraint in the activity of forming reasons. It requires that agents build their reasons in an ideal dialogue with others and rule out considerations such as "because I say so!" This phrase does not serve as an explication of the agent's action, and even less may it serve as a justification of the agent's action. Clearly, this is not to say that it does not have any normative relevance. For instance, it may be an injunction, or a statement that protests in favour of the agent's entitlement to do whatever she likes, without responding to the demands of others. But this is exactly the feature that makes this normative statement *not* a normative justification addressed to others. Reasons are just some normative items in our normative language; even though they play a crucial role, they do not have to be considered the only tools we have to exert and express our normative capacities.

The point established is that when we construct reasons that explain and justify what we do, we also define who we are, practically speaking, and in doing so we address a distinctive audience, that is, the audience of "relevant others." In practice, we negotiate and build up our identities in an ideal dialogue with them. Because our reasoning implicates others in constitutive ways, we are also constitutively vulnerable to others. This vulnerability is especially evident when we deal with immoral agents and power structures.

Reasons According to Mobsters

The philosopher's project is not to oppose violence and illegality via the production of reasons but to understand how we can reason together about the best prospects for a shared life. To this purpose, it is crucial to understand "how a mafioso reasons." This is not an intellectual curiosity but an important move from a practical point of view, since reasons are supposed to guide human agents and account for their identity and agency. Rational guidance is a tool for humans to act effectively and intelligently, not only in the pursuit of our particular goals, but also in cooperation with others and for the sake of shared ends. Within this perspective, it is an open question whether and how we can rationally engage the mafioso, or any other kind of immoralist. Is it possible to engage with immoralists through rational argument? Can we show that they are wrong by sheer rational argument, and compel them by sheer rational argument to join the moral community? These are questions that have been outstanding since Plato's first formulation in the *Republic*. Such questions do not concern only the powers of rationality, but also the legitimacy of state coercion, and the answers to these questions strongly affect the morally and politically legitimate forms of responses to the mafia and other sorts of immorality.

In recent philosophical literature, the mafioso makes his appearance as a test for the capacity of reasons to guide action. Philosophers use an "idealized" mafioso who lives by a code of honour, while using violence and manipulation in order to defend his interests (Cohen 1996, 183). According to Christine M. Korsgaard (1996), for instance, the mafioso presents a philosophical problem insofar as he understands reasons, but he is unconcerned with the claims of others. In the language introduced in the previous section, we may characterize the mafioso as thinking and acting on the basis of reasons that respond to a particular community. His failure, according to Korsgaard is that he is not reflective enough to produce genuine reasons. This is because for Korsgaard reasons are inherently public, and thus address all others, without qualification (134–5).

To see the point of this argument, it is necessary to clarify what sort of "publicity" is at stake here. The term "public" is a term of art and indicates that the considerations legitimately counting as "reasons" ought to be produced by a process of reasoning that is public rather than grounded on special or particular interests. Public reasoning is driven by the recognition of others as having equal normative standing. This is a minimal requirement, which does not guarantee accord but allows reasoners to correctly identify the scope of agreement and disagreement. A first broad distinction can be drawn in terms of semantic versus ethical publicity (LeBar 2001). In the semantic sense, publicity means shareability (Korsgaard 1996, 135). Reasons are discursive items that deploy concepts. Insofar as concepts are public, reasons are also public. There cannot be private reasons in the sense in which there cannot be private concepts and meanings because their intelligibility depends on their publicity. In a nutshell, this is the basic lesson drawn from the so-called Wittgensteinian argument, which establishes the inconceivability of a private language. However, appeal to the Wittgensteinian argument against the private language fails to show what is wrong with the mafioso's reasoning. The mafioso produces reasons that are intelligible and understandable also by people who do not share anything with the mafioso. Furthermore, there is a sense in which "understanding" the mafioso's reasons has very little to do with semantics. The sort of intelligibility we care about in this context is epistemic rather than semantic, in that it concerns the explanation of the link between agents and their actions. The reasons the mobster offers are reasons that we understand not only because we share his language enough to master the meaning attached to them (it thus differs from mere noise), but also because these reasons are intelligible explanations of why he does what he does. We understand the mobster's reasons on his own terms, even when we do not share his position, interests, and values. This epistemic sense of publicity is very important and its identification represents a step forward in the conversation with the mafioso, because it allows *us* to see things from his particular perspective. By giving an explanation of what he has done, he enters into a relation with us as a reasoner. This relation is constrained by some norms, by which he appears to abide. For instance, he knows that in offering an explanation of what he has done he ought to produce reasons that are credible enough and function as an explanation. If he said that he smashed the store window simply because he did not like the colour, this would have a certain impact on the hearer; it would not be necessarily incredible, since the act can be read as an exhibition of sheer force, which may have its rationale in the mafia system, as a demonstrative act. Reasons on the account of which agents say to be acting are important normative items in dealings with others, even when they are false or self-deceptive. They position the others on the normative map.

Like the semantic claim, this epistemic claim says nothing about the limited appeal or the moral status of the mobster's reasons. There are immoral reasons that are perfectly intelligible. Thus, such reasons are not only intelligible in the semantic sense of the term, but also understandable in the practical sense of the term, insofar as one may recognize that such considerations count as reasons for acting one way rather than another. Suppose we read a police report where a young mobster explains that he smashed a store window as an act of retaliation. The explanation is intelligible, and serves to identify the reasons that motivated the mobster to act as he did. But they are also understandable as reasons insofar as one recognizes that these are actually binding reasons for the gangster. This sense of publicity is not semantic, and yet it does not pick out the thicker sense of publicity that is required to rule out the mobster's reason as immoral.

Furthermore, this epistemic and practical sense of publicity also identifies reasons that are particular, but sound like moral reasons. For instance, suppose Rita explains that she informed the police about the conversation she overheard because she wanted to protect her brother. This account of the action makes her action intelligible and counts as a good reason to act as she did. One understands her point of view that favours the action protecting her brother. These two examples show that the semantic and the practical sense of publicity pick out different aspects of reason producing practices.

These considerations are often used to show that the feature of publicity is not sufficient to explain the difference between moral reasons and the mobster's reason (Cohen 1996; Lebar 2001). In fact, this seems to be revealed also by Korsgaard's (1996) treatment of the mafioso case. She insists that the mobster fails to provide public reasons. The natural follow up of this line of reasoning would be to deny that mobsters are bound by genuine reasons and obligations. This is not, however, the course Korsgaard takes. Instead, she claims that mobsters do have reasons and are bound by special obligations, which spring from their particular practical identity as mafioso, that is, the identity under which they understand and value themselves. These particularistic reasons and obligations, even though they are "shallow," eventually conflict with the "deeper" reasons that spring from one's moral identity. Korsgaard's treatment of the mafioso case is interesting because it shows that the crucial notion of publicity at stake is neither semantic nor epistemic. If it were semantic, the response would be that the mafioso does not have proper reasons. But her solution suggests instead that the mafioso has genuine reasons deriving from his practical identity. Her resolution of the case rests on the argument that the unqualified moral identity is deeper and more fundamental than any other practical identity under which individuals understand and value themselves. Thus the experience of a conflict between the moral identity and the practical identity is damaging in a radical sense, because it undermines the agent's metaphysical integrity. My present interest is to call attention to the fact that Korsgaard crucially deploys the notion of practical identity in explaining how reasons are generated in the mafioso's case, even though she originally articulates the problem in terms of publicity. To this extent, her proposal in terms of practical identities does not really address the problem of the public nature of reasons.

In previous work, I have argued that many of the mafia practices are grounded on an implicit agreement and produce obligations that are binding even in the particular occasion in which they are not in the interests of any one singular individual. This indicates that mafia affiliates cannot be understood as mere egoists. They do not act solely in view of their particular interests, and while their hierarchical structure indicates that their practices favour subjection, it also indicates that there are duties of loyalty and reverence for the special status of the ones in power. Therefore, there is an important sense in which mobsters act on principles in the sense that they are bound by obligations to their superiors, and are bonded by mutual accountability. However, such bonds and obligations are conditional upon membership in a local community. Because the normative relations are subjected to membership, and grounded in the interests of the members, they are also vulnerable to shifts and changes in their grounds. As a result, the kind of cooperation available is limited and constrained. The interests at stake in mafia relations are not only material (black market, finance investment, control of local stores), they are also, and more important, symbolic, and concern social status and the currency associated with it such as public goods like assistance, shelter, and occupation. The stability of obligations and social bonds is maintained by threats and acts of violence: external competitors on the market, internal competitors for leading positions (Bagnoli 2009). Alliances fluctuate according to shifts in interests and, since everyone is represented as "having a price," such character traits as duplicity, secrecy, concealment, and silence become necessary virtues alongside loyalty and fidelity. Nonetheless, it would be too simplistic to assert that mobsters do not think or act on principles, hence failing to produce public reasons in the semantic or epistemic sense.

To adequately address the problem, I suggest that we introduce a third sense of publicity. In this third sense, reasons are public insofar as they are generated by a reasoning constrained by the claim that others have equal normative standing (Bagnoli 2007). To relate to others as equals does not correspond to adopting reasons that work for everybody without qualifications, as happens in formalist interpretations of the requirement of universality. Public reasons have a grip on us insofar as we relate to others as equals. In this reading, respect as mutual recognition of status is a constitutive constraint on reasoning and ensures that reasoners produce effective reasons; that is, reasons are genuinely public. Reasoning is conceived as a communal practice that practical subjects enter to solve communal problems. Respecting others and ourselves as having equal standing is a constitutive feature of the practical standpoint and plays a crucial role in responding effectively in the world. To be effective, we need to take into proper consideration that we live in a world shared with other people like us, that is, similarly equipped and similarly vulnerable and dependent (O'Neill 1996, 99–106).

This third sense of publicity usefully distinguishes reasons that are moral insofar as they address others as equals, and reasons that appear to be moral but have limited applicability. This third sense of publicity also shows what is wrong with particularistic reasons: their efficacy and normative authority is limited. They are items that count as valuable only in the exchange with members of the same community, sensitive to the same considerations that are grounded on a shared sense of what is in their interest as a member of that community.

The promised advantage of this proposal is that it produces reasons that claim universal authority. Reasons that are public in the third sense are not anchored to any one particular interest, and thus they cannot serve as special motivations for special people. Critics hold that this represents a weakness of the universalist proposal, because it severs the linkages between reasons for action and particular motives, derived for instance from membership in a particular community. But I hope to show that this feature is indeed an aspect of strength precisely because it does not restrict its appeal to particular communities. I do not mean to neglect the problem of the linkages between reasons and special motivations, however, because the threat of producing reasons that are universally valid but ineffective is a real challenge. My way of addressing the challenge is to show that reasons are not separated from our interests and concerns, even though they are not anchored on one particular set of interests and concerns. It may be that such universal reasons fail to be motivating in the case of conflicts of interests, but they do serve an overarching role in structuring normative relations and they have paramount importance precisely in the context of conflict resolution strategies. Mafia conflicts can be explained and treated in this way.

I have argued that in forming reasons for action, agents necessarily refer to relevant others to whom they address their rational justification. The scope of relevant others is neither fixed by nature nor by logical or semantic considerations. It is, instead, a normative *task*, and there are different (philosophical) proposals as to how to carry out the task effectively. The constructivist view I defend is that this normative task can be carried out most effectively by producing reasons that address others as equals rather than as members in a particular community. This proposal is meant to generate reasons that justify a course of action publicly rather than relatively to special communities.

Beyond Territorial Bonds: The Virtues of Virtual Communities

In traditional communities, geographical boundaries are important normative sources. Belonging to a place does not immediately translate into belonging to a distinctive community, but it is a fact of normative relevance. When we ask where people are from, the question is rarely prompted by geographical interest. It often arises in contexts where the issue of the relevant membership is crucial. It is exactly because placing oneself is crucial that people employ stereotypes and prejudices: they serve as heuristics to solve the problem of the relevant others. They are in the most generic and trivial sense discriminatory, insofar as they serve to direct the placement of others inside or outside the boundaries. How to define the boundaries, however, is a practical exercise. Placing oneself in a certain community is a normative act that identifies bonds and responsibilities within that community. For instance, there are special obligations to neighbours that do not apply to complete foreigners. There are norms of etiquette and good manners that are especially directed to govern physical proximity. Where you are placed matters not only to define the bounds of your relevant community, but also to identify the sorts of reasons that count as such for your relevant others.

Territorial bonds, bonds created by the transformation of territorial spaces into places, provide the baseline for forming reasons that have a local authority and thus limited effect. The lead I want to follow is that while in traditional societies territorial considerations fix the reference to relevant others, in the web era the boundaries are more flexible and porous, largely disconnected from reference to geographic territory. This fact indicates that territorial bonds represent a less significant normative source than they have been in the past, and I want to suggest this is a relevant factor that potentially plays in favour of the development and expansion of antimafia culture.

Virtual communities are not different from traditional communities in some relevant respects. To state that a place implicates a "configuration of positions" (Augé 1995, 21) has distinctive normative implications. To situate oneself in a place is to situate oneself in a web of normative relations. Narratives of the self are normative narratives. Likewise, narratives that traverse and organize places are normative ways to build communities and form ties. Placing oneself in a web community is taking oneself to have responsibilities and duties relative to a specific membership. To this extent, membership in a virtual community is perfectly like membership in an offline community governed by norms. Reference to norms makes it apparent that the selection of the relevant others in web communication is not ultimately "individualistic." Yet the construction of the antimafia web community is subjected to constraints that are less substantial than traditional group forming constraints. For instance, one may encounter the antimafia website by chance, enter for reasons that have nothing to do with one's birthplace, ethnic origin, personal history, family ties, and so on. One may enter simply because she or he is attracted by the "principle of justice." Second, reasons for joining the community may be less strong and permanent. The strength of such communities is that they offer the opportunity to form and endorse identity outside the confines of a place defined by boundaries of physical contiguity (Augé 1995, 27). This indicates that the spatiotemporal dimension of community is a dynamic dimension, defined by negotiation through normative practices. In global communication, people can situate themselves more discretionally, and consequently fix more discretionally the class of reference. Territorial bonds do not represent a strict normative guidance. In addition to this discretional feature, opacity plays an important role. Opacity favours the possibility to sign up with a fake identity and dare to do things that one would not do in physical presence or knowing that there is a high risk of being discovered and publically exposed. In direct communication you are face to face with the other, and thus you can read facial expressions and capture messages that are not mediated by language but are expressed through bodily and non-verbal communication. In web communication users have more control over the information they want their interlocutors to know. To this extent, opacity works in favour of protecting one's real identity, if desired. This feature is Janus-faced and can work either way. On the one hand, it offers protection to mafia worshippers and sympathizers. Apparently, there are sites where hundreds of young admirers of violence, mainly fanboys of mafia bosses, reportedly discuss the bloody practices of real or fictional mobster figures. On the other hand, however, the opacity of web communication may work in favour of legality because it can protect from retaliation and, more importantly, because it serves as a repository of knowledge about the structure and consequences of illegality, while offering concrete resources to counter its effects. Resistance to illegality may profit from opacity and thus thrive on the internet.

The web era has facilitated the advent and consolidation of non-profit antimafia organizations, which invest in fighting ignorance, collecting and protecting the memory of the past, and educating by redirecting individuals to worthwhile activities. Perhaps more important, web communication amplifies and broadens the spectrum of people interested in the culture of legality. In the beginning, people who launched antimafia initiatives often had been personally wounded by the mafia, as in the case of Rita Borsellino, whose brother, Judge Paolo Borsellino, was slain by the mafia. Other people started cooperating with the justice system after losing family members in mafia battles, as in the case of Rita Atria. Raised in a mafia family, she became a witness for the Italian state seeking justice for the murders of her father and brother during the years of clan warfare in the 1980s and early 1990s. Arguably, at the outset, people actively involved in antimafia movements often act out of personal interests, broadly speaking; that is, people acting in the pursuit of an amelioration of their own territorial community. By contrast, in the web era, antimafia sympathizers do not necessarily live in areas controlled by the mafia. Their interest in joining the activities of non-profit organizations can be explained in a way that does not refer to their membership in a particular community: they strive for a better world, and operate for a more civilized and peaceful society. In short, they are driven by civic virtues rather than by interests grounded in a special membership in a territorial community. However, civic virtues are not abstract qualities that deprive citizens of their origins and culture. In fact, morally oriented reasoning is public in nature, but it does not encourage uprooting one's culture and denying one's particular identity. The claim is, rather, that reasons are public items serving the purpose of mutual justification. Mutual justification is crucial in any dealing where conflicts of interests are amenable to rational resolution. Furthermore, for the purpose of this argument, legality is broadly assimilated into publicity. This is because legality is a normative notion, distinct from the legality of positive law. In the account I have given, legality rests on its public, hence rational, foundation. It is not a consequence of this argument that legality requires abiding by any positive law, since there might be laws that are immoral. In this latter case, legality as based on publicity provides a normative criterion for distinguishing between morally legitimate and illegitimate laws. An implication of the argument is also that public reasoning does not amount to what people de facto share. Public is a normative concept that provides the criterion for selecting the considerations that legitimately count as reasons.

Structural Forms of Recognition, New Modes of Empowerment

I have suggested that the weakening of territorial bonds, which is characteristic of social networking and formation of practical identities in the web era, is a resource for antimafia culture. The novelty of the modes of empowerment that web communication allows should not be exaggerated, however. The possibility of empowerment depends on structural forms of recognition that are common to all forms of resistance to illegality. Structurally, there is nothing new about the virtual modes of fighting the mafia, insofar as they are modes of building a moral community based on mutual respect and recognition rather than on territorial or communitarian bonds. But the effectiveness and practical impact of these structures also depend in key ways on the new opportunities that technology indicates. I want to end this exploratory argument in a constructive spirit by examining a successful example of community empowerment, constructed by Libera, which deploys web communication in notably effective ways.

As of December 2015, Libera coordinates some 1,500 units, comprising associations, groups, and schools. Since its founding, Libera has understood and emphasized the importance of education and information in the fight against the mafia. Its basic idea is that punitive interventions and corrective policies, while necessary and appropriate, do not suffice to effectively combat and eradicate the culture of illegality. Empowerment is viewed in terms of many different and capillary activities that aim at alerting, informing, and mobilizing civil society in the fight against the mafia, while also promoting legality and justice. To fulfil these purposes, Libera uses new technologies and social networks extensively and knowingly, articulating the awareness that these are important tools for informing and connecting citizens. Libera's website both performs and offers a variety of concrete activities. For example, it provides information about the social use of goods and properties confiscated from the mafia; conducts didactic and pedagogical projects that involve schools; organizes research that involves universities; and provides volunteer camps open to individuals, families, groups, and associations. The network also conducts large campaigns to inform visitors and members about freedom, loansharking, extortion, and exploitation. In addition to its website, Libera is present on the major social networks such as Facebook, Twitter, Gmail, Pinterest, and YouTube. The website is designed to inform, keep alive the memory of the past, educate about legality, and promote engagement and commitment.

While Libera coordinates units that operate in specific territories, the recruitment policy that it adopts is not territorial. Its cultural campaign does not target specific territories or social categories. What I find most interesting is the way the prospective members are addressed: "And you? Which side are you on?" The question is directed to any anonymous user, not because of their identity, history, and tradition, but as moral agents. This specific form of address to visitors' functions in what Paula Salvio analyses as a set of complex engagements that articulate Libera's online and offline actions (see her chapter elsewhere in this book, especially pages 85–6). In this system of address, a moral judgment is implied.[3] The implication of the address is that by not actively operating for legality and empowerment, one implicitly favours the mafia. The moral judgment is meant to alert the prospective members against the dangers of indifference, ignorance, and negligence. This is an interesting aspect of a strategic interaction, because it shows that Libera does not take for granted its intended audience. Rather, it builds up an audience, first by sensitizing the anonymous users to the civic, moral, and political dangers of indifference, lack of engagement or withdrawal, and then by pointing to the concrete results of cooperative action.

A second interesting feature of the website is that it highlights activities of the association as a result achieved through a *cooperative effort*. To underscore cooperation as the key in the fight against the mafia achieves different results: it solicits communal interest in joining the community and it combats the individual psychological tendency to feel alone and powerless against a too pervasive and powerful force. This is not a fight in which individuals can engage by themselves. Joining a communal effort differs from adding one's single act to many other single acts. In other words, the message conveyed is that the fight against the mafia works as a shared goal rather than as an individual activity. In fact, the website also emphasizes that this association is part of a much larger plan and shows links to governmental institutions, such as Interpol. Showing connections and linkages to other governmental sites is a powerful way to demonstrate that there is a ramified activity against illegality rather than individual, scattered, and sporadic action. Furthermore, bridging different institutions and associations, which work towards the same social cause, has the effect of building a sense of community, independent from territorial bonds. The bounds of the community are drawn by a communal sense of purpose. To this extent, Libera creates social identity by an intelligent use of social networks. At the same time, the social network provides motivational support to its prospective members, an important safety net for individuals that are motivated to work collaboratively against the mafia, but cannot count on the moral support of their environment.

The third notable feature of the website is how it maps and illustrates the activities in detail, so the occasional user gains an immediate and vivid impression of what the association concretely does for promoting legality. Web communication makes these activities traceable in time and testifies to their existence and continuity through time. In this respect, the protection of memory is an important feature, which gives the members a sense of restitution, and it also demonstrates how ideals of justice can be put into practice to effectively transform territorial realities. Tracking this transformation in time and showing the continuity and permanence of intervention are particularly important tasks. They are not only demonstrative and inspirational for the prospective members, but also play a motivational role for the active members of the moral community. Such members are vulnerable to the sense of isolation and despair, especially when they lack external cooperation. The normal sense of impotence that one might feel in massively corrupted social realities is amplified by the discontinuity of governmental political support. This is a well-known aspect of the failure to oppose the mafia through activities that rely solely on state funding and that are subject to the change of governmental policies. Taking action through the social network, instead, gives the user a sense of membership in a community that shares ideals and resources, is not temporally bound, and counts on mutual support and recognition.

I have commented on the moralistic tone of some posts and forms of address. In its recruiting policy, Libera clearly starts from the individual. It exhorts the anonymous users to consider what they have done to fight against the mafia. It stigmatizes omissions and lack of activity as passive forms of co-responsibility on which illegality thrives. Exemplifying this point is the post, "The first real reform to enact is in *our conscience*. We can't ask others to act if we don't assume our share of responsibility" (italics mine).[4] The presumption of this rhetoric seems to be that transformation of the individual conscience is the starting point for public transformation. The claim is that transformation is a cultural change that ought to be operated at the individual level. At its moralizing peaks, the prose uses the first-person plural, which entails that the occasional reader is already a prospective ally: if you are visiting this site, you are with us in the fight against the mafia, and more broadly, in the larger war for freedom, equality, and social justice. Libera tells us,

> We have to understand where we made a mistake in order to push forward and defeat mafia organizations and corruption, to really affirm in Italy, Europe, and the rest of the world the values of freedom, equality, and social justice ... We have to rethink solidarity, so it's no longer an excuse

for people who don't want to discuss inequalities and privileges so they
can affirm their own rights ... We have to live by ethics so that integrity
and transparency are truly the heart of politics and the economy.[5]

Here, the moral address also creates a sense of expanding the boundaries of the relevant readership, from the national boundaries of Italy, to
Europe, and to the rest of the world. The insistence on the geographical
progression (Italy, Europe, the world) implies that the problems of the
mafia are not peculiar to and distinctive of Italy. The suggestion works
as a diagnostic tool insofar as it presents the Italian situation as affected
by the same structural problems as those of other regions of the world
where illegality thrives. This presentation may be strategic insofar as it
normalizes the Italian case, at least undermining the image of Italy as
a peculiar study case that resists classification under any more general
category. This "normalizing approach" also suggests that if the problem of Italy is the same problem that affects other regions of the world,
then the solution that is applicable to the Italian situation may be similar to the one effective elsewhere. The merit of this approach is that it
elicits a sense of human fellowship, presenting the fight against the Italian mafia as a part and parcel of a larger war against illegality and for
a culture of freedom and justice. The emphasis on good practices and
continuing education aims to encourage and sustain active membership in the larger community of legality.

In short, the case of Libera shows that an intelligent use of social
networks serves the purpose of developing, educating about, and
expressing civic virtues, and represents a powerful tool in the fight
against the mafia.[6] Territorial membership is a source of vulnerability
insofar as deviance from the norm is more easily detected, exposed,
and punished by the mafia. By contrast, web communication refo-
cuses on other virtues that are unrelated to loyalty to clans and territory. Through social networking, Libera articulates and spreads the
conceptual vocabulary of legality that is crucial in promoting moral
and political awareness; it teaches the concepts of freedom, dignity,
citizenship, responsibility, information, democracy, legality, transparency, justice, truth, solidarity, and development. These terms are not
simply words but concepts that constitute an alternative framework
to the mafia. They are not merely hermeneutical instruments that help
the citizens to understand and interpret their social reality, but also
tools to change it. These concepts play a crucial role in the attempt to
build the social structure and strengthen the social fabric. Thus, as this

exploratory study demonstrates, the process transforming (cyber)space into antimafia places, as well as the norms, tools, and practices of legality employed by citizens actively constituting them clearly merit further close scrutiny.

NOTES

With gratitude I dedicate this essay to Fabio Viti, who despite himself is responsible for my scattered readings in anthropology.

1 In 2008, *Eurispes* cited Libera as one of the Italian excellencies. In 2012, *The Global Journal* inserted the organization among the first hundred world NGOs. For a brief history of Libera and its activities, see Salvio's chapter "'A Taste of Justice'" in this volume.
2 See for instance, Fricker (2011).
3 Baris Cayli devotes extensive analysis to the moral dimension of antimafia communication in the discussion he conducts here on Giuseppe Fava's ethical code and, in his 2013 article "Creating Counterpublics against the Italian Mafia," on the scope of Libera Informazione.
4 See http://www.libera.it/flex/cm/pages/ServeBLOB.php/L/IT/IDPagina/1. "Ecco perché la prima vera riforma da attuare è quella delle *nostre coscienze*: non possiamo chiedere ad altri di agire quando noi non ci assumiamo la nostra quota di responsabilità" (italics mine).
5 See http://www.libera.it/flex/cm/pages/ServeBLOB.php/L/IT/IDPagina/1. "Dobbiamo capire dove abbiamo sbagliato per andare oltre e vincere le mafie e la corruzione, per affermare davvero in Italia, in Europa e nel resto del mondo i valori della libertà, dell'uguaglianza e della giustizia sociale... dobbiamo ripensare la solidarietà, perché non sia più la scusa di chi non vuole mettere in discussione disuguaglianze e privilegi per affermare diritti ... dobbiamo vivere l'etica, perché integrità e trasparenza siano davvero il cuore della politica e dell'economia."
6 I speak of civic virtues, and these are related in important ways to ethical values, such as truth, justice, and freedom. In chapter 2 of this volume, "When a Journalist Defies More Than the Mafia," Cayli demonstrates how these values form the foundation of Giuseppe Fava's professional code that serves as a legacy shaping contemporary web-based antimafia journalism.

2 When a Journalist Defies More Than the Mafia: The Legacy of Giuseppe Fava and Italian Antimafia Culture

BARIS CAYLI

Two Shots and Five Bullets in Catania

Giuseppe Fava, a newspaper editor, author and playwright who was regarded as one of Italy's most outspoken campaigners against organized crime, has been slain, the police said today. Mr. Fava's body, shot twice, was discovered Thursday night in his parked car here. The police said he had gone to pick up his granddaughter, who was rehearsing a part in a theater comedy. Mr. Fava, 59 years old, wrote several books dealing with Sicily.

Only last week he appeared on a nationally televised talk show to discuss the Mafia.

Antimafia campaigner, New York Times,
7 January 1984

With its first report on 7 January 1984, the *New York Times* announced the death of the internationally acclaimed journalist Giuseppe Fava. Two days earlier, five bullets ranging from 5 to 7.65 millimetres took Fava's life on the street next to the Verga Theatre, where his plays were frequently performed (Ward 2007, 8). Just the week before his death, on 28 December 1983, Fava was the guest of Enzo Biagi's popular TV program on *Retequattro*. Fava was one of the few people who boldly denounced the criminal networks, the names of the mafiosi, and the changing character of the mafia in Sicily. In his last interview with Enzo Biagi, Fava's shocking revelations once again created trouble for the leading mafiosi figures on a nationally broadcast television program. Mincing no words, he charged:

Mafiosi are in the Parliament, sometimes they are ministers, sometimes they are bankers, mafiosi are those who are in charge of the nation right now. You cannot define a "mafioso" as a small time crook who forces you to pay a cut of your small business. This is small stuff that exists in all Italian cities, in all European cities. The problem of the mafia is much greater, much more tragic. (Fava 1983a)

The assassination of Fava was not an entirely surprising event, given his unrelenting, concise disclosures about mafia crimes in print, television broadcasts, and film. His attacks against the mafia's expanding power in Catania reached their peak in the early 1980s, when the different mafia clans increased their illicit revenues through their entrepreneurial skills and collaboration with corrupt politicians and bureaucrats. Perhaps Fava's (1983b) famous article "I quattro cavalieri dell'apocalisse mafiosa" (The four horsemen of the mafia apocalypse) should be noted as a milestone that paved the way for his murder. Fava publicly condemned the mafia's social and political networks in Catania. The article, published in *I Siciliani* on 1 January 1983, revealed precise information about the criminal business deals of the Santapaola clan, which was the notorious mafia syndicate of Catania. The mafia wars in Sicily and the murders of prominent public figures in the early 1980s created widespread despondency among Sicilians. The ruthless power of the mafia clans was at a height when the hit man of the mafia boss Nitto Santapaola killed General Carlo Alberto Dalla Chiesa, the most powerful official in the antimafia fight, on 3 September 1982. After this shocking murder, Fava represented a relatively easy target for Nitto Santapaola, whose orders to assassinate the journalist were carried out by the hit man Maurizio Avola, the boss's nephew.

However, it took more than ten years to discover the perpetrators behind the murder of Fava. On 18 May 1993, Nitto Santapaola was arrested. This arrest was made possible by Maurizio Avola's decision to become a *pentito*, in other words a mafioso who turns state's evidence, ostensibly repents, and provides evidence against the mafia. Eventually, Avola confessed to the murder of Giuseppe Fava and revealed the names of those who ordered and organized his killing. Fava's slaying was truly a demoralizing event among the fellow Sicilians who shared his same principles, which were fundamental for building the future of their homeland. Yet his death spurred new ethical codes of truth, democratic freedom, and justice, which were Fava's guiding principles for ruling the polity and shaping sociocultural life.

In the following discussion, I focus on Fava's ethical codes and explore how they constitute a legacy of socially committed journalism, which functions as both a weapon to defeat mafia organizations and culture, and contributes to the formation of antimafia writers working in online journalism today. In order to understand the significance of Fava's ethical practices of investigative reporting on the mafia in the 1970s and the early 1980s, it is beneficial to situate him in relation to a few of the Italian journalists who conducted inquiries into Cosa Nostra in the postwar period. For example, after contributing articles to such dailies as *Il tempo di Sicilia* and *Il mattino di Sicilia*, the award-winning Mauro De Mauro (1921–1970?) earned recognition at the newspaper *L'ora* for his investigations of the relations between Cosa Nostra and major political figures, the drug industry, and illegal construction. Dubbed the "inconvenient journalist" (*il giornalista scomodo*), due to his public revelations about mafia criminals and corrupt politicians, De Mauro was kidnapped on 16 September 1970. His remains have never been found, fuelling conspiracy theories to this day about his death and the potential collusion between members of Cosa Nostra, the Italian government, and the secret services. Mario Francese (1925–1979) is best known for his socially committed investigative articles published at the Palermo newspaper *Il Giornale di Sicilia*, which examined such important subjects as the mafia Ciaculli massacre on 30 June 1963, when a car bomb killed five carabinieri and two members of the Italian Army; the power structure of the various mafia clans and the names of bosses ruling them; and the Corleonesi clan in particular, headed by Salvatore Riina, later convicted of ordering the murder of Francese. Francese was killed in front of his Palermo home on 26 January 1979. Although Michele Pantaleone (1911–2002) worked for achieving civil democratic rights, justice, and the defeat of the mafia in his capacities as a politician in the 1940s and the 1960s, and a journalist at *L'ora* in Palermo, he is likely most renowned for his numerous books that analyse a range of problems produced by the Sicilian mafia. Among his important studies are *The Mafia and Politics* (1966), *Mafia e droga* (1966), *Mafia e antimafia* (1992), and *Omertà di stato* (1993). Though his career was brief, the poet, antimafia activist, and journalist Giuseppe Impastato (1948–1978) is particularly noteworthy. Born in a mafia family in Cinisi, in his personal and professional life Impastato performed radical critiques of mafia power, politics, and business. Among his accomplishments is the creation of the independent radio station Radio Aut in 1976, where he broadcast constant attacks on the mafia that challenged the mafiosi

and the public image they aim to project as so-called men of honour demanding respect. Significant here is the radio program "Onda
pazza" (Crazy broadcast), in which Impastato employed sharply witty
satire targeting the Cinisi mafia boss Gaetano Badalamenti, along with
the multiple crimes he and fellow mafiosi committed, often in collusion
with city leaders and business people. On 9 May 1978, Impastato was
murdered by the mafia, his body staged to make it look as if he had set
a bomb in a failed terrorist attack. In 2002, Gaetano Badalamenti was
finally found guilty for ordering the murder.

   While keeping in mind the varied contributions made by journalists
who published valuable investigations into the mafia and its crimes, I
want to focus here on the particular ethics and works that distinguish
Fava's contributions to both the field of antimafia journalism in the
seventies and the eighties and, subsequently, the practices and roles of
web-based antimafia journalism, as the current practitioners endeavour to change the sociopolitical and cultural landscape of the country.
The analysis draws upon the full range of Fava's journalistic productions, which include documentaries that he produced, his books, and
the articles he wrote for *Il Giornale del Sud* and *I Siciliani*. After examining the multiple perspectives on the mafia, Italian society, and politics that Fava crafted and his primary ethical codes, I focus on how his
legacy shapes contemporary web-based antimafia journalism as exemplified by two significant online news sites: I Siciliani giovani and Libera Informazione. Fava is a pivotal figure in relation to these antimafia
online news organizations. I Siciliani giovani was formed specifically
to sustain Fava's ethical principles of journalism and civil life, as incorporated in his publication *I Siciliani*. Similarly, Libera Informazione has
solid connections with I Siciliani giovani, and has organized events at
which Fava's legacy is recalled to cultural memory in order to mobilize the participants around his principles of civil responsibility and the
antimafia fight against all crimes, corruption, injustice, and oppression.

Giuseppe Fava's Three Ethical Codes: Truth, Freedom, and Justice

Three years before his death, Fava introduced new epistemological dynamics into journalism as a profession. On 11 October 1981, he
stated, "I have an ethical concept of journalism" (Fava 1981). This concise, powerful declaration indicates how Fava constituted the foundation of his philosophy as a journalist and pioneered a reforming path of
journalism by making ethics the keystone of informing the public about

difficult social problems and their solutions. However, neither Fava nor scholars who examine his works have analysed the principles of his professional ethics, or how he conceptualized and enacted them. Based upon Fava's numerous articles, interviews, films, and documentaries, I propose that there are three utmost ethical principles comprised by Fava's guiding concept that he put into practice while working as an investigative journalist. These three principles are truth, freedom, and justice, which also create the realms of Fava's socially committed journalism. The truth is the primary principle that should form the polity in society. Hence, with the help of truth, every citizen has the opportunity to learn the core mechanism of political decisions, apparently mysterious policy changes that influence everyday life, and the mutual collaboration between the state and non-state forces. Nevertheless, it is necessary to consolidate the second principle, freedom, in society to pave the path of truth because only a free society, whose members are not suppressed by the powerful, is able to sustain the truth as the fabric of ethical and moral culture. Thus, the two ethical principles of truth and freedom are functionalized to bring justice into the sociocultural sphere of society and legal regulations of governance. Indeed, justice comes to the fore as the final ethical tenet and governing force of the conflated power of truth and freedom. Therefore, justice, the third ethical principle, is an outcome of the complex interrelationships between truth and freedom, as these two ethical precepts constitute the essential dynamics of justice. Fava referred to each of these principles as a metanarrative while telling his story, in which the mafia functioned as the main antagonist. In this specific context, the roles of truth, freedom, and justice may be understood as the responsibility to tell the truth about the mafia and the numerous problems it produces in social, economic, political, and cultural life; freedom from mafia oppression in the aforementioned spheres, levied through acts and threats of violence; and justice in the sense of transparent, honest, and equitable action in the system of law and its enforcement, and in the sense of equality for all citizens, guaranteeing equal access to human rights. These ethical principles as practised by Fava contribute to both socially engaged forms of journalism and the culture of legality in daily living.

Fava's ethical approach to journalism was neither superficial nor illusory. He knew the strengths and weaknesses of the mafia clans and eventually recognized the realities of this chronic social problem, underlining the importance of the state's contribution to fighting the mafia. With the engagement of the state in the antimafia campaign, it would be possible to defeat mafia culture and bring the third ethical principle, justice, into the core governing mechanism of society. Accordingly, he stated:

> If five million Sicilians rebelled against the Mafia, nothing would happen at all ... The real enemies of the mafia are a true State, the rule of law, the judges who really bring justice, incorruptible officials, and politicians authorizing their duties with the interpretation of absolute morality. (1983c)

Fava's recognition of the vital importance of state power and its institutions to dismantle mafia organizations and unflinching critiques concerning the state-mafia collusion indicate his analytical acuity and commitment to rebuilding civil society.

On 5 April 1976, Fava's use of the metaphor of cancer to express the character of the mafia and its sociocultural effects drew public attention. Referring to the mafia as a deadly disease, he aimed to reveal the destructive power of the syndicate in the entire city of Catania. He tells readers, the mafia

> is not simply crime committed in the background of extortion, corruption, and bad governance. Catania is the city wherein small groups of young people living with the impossibility of continuing their assaults against the banks, post offices and the jewelers, have devoted themselves to a darker, more sordid and tranquil kind of criminal speculation, which is extortion aimed at public institutions. This is happening in Catania and this is the mafia. Whatever one may say, this is the mafia. The mafia is the struggle between conflicting criminal interests that plunder the economic benefits of a city and create a monopoly of violence and fear to subdue citizens. ("Gli anni dell'Espresso sera")

This definition of the mafia invokes the mafia's omnipotent status as a disease that prevents attempts to attain truth, freedom, and justice. Expanding upon the pathology of the mafia's causes and development, Fava defined the sociocultural situation of Southern Italy and particularly of Catania with the coinage "Catania syndrome" in his famous article "Sindrome Catania" (1983c). This syndrome consists of the sociopsychological dynamics of a decayed society that lacks the necessary qualities to reveal the truth. The detachment from the truth summarizes the precarious sociocultural context in which the mafia determines the macro dynamics of social order.

Fava's analysis of the Catania syndrome draws out its many symptomatic elements and effects, which include the socio-economic gap between the rich and the poor in the urban centre and peripheries of the city. Fava underlines the settlement of the 200 richest people of Catania along the entire coastline of Acitrezza, from San Gregorio and Gravina to Mascalucia and Tremestieri. The luxury villas, buildings, and villages of the upper-crust of Catania represent symbols of power and bring into relief dramatic contrasts with the emigration of Catania's poor and unemployed to the ghettos and slums of Turin and Milan to seek a better life. Fava continues his social critique of the Catania urban text, informing readers,

> The changing character of the urban settlement pushed the poor people of Catania into the maze of streets and crumbling buildings of the new neighborhoods such as San Berillo, Librino and Monte Po. Two hundred thousand deprived people of Catania live where the social and public services give the image that nothing has changed in one hundred years in this part of the country ... The marginalized population of Catania perhaps could be better understood through increasing delinquency among its young people who could not find even a place to play football. (1983c)

The social realities of the Catania syndrome lie in the dependency and submission of the residents of Catania to the mafia's enduring power. Fava astutely calls attention to the mafia extortion racket as key to the criminal clans' power and the Catania syndrome in everyday life. Accordingly, Fava tells us:

> You can either accept or deny it, but you cannot change the fact that ninety percent of the business and commercial sector pay extortion money to the mafia clans in Catania. Yet more tragic outcomes are followed by the bloody clashes between rival clans that compete to gain the control of the drug trafficking. The victims of these clashes are the people of Catania, not the outsiders. Catania is a city where a small town politician can become a governor of the territory and an obscure provincial contractor can become a Knight of Labor so everything he touches turns to gold. An affable entrepreneur, the friend of good bourgeois salons, who shook the hands of the prefects and deputies, could be accused of killing Dalla Chiesa within a few months. This is the Catania syndrome. (1983c)

Fava's multidimensional struggle to articulate the social and cultural dynamics of Sicily reached beyond his articles in the newspapers. Fava moved to Rome at the end of the 1970s, and worked for RAI, the national Italian broadcast association. There he made films and documentaries related to Sicily, its history, and people. Among the documentaries, *Da Villalba a Palermo (Siciliani, Cronache di mafia)* is striking for the way Fava masterfully demonstrates how the mafia and its culture are embedded within the social structure and shape the beliefs, words, and actions of the local people in their everyday lives. Co-directed by Fava and Vittorio Sindoni and filmed in 1980, the documentary puts before viewers' eyes the local power of the mafia, which seems impossible to challenge from the local people's perspectives. In one scene, Fava approaches a group of young people standing in the middle of the street in Palermo, and asks one of the young men, "Why does the mafia exist in Palermo, Sicily?" The young man seems puzzled at first and says, "I don't exactly know the reason but it's an ancient problem." Fava probes the issue of the "ancient problem" and immediately directs one more question to the young man. In an authoritative voice, he asks, "Do you think the mafia still exists today?" This time, the young man has no doubts and responds very precisely, "No, no!" Such an accurate and disappointing answer is no surprise at all. The young man's response shows not only the detrimental silence the local people observe amidst the mafia's dominating power, but also reveals the denial of the very existence of the mafia. After this negation of the mafia's existence, Fava approaches another boy to discover his reactions to the idea of collaborating with the police and state forces if a crime is witnessed. Fava asks, "If you see a person who is shot and murdered by someone that you know, in broad daylight in the middle of the street in Corleone, do you go to the magistrate and say who the killer is?" The young boy says, "I prefer not to answer."

It is evident in the documentary that Fava's ethical code of truth in particular, and how it is exercised in a free society, depends on the factual realities lived and known by the local people and the free dissemination of the facts regarding them. More important, the realities of the local people shape the very form of the truth, as either distorted or accurate in relation to factual information. The urgent need for truth and its presentation to the public structured the mission that Fava embraced in his subsequent enquiries. Shortly after this documentary, Fava directed the then newly established *Il Giornale del Sud*. He put into practice a transparent, direct, and explicit approach while editing the newspaper. Other newspapers in Sicily periodically reported on the businesses of the mafia clans and corruption cases in their pages. However, exposing the specific names of those clans and their members was relatively limited. When I interviewed Gaetano Liardo from Libera Informazione, he informed me that the editors of the regional and even national newspapers would sometimes censor the news if the case involved mafia clans, as well as their relationships and networks with the leading political figures. This kind of censorship was one of the main reasons for establishing an independent, web-based news establishment (interview by author, 5 January 2011). The censoring of so-called sensitive information was contrary to the journalistic efforts of Fava and his ethical code. Thus, when the first issue of *Il Giornale del Sud* was published on 4 June 1980, Fava ambitiously explained three fundamental words shaping the mission and goal of the newspaper: people, justice, and truth in his article "Con amore collera e speranza." With this explicit scope, Fava published meticulously researched inquiries into the expanding criminal industries of the specific clans, mafia bosses, and the politicians and bureaucrats who colluded with them. This consistent public scrutiny created difficult conditions for the mafia organizations and their collaborators, who were already known by the majority of the public. Indeed, their names found a huge space in the pages of the local newspaper *Il Giornale del Sud*. The dangers of such reporting cannot be minimized. In 1958, *L'ora* newspaper published the names of the powerful mafia bosses, their major business connections, and the political figures with whom they colluded. The newspaper's offices were bombed, as John Dickie notes (2004, 319).

Although local struggle is necessary to defy the territorial power of the mafia, Fava was among the first to publicly recognize that the crime organizations also constituted a national problem. Nevertheless, the mafia was predominantly perceived as a regional issue rather than a national one. From Fava's perspective, the notion of the mafia as a provincial issue presented various problems for the nation and the struggle to fight the mafias. He proposed the three principles defining his ethical code needed to be employed at the national level, an idea developed in his prominent book *Mafia. Da Giuliano a Dalla Chiesa*, published in 1982. This study made a profound contribution to understanding the historical evolution of the mafia in Italy. Through his brief presentation of the history of the mafia, a destructive power in Southern Italy for over 100 years, Fava argued that it was erroneous to think of the mafia as only a regional problem. Instead, in "I quattro cavalieri dell'apocalisse mafiosa" (1983b), he illustrates how the criminal organization produces a sociopolitical tragedy of national proportions generating material

problems throughout the entire country. Furthermore, the representation of the mafia as an isolated problem of Southern Italy aids mafia
clans by covering its adaptable character. The adaptability of the mafia
groups makes them particularly effective at profiting from new opportunities to conquer territories in Northern Italy even in the 1970s.
Viewing the mafia as restricted within the borders of Southern Italy
was popular in mainstream media, particularly after the Second World
War. The orientalist approach towards the definition of the mafia as a
"Southern Question" and its power in Southern Italy not only radical-
ized the problem, but also veiled the immense expansion of the mafia
groups across Northern Italian cities and communities in the 1970s and
the early 1980s. In this sense, the broader perspective Fava adopted in
his conception and approach to the mafia phenomena and their national
effects was foresightful, challenging, and reformative.

As part of Fava's socially committed journalism, several articles demonstrate his deep concern over the way truths are distorted as decep-
tions in Sicily. In the very first issue of *Il Giornale del Sud*, he expressed
his rage about buried truths and how the obstacles to uncovering them
were orchestrated and camouflaged by mainstream newspapers, official media outlets, hundreds of pages of court decisions, and police
reports. According to Fava in "Con amore collera e speranza" (1980), if
one is eager to learn the truth, it needs to be sought where those truths
lie in their diverse forms. His idea of truth and the effects of its repression in the sociocultural context of Sicily motivated his investigative
journalism. The mafia was a socio-economic, cultural, and historical
reality plundering society in every field, from sports to culture, politics to environmental problems. Thus, Fava declared that his editorial
mission at *Il Giornale del Sud* was to fight the mafia and its influence
on social and cultural spheres through each section of the newspaper,
which consisted of a total of thirty-two pages (1980).

The disinterest shown by the public reaction in northern Italian
towns towards the ongoing scandals in the southern part of the country
was pervasive. Fava believed it was imperative to close the social and
cultural gap between the south and north. Guided by this aim, Fava's
socially engaged journalism targeted the social problems of the country
in which the mafia was the primary cause of social erosion, produced
through its cultural mentality, socio-economic networks, and expanding power over different sectors of the country. These social problems
included different subjects examined from a wide range of perspectives.
Indeed, Fava covered environmental concerns of the small towns and

the catastrophic social outcomes that might have posed certain risks to Sicily in his articles. For instance, in "I Siciliani, perché?" (1983e), Fava wrote that the level of pollution in Priolo, which is a small industrial town in the province of Syracuse in Sicily, threatened the thousands of peoples' lives who had to live in this territory. He added that Comiso, miles away from Priolo, was under a severe threat as the United States Air Force had decided to deploy Ground Launch Cruise Missiles at the town's airbase in the early 1980s and had completed its deployment in June 1983. The second biggest nuclear heads in Europe were in the heart of Sicily, and if the airbase were destroyed, half of the entire island of Sicily would be erased from the map within minutes. Fava's microgeographic journalism dealt with a social problem even in a small town, and at the same time, proposed it must be addressed accordingly by the entire nation. Likewise, if the same or similar problem was created partly or completely by the mafia and through violating the moral codes of society, the public reaction should be at the national level. Fava's holistic approach was understandable at the time when Southern Italy was marginalized by the political figures with the power that could address its economic and social problems. Despondency thus prevailed among the citizens of the region. Accordingly, Fava claimed that "everything that happens in Milan, Rome, Venice, Turin for better or worse, belongs also to the South, to the Sicilians. What happens in the South and in Sicily, good, evil, fear, pain, poverty, violence, beauty, culture, hope, dreams, belongs to the whole nation" (1983e).

In addition to putting the mafia's economic affairs under public scrutiny, Fava also drew attention to the extensive and deep social networks of the mafias that eventually paralysed both Catania and its residents in the 1970s. This embedded mafia disease creates social and economic disaster, and likewise, hopelessness among the local people. In doing so, the mafia consolidates its persistent power, while tearing apart the social, cultural, and historical legacy of the society. Fava explained this contradictory interrelationship between the power of the mafia and the weaknesses of society by emphasizing how the Mediterranean basin, the birthplace of many admirable civilizations, was erased as uncivilized variants of the mafia and its culture territorialized the regions. Fava's (1980) dejected perspective is discernible in his statement:

We live in a country stained with blood ... from stupidity, vanity and the violence of the Powerful ...We, I mean the Sicilians, five million human beings, continue to delegate the less capable people to decide on our own destiny. Five million smart people who may be at the center of the Mediterranean civilization could not manage to organize and decide on their own destiny.

Fava continued underscoring his daily mission to renew Sicilian culture, driven by diverse emotions such as anger, love, and pride disseminated through the articles, reviews, and opinions in *Il Giornale del Sud*.

Il Giornale del Sud unquestionably became one of Fava's pioneering venues for spreading information about the mafiosi and denouncing the scandalous political-criminal nexus, as well as mafia expansion and diversification in business. Pino Arlacchi (1986) also addressed the emergence of the new mafia strategies in Sicily in the early 1980s, noting how they fostered relations with the business sector with a vigorous entrepreneurial spirit (5). Nevertheless, it was hard to find an institution or organization in which the mafia did not exert dominating power in the early 1980s. Similarly, Fava wrote extensively about the new areas, geographic and financial, that the mafia was developing. He particularly analysed how the mafia business network effectively infiltrated the legal economy. This infiltration was not limited to the business sector alone. It was running deep even in Fava's workplace. It became clear, as Alexander Stille (1996) notes, that the owner of *Il Giornale del Sud*, Gaetano Graci, had solid connections with corrupt politicians, judges, and the mafia (40, 71–2). Therefore, Fava and his young team left the newspaper, and undeterred, established their independent newspaper, *I Siciliani*, in 1983. The philosophy of journalism that Fava applied at *Il Giornale del Sud*, reporting astounding scandals and corruption news, also shaped the mission of *I Siciliani*. He conceived of *I Siciliani* as a newspaper that would cover all areas of life, people, and the region, including politics, current events, sports, local culture, entertainment, and art. In contrast to other newspapers, the form of *I Siciliani* was structured through its critical perspective that was based on exposing all facts and speaking truthfully about power. As a result, the writing in *I Siciliani* achieved recognition as cutting edge and authoritative, of equal if not greater stature than *Il Giornale del Sud*. For example, in his by now famous article "I quattro cavalieri dell'apocalisse mafiosa" (1983b), Fava exposed the business dealings between the businessmen Carmelo Costanza, Mario Rendo, Francesco Finocchiaro, and Gaetano Graci and the mafia, especially the crime boss Nitto Santapaola, and explained how the resultant financial network enabled the mafia to dominate the local economy of Catania.

Although the recent attention attracted by Roberto Saviano's 2008 non-fiction novel *Gomorrah*, applauded for the way it exposed the day-to-day business of the camorra in Campania, may lead one to believe that crime organization is a relatively recent development, in 1983 Fava published a detailed inquiry into the expansion of both Cosa Nostra and the camorra in terms of geographic territories and criminal undertakings with the Italian state and its institutions. His article "Mafia e camorra: chi sono, chi comanda?" (1983d) tersely argues that the state has functioned as an enemy for over a century in Sicily. Perceiving the state as a nemesis has historically been shaped by certain rational paradigms and oppressive governing methods of the state. These methods included the tax system, tariffs, obligatory military enlistment, and confiscation. The unification of Italy was neither able to win the citizens' hearts nor decrease their degree of hostility against the state. Indeed, persistent disappointments among the citizens of the new state brought a "bitter solitude" (1983e). He added that the political developments within the last forty years made it clear that Palermo, the capital city of Sicily, was a colony of the Roman power. The dramatic failure of the *Cassa per il Mezzogiorno* (Fund for the South), plundered by embezzlement, fraudulent use of public works funds, corruption, and violence made the local economy collapse and tore apart the region. Finally, the dreadful crisis of the justice system came to the fore with the mafia assassinations of the magistrates Pietro Scaglione, Cesare Terranova, Gaetano Costa, and Giangiacomo Ciaccio Montalto. All these tragic developments strengthened the notorious belief that the state was absent in Sicily and the Sicilians were left alone with their troubles.

I Siciliani gained numerous enemies and rivals in a very short time. Fava's articles defeated the mafias, politicians, and businessmen in the moral sphere, if not the economic and political spheres, with the three ethical codes of truth, freedom, and justice constituting the basis of his struggle. Fava and his passionate team defied the mafia through their socially committed journalism in *I Siciliani*. Unfortunately, they were able to perform this highly prolific and equally perilous role for only one year, up until Fava was murdered in 1984. Fava devoted his life's work to making the truth, freedom, and justice the leading ethical forces in Sicilian society, supplanting corruption, violence, and injustice. The mafia groups still have undeniable power in the local and national economy and political life in Italy today. On the other hand, since the assassination of Fava, numerous journalists and media outlets have been writing and working in Sicily and other parts of the country.

Although Fava's writings did not produce fundamental change in the economic and political spheres, his eminent role as an investigative journalist and his ethical code form a legacy that works as a source of inspiration for the next generation of journalists following Fava's challenging, socially engaged path. Among the online news sources evidencing Fava's legacy are I Siciliani giovani and Libera Informazione, both founded after his tragic death. These journalistic outlets wield influence in the antimafia movement thanks largely to their decisive role in web-based media. They also testify to the mafia's failure to silence news media in the face of what I suggest are serious threats to the diverse mafias in Italy today posed by web-based media.

The Ethical Legacy of Giuseppe Fava and Its Influence on the New Generation of Antimafia Journalism and Culture

Today there are numerous antimafia media establishments across Italy. Some of them operate at the local level and others engage in the fight against the various mafias at the national and international levels. The developments in media, technology, and the methods of spreading information have clearly played a great role in the growth of antimafia operations in cyberspace and their endeavours to produce online and offline spaces in terms of a culture of legality. However, if we do not take into account the evolution of the antimafia movement, its historical dynamics and, most important, the huge costs that were paid by dauntless journalists such as Fava, these developments in journalism designed as weapons against the mafia and practices of social renewal cannot be fully understood. Fava's legacy extends beyond his ethical code. What is more, Fava's legacy includes his persistent struggle to stand against the mafia whatever the cost to be paid for this revolutionary act, as evidenced by his murder. As in the cases of Judges Giovanni Falcone and Paolo Borsellino, the mafia killed Fava, but not his ideas. His assassination and the threats against other journalists following Fava's path have rendered the antimafia fight more durable and powerful. Amy Boylan's "Democratizing the Memorial Landscape" in this volume underscores the importance of commemorating the sacrifices of all victims in cyberspace. In this context, Fava's heritage as an inspiration for the next generation of journalists in the media and commemoration of mafia victims on the virtual landscape constitute parallel dynamics of antimafia struggle. Fava's socially committed journalism functions as a historical model. Similarly, the creation of a cyberspace for mafia victims serves as a model of vital mistakes of the past that must be avoided. Indeed, Boylan describes such a despairing commemoration as "a house of memory for the dead" in cyberspace. As a result, both the struggle of Fava and commemoration in virtual spatialities show dreadful and sometimes contradictory aspects of anti-mafia culture. Yet these formidable aspects are deeply rooted in the ethical legacy of prominent social figures in Italian society. I also propose that Fava's legacy and its incorporation within the developments in web-based media have made the voices of the public both more visible and less obedient to censorship and deterrence. In this context, I Siciliani giovani and Libera Informazione are two noteworthy examples illustrating how cyberspatialities of antimafia journalism, based upon Fava's ethics and practices of social commitment, may deeply affect, if not determine, the mafia's fate.

I Siciliani giovani endeavours to realize the mission of Giuseppe Fava and his newspaper *I Siciliani*. It is clear from the name of the organization that this is a renewed news agency with a young cadre of reporters; *giovani* literally means young in Italian. However, its goal aims to attain ideals very similar to those guiding Giuseppe Fava and *I Siciliani*. The slogan of I Siciliani giovani, which appears under the title of the printed magazine and website, articulates the purpose of their struggle and indebtedness to Fava. Invoking Fava's well-known words, the slogan states: "What purpose is living, if you don't have the courage to fight?" The phrase serves as remarkable motivation and a reminder that the primary principles of Fava's ethics of journalism reach millions of Sicilians through I Siciliani giovani. The printed magazine is disseminated monthly. The website of I Siciliani giovani is updated daily. Similar to the program instituted by Fava, the website and the printed magazine cover diverse issues related to the social, political, economic, and cultural issues of Catania, Sicily and Italy. The mafia and its activities form the primary content of I Siciliani giovani. The website features diverse sections that represent differentiated cultural products of legality. Among these are editorials, articles on politics, investigative inquiries, reports, interviews, articles on history and the economy, local and national breaking news, culture, and ebooks. The website is available only in Italian. Nevertheless, it is possible to comment on the news and entries, subject to editorial approval. One of the most crucial missions of I Siciliani giovani is to sustain the antimafia fight and make it more effective by using its public power in conventional and web-based media.

The role of I Siciliani giovani has vital importance, as underscored by the recent scandals that broke in Italy in March 2015, and raised the problematic issue of how certain individuals benefited from their associations with the antimafia movement, using them as cover for their businesses and collaborations with the local mafiosi. The Antimafia Commission of the Italian Parliament has opened a new investigation for the claims that Antonello Montante, the president of the Sicilian branch of the employers' organization Confindustria, has had relationships with Sicilian mafia bosses. The widening scandal gripped the country after the investigators discovered in early March 2015 that Roberto Helg, Palermo's chamber of commerce leader, received €100,000 as extortion money from a local businessman. These two shameful incidents are tragic developments since both Montante and Helg have appeared many times at antimafia events and have expressed their efforts to fight the mafia. Rita Borsellino (2015), the sister of the assassinated magistrate Paolo Borsellino, made a sobering statement about the scandals and antimafia movement, saying that

> the movement sprang up spontaneously in Sicily on the wave of emotion after the massacres of 1992 … There are many people who have stuck with it, who have sacrificed their time and their work … But unfortunately, even though it's painful to say, others have evidently hidden under this banner to pursue their own interests.

Although the Montante and Helg cases have damaged the reputation of the antimafia fight, they have also prompted immediate, salutory self-scrutiny, enabled largely by web-based media. I Siciliani giovani published a news campaign called "La Mafia dell'Antimafia" (The mafia of the antimafia) to protest the discredited names and, moreover, declare ten objectives in its April 2015 issue. The objective was to make the antimafia fight more effective and to develop new solutions for the problems in the antimafia movement:

1 Eliminate bank secrecy.
2 Confiscate all mafia assets and goods, including those attained through corruption and tax evasion.
3 Assign all confiscated goods to the cooperatives of young labourers; assist the people who support cooperatives.
4 Effective registration of the confiscated property.
5 Sanction relocations, the abuse of insecurity, and the failure to comply with the Statute of Workers' Rights or working regulations.

6 Achieve separation of the financial and industrial capital; cap on investments in publishing; enforce the Tobin tax (a tax on all spot conversions of one currency into another to punish short-term financial round-trip excursions into another currency).
7 Public management of the essential public services (schools, universities, defence, water, energy, technological structures, international credit).
8 Support the project of the national safety of the territory, as an economic driver especially in the South; prohibition of other uncontrolled developments; banning polluting industries; restructuring of existing land and land reclamation at the expense of the polluter.
9 Improve control of the territory in high-intensity mafia areas.
10 Strengthen application of Article 41 of the Constitution. Article 41 reads: "Private-sector economic initiative is freely exercised. It cannot be conducted in conflict with social usefulness or in such a manner that could damage safety, liberty and human dignity. The law shall provide for appropriate programs and controls so that public and private-sector economic activity may be oriented and coordinated for social purposes."

I Siciliani giovani's campaign against the recent scandals and its news about the risks of the mafia both at the regional and national level show how they put into practice the elements of Fava's socially committed journalism. The ten objectives of the antimafia movement illustrate how the journalists working at I Siciliani giovani employ a critical perspective to detect problems of illegality, even in activities operating in the purview of the antimafia, and bring new strategies to make the movement more effective in the legal, political, social, and cultural spheres. I Siciliani giovani is hardly anomalous. Dozens of antimafia establishments in web-based media complement the mission of I Siciliani giovani, with Libera Informazione among them.

The foundation of Libera Informazione must be located in the history of Libera, which is the largest non-state antimafia organization and network in the country. Libera Informazione was established in 2007 as one of the branches of Libera, upon the initiative of the journalist Roberto Morrione. The aim was to create a media network among journalists, freelance media workers, newspapers, television and radio sectors, online media, and the citizens, which would inform the public about organized crime activities both at the national and international levels. The Internet portal of Libera Informazione (www. liberainformazione.org) is updated regularly. In contrast to I Siciliani giovani, Libera Informazione only covers the news and activities of organized crime and the antimafia movement. As a result, it has a more articulated focus on the mafia. The presentation of the multiple facets of the mafia organizations in society and the state is a challenging mission. Libera Informazione aims to achieve a broad flow of information through its collaborations with various antimafia associations, bloggers, local journalists, and individual activists. In doing so, they work to create and apply public pressure on both the policy-makers and the mainstream Italian media to allocate more space for news about the mafia. There is no doubt that the strong, extensive network of Libera helps realize the goals of Libera Informazione. On the other hand, the news at the website of the foundation also directs attention to the local news related to the mafia. When I interviewed journalists working with Libera Informazione in 2011, I was told that the website was open to comments in 2007, but after the increase in inappropriate comments, attacks, and threats, they decided to close the website to visitor comments. More alarming, the website was hacked in 2010.

The structure of Libera Informazione's website is organized into eight sections: breaking news located on the home page, interviews, videos, publications and archives, investigative files, the network of the foundation, and the news section for each region of Italy. The most influential contribution of the organization is the publications that can be downloaded free. The investigative files also inform the public so the citizens have the opportunity to learn more about the recent corruption scandals through in-depth articles. This service is especially critical due to the mafia infiltration of news organizations and the lack of information on mafia activities in mainstream media. Furthermore, the sections on mafia news and the antimafia events for each region render the organization's mission more effective by performing mass dissemination of factual insights from the local areas through its local volunteer journalists. This local connection, which Fava examined in his writings and documentaries, exposes the territorial power of the mafia and its silent but deep influence over the people in microgeographic sociocultural relations.

The network of Libera Informazione is a significant instrument for making the antimafia movement stronger and more diversified. One of their most important collaborations is with *Narcomafie*, which is a monthly magazine founded in 1993 by don Luigi Ciotti, who is also the founder of *Libera. Narcomafie's* magazine and website disseminate information about the mafia and particularly drug trafficking, which brings the most revenue to the mafia syndicates. *Narcomafie* has published a remarkable number of investigative files about the mafia and drug trafficking. One of its most notable publications came out in 2008, titled *Nuovo dizionario di mafia e antimafia* (New dictionary of the mafia and antimafia). Recent issues in 2015 and 2016 provide detailed information about the power of 'ndrangheta in Lombardy and the Veneto regions.

Both I Siciliani giovani and Libera Informazione are indispensable instruments of democratic formations in web-based media, functioning to raise concerns in the name of the public while fighting against the mafia. Amitai Etzioni (2004) argues that virtual democracy consists of the participation of online communities to widen the scope of democracy and express their concerns. He explains that "the Internet could not only fully duplicate offline democratic procedures and outcomes, but it could improve upon them. It would be much easier online than offline for millions not merely to gain information and to vote, but also to participate in deliberations and in instructing their chosen representatives" (98). From this perspective, web-based media employed by the antimafia movement widen the scope of virtual democracy in Italy while defending the public good by taking Fava's ethical codes of truth, freedom, and justice as their guiding principles. It must be noted that the type of information disseminated may be a determinative force for mobilizing the masses. The information, especially *radical information* such as Fava's news about the mafia, has the potential power to change the political landscape by exposing in news writings and videos the embezzlement of public funds, corruption, and unethical behaviour of the politicians, or even informing the public about the limitations of the citizens' sovereignty. These are the hard social problems of the country. In theory, public engagement serves public deliberation and lends its voice to active citizenship, which opens gates to alternative spaces for the representation of public voices. In doing so, the web-based media arm of the antimafia movement offers new remedies to these hard social problems by exposing truths, shaping the form of freedom, and seeking justice.

The mafia poses certain risks to targeted victims, including journalists, through its relentless violence and threats that are a more dramatic deterrent at the local level where the mafia has a strong power base. On the other hand, if the voice of the people does not fall on deaf ears, the mafia is not an invincible force. This is the reason that the local sites and connections of mafia infiltration warrant national attention, as proposed by Fava in the early 1980s. The roles antimafia web-based media can perform to draw such attention can be best understood in the critical frame offered by Ulf Hannerz (1992) and his definition of Global Ecumene as a network of the networks (34). As a dominating force, Global Ecumene is more visible where the cultures between the periphery and centre are highly connected. In this respect, in the last decades, antimafia media outlets have provided such connections by creating a public space for local journalists and making confidential information about the mafia clans and their political networks available to everyone who has internet connections and thus access to the websites. Indeed, online antimafia media's struggle seeks to create a Global Ecumene of the antimafia movement. This is to say that the cyperspatial practices and resultant spaces of antimafia culture in Italy aim to transform the direction of the risks posed by the mafia by spreading ample, concise information among citizens about the criminal organizations. The antimafia agencies in web-based media wield profound influence over the public domain of society, which eventually becomes the interplaying area for the development of the Italian antimafia culture of legality.

Public opinion cases regarding crime generally do not take into account the role of community influence on individual reactions (Stack et al. 2007, 295). In this context, antimafia journalism in cyberspace represents a powerful instrument for developing the public sphere as a site for increasing individual awareness. This struggle conveys the message that the citizens are not alone to show their opposition to various forms of oppression and threats produced by the local mafiosi. Pertinent in this respect is Michael Schudson's (1998) notion of the "informed citizen" as a crucial instrument for detecting "political dangers" in the available flow of free information rather than government-based information sources (52). More to the point, in contrast to conventional news sources, the internet offers a public space that is relatively free from censorship, which poses certain advantages in regions where the mafia structures the hierarchy of power and often politics. Gaetano Liardo of Libera Informazione underscores this point, asserting that the publication of news related to the political-criminal nexus still presents a challenge in mainstream television broadcasting and print media (interview with author, cited in Cayli 2013a, 65). Moreover, such news outlets tend to devote limited space to local news concerning mafia activities and power, unless they pose an explicit national threat, as in the cases of the murders of Giovanni Falcone and Paolo Borsellino. Other pertinent issues include the very formation of journalists. Daniel Hallin and Paolo Mancini argue in *Comparing Media Systems* (2004) that there is a rather slow development process of "journalistic professionalism" in southern European countries (138). In these countries, strong clientelism and political culture set the main barriers to creating professional journalists who should be independent and working in the service of truth rather than certain powerful groups. In line with this statement, important agents of mass media and politics have found new, uncontested milieus in the political life of Italy, especially with Berlusconi's entrance into the political arena in the 1980s, bolstered by his media power (Mancini and Mazzoleni 1995; Mazzoleni 1995). Thus, I argue that the critical, alternative media – particularly web-based media – presents remedies, or at least constructs a public space for the production of those remedies, as evidenced by antimafia media establishments. This kind of cyberspatiality creates public space and makes it functional so as to mitigate the mafia's power over the public domains of society. Such cyberspatialities function as products and producers of radical, yet critical journalistic professionalism that employs counterpublic practices and helps realize the ideals of ethical journalism in Fava's sense. Hence, each of these practices offers a new tool to diminish the power of the politics-media-mafia triangle.

These antimafia initiatives in new media frequently direct public attention to the poor administration of state institutions and egregious political impotence that empower mafia clans comprised by Cosa Nostra, the camorra, 'ndrangheta, and the United Sacred Crown. The power of web-based media has created a determinative space by keeping the public informed about "political scandals" and challenging the "political legitimacy" with surges of critical power within the new communication sphere (Castells 2007, 250). Moreover, web-based media gains more importance in socio-economically advanced countries such as Italy where 58.5 per cent of the population uses the Internet actively (Internet Users in Europe 2015). Perhaps more important, new media does not only help the fight against the mafia, it also triggers the settlement of democratic communication (Tambini 1999) and stimulates mass democracy (Bucy and Gregson 2001).

Fava was among the relatively few Italian journalists who ventured to defy the mafia publicly in the 1980s. Today, the mafia still poses particular risks to the local journalists not only in Sicily but throughout the entire country. However, what makes today's antimafia culture different from that of the 1980s is the increasing number of agencies, institutes, volunteers, and journalists that fight persistently. We can note that Italian antimafia culture has produced the most innovative and diverse methods in the world to combat the mafia. This relatively successful fight cannot be accurately understood if we ignore the previous journalists, like Francese, De Mauro, and Fava, who immensely contributed to this struggle and provided an extraordinary example for the next generation of journalists. As clearly evidenced by the expanding web-based media outlets, Fava's ethical codes of truth, freedom, and justice have shaped the principal character of antimafia journalism. The courageous attempts demonstrated by Fava and today's antimafia journalists form a fundamental weapon for defeating the mafia and its culture. Fava and his team's *I Siciliani* continue to inspire and inform this fight under the publication title *I Siciliani giovani*, and are joined by such important online news sites as Libera Informazione and *Narcomafie*, among numerous others. The power of web-based media strengthens the antimafia mission by providing timely, accurate information about the various mafia organizations and their activities throughout Italy and the world. This does not mean mafia threats on journalists can be taken less seriously. Roberto Saviano, Giuseppe Maniaci, and Michele Albanese are only a few names among eighty-nine journalists who have been threatened by mafia groups (Walker 2014), several of whom must live under constant bodyguard protection. It is not a surprise that these journalists are based in Sicily, Campania, and Calabria, where the mafia groups have a strong territorial power. The fight against the mafia serves to protect the right to speak and the right to know. More important, defeating the mafia and mafia culture fosters the hope that an ideal society is attainable in Italy, because the mafia symbolizes hopelessness, oppression, inequality, moral deprivation, and injustice. These unjust conditions produced by the mafia are the poignant reminders of Italy's social problems that have marginalized the ideal society concept since the unification of the country. However, the national mafia problem also opens a new chapter in the lives of the foreigners who visit Italy's virtual or geographic territories and engage with the antimafia movement and its cultural production. Such encounters can create an ethics that enables travellers to embrace global values of justice and the struggle to attain it. Moving from the canvas of the mafia's symbols to the fight to renew Italian culture and attain an ideal society is a journey of sociocultural transformation. Fava's ethical codes, mafia victims, and the new generation of web-based media

articulate the motivations and practices that such a sociocultural transformation needs. This is the reason that the fight against the mafia is
grounded in the project to renew Italy through democratic channels,
civil resistance, and bottom-to-top social mobilization, markedly
empowered by the increasing employment of web-based media.

3 "A Taste of Justice": Digital Media and Libera Terra's Antimafia Public Pedagogy of Agrarian Dissent

PAULA M. SALVIO

Introduction

On 14 May 2014, National Public Radio featured the first of several instalments of a new season of *Hidden Kitchens*, produced by "the kitchen sisters," award-winning journalists Davia Nelson and Nikki Silva. The program, "The Pizza Connection: Fighting the Mafia through Food," profiled Libera Terra (Free land), which is a branch of Libera, the largest non-profit antimafia organization in Italy. Founded in 1995 by don Luigi Ciotti in collaboration with relatives of victims of mafia violence, Libera was created to fight the mafia through education, employment, and agriculture. The initial aim of Libera Terra as stated on its website was to cultivate historically "difficult" territories throughout Italy that had been previously owned and neglected by the mafia and, in turn, redistribute this land to the public for social use (http://liberaterra.it/en/).[1] Libera Terra began its work by promoting organic, self-sufficient, cooperative farming. Its collective efforts continue to be directed at creating what it describes as "work places that establish a moral economic system based on legality and social justice." Today, small organic cooperatives established throughout Italy on farm land confiscated from the mafia bring these goods to a global market (Kitchen Sisters 2014).

The Sicilian tradition of non-violent dissent against the mafia, revitalized under the direction of don Ciotti, grounds itself in the symbolic and physical practices of organic farming and cooperative economics that characterize an agrarian history in Sicily that has long valued what Michael Hardt and Antonio Negri label as "the commons" in their work *Empire* (2001). They use this term to describe the production and liberation of a diverse multitude, to render suspect or illegitimate claims to private property, and to challenge the continuous movement throughout the modern period to privatize land, water, air, and space (300–3). Like many activist organizations, Libera Terra makes use of social networking and trans-media practices to inform a transnational public about projects that are committed to strengthening the commons. Libera Terra shares with Hardt and Negri an abiding concern with the multitude or the working poor (redefined as the "party of the poor" and, in Spinoza's terms, the only true subject of democracy), as well as a belief in the labouring class to create an alternative world apart from that given by capital (Harvey 2011). For Libera Terra, this commitment to the commons includes developing and expanding resources for citizens and residents of Italy, not only to free society from the grip of mafia violence, but also to support those who are marginalized from society due to poor health, unemployment, underemployment, and disabilities. These public services and projects include workshops and educational curricula on participatory democracy, free access to news on mafia and antimafia activity, commemoration projects designed to remember mafia victims, and employment opportunities to produce products crafted by Libera cooperatives that include wine, olive oil, and marmalades.

If, as Hardt and Negri (2001) argue, "those who are against" the empire's pursuit to exploit and dominate the multitude "must continually attempt to construct a new body and a new life" (214), then Libera Terra might be understood as a collective of ideal citizen subjects who refuse to submit to the corruption imposed by generations of mafia infiltration into politics, social life, and the economy. Their continued efforts to create new "bodies and new life," to radicalize and to transform society is in line with Negri and Hardt's methods for creating experimental zones of becoming (214). These efforts continue as corporations, politicians, and wealthy elites yield exorbitant amounts of influence on both electoral politics and public policy.

In "Creating Counterpublics against the Italian Mafia" (2013), Baris Cayli conducts an astute study of Libera's use of web-based media to create counterpublic spaces, and examines how the antimafia organization uses social media to exercise its commitment to democratic ideals of access, inclusion, deliberation, and participation in projects directed towards and engaged in social renewal. Cayli's study focuses primarily on one branch of Libera established in 2007, Libera Informazione. The youngest of the five main projects of Libera, Libera Informazione is a collective of journalists and volunteers working throughout Italy who use Facebook, Twitter, and blogging to write and disseminate news about mafia and antimafia activity that would otherwise be kept out of the press or be marginalized in the mainstream news media. This branch of Libera, argues Cayli, successfully renews contemporary culture through media channels in the public sphere by informing communities at the local and national levels and raising consciousness about the criminal-political nexus and activities of mafia groups. Antimafia cyberspatialities, as Cayli maintains in his chapter in this volume, create radical spaces of dissent and interrupt what he describes as "the politics-media-mafia triangle" (chapter 2, 82). The story of Libera Informazione, he concludes, is one of public engagement and participatory, reformist culture that challenges conventional journalism by introducing a counterpublic sphere that exists apart from profit. Moreover, because journalists, when acting alone, continue to experience threats when exposing mafia activity, Libera Informazione offers protection through solidarity with other organizations and member groups.

The fact that many of Libera Terra's activities use social networking to promote its projects raises serious questions, particularly given the ways in which the mafia makes use of social networking to leverage their wages and wage their wars, capitalizing, as noted by Robin Pickering-Iazzi in the introduction to this volume, on the multiple ways in which multimedia platforms work to expand not only their profit but also their ideal public image. These global, capitalist communication networks are unavoidably and inextricably entwined with what political theorist Jodi Dean (2010) describes as the practice of communicative capitalism. "Just as industrial capitalism relied on the exploitation of labor," argues Dean, "so does communicative capitalism rely on the exploitation of communication" (4). Dean is skeptical of the extent to which social networking systems that create a profit for the few and produce severe economic inequality for the many can work to democratize social movements. And while communicative capitalism may incite and facilitate what Hardt and Negri (2001) describe as a "capacity to construct a new social body and a new life," these methods are those of Empire: do more, go further, be flexible, inventive, innovative and always on the cutting edge (cited in Dean 2010, 78–9). Fantasies of activity and participation drive communicative capitalism and the belief, according to Dean, that "the values heralded as central to democracy take material form in networked communications ... ideals of access, inclusion, discussion and participation come to be realized in and through expansions, intensifications and interconnections of global telecommunications" (4). In the process of using ever more innovative upgrades to create a common public sphere for deliberation and open participation, the use of social networking systems such as Facebook and Twitter not only fail to provide democratic ownership of their platforms, but also, Dean argues, create an *ersatz* sense of political engagement. "Busy people can think they are active," observes Dean (2005):

> ... the technology will act for them, alleviating their guilt while assuring them that nothing will change too much ... By sending an e-mail, signing a petition, responding to an article on a blog, people can feel political. And that feeling feeds communicative capitalism insofar as it leaves behind the time-consuming, incremental and risky efforts of politics ... It is a refusal to take a stand, to venture into the dangerous terrain of politicization. (70)

The "low-risk" political involvement Dean describes is also critiqued by Malcolm Gladwell (2010) and Evgeny Morozov (2009), both of whom speak to the argument of "slacktivism" as a form of what Morozov describes as "feel-good online activism that has zero political or social impact. Slacktivism gives those who participate in 'slacktivist' campaigns an illusion of having a meaningful impact on the world without demanding anything more than joining a Facebook group." Morozov (2009) characterizes online activist activity as ideal for what he describes as a lazy generation. "Why bother," he asks, "with sit-ins and the risk of arrest, police brutality, or torture if one can be as loud campaigning in the virtual space?"[2] Many of the critiques of digital media, including Gladwell's and Morozov's concerns about "slacktivism," assume a traditional practice of citizenship modelled on the image of the "dutiful citizen" engaged in traditional forms of political participation such as voting and face-to-face protests. More contemporary concepts of citizenship highlight civic action through community work, unconventional political action, and digitally mediated forms of political expression.[3] Contemporary concepts of citizenship also take into account the way in which social media is used to mediate acts of social renewal.

Is it possible to use social networking to create a political sphere of communication that has emancipatory potential for cultural and social renewal given its ties to the exploitation of labour and neoliberal markets? Do the social networking practices associated with the work of Libera Terra significantly impact public consciousness about mafia violence and serve the commons? Or, does Libera Terra's use of social networking systems serve as a clear case of the insidious ways in which antimafia digital platforms promote a kind of "slacktivism" and actually displace attention from the profound inequalities produced and amplified by global financial networks, many of which are tethered to mafia profit and prosperity and tied to social networks?

In this chapter, I draw on critical theory of contemporary media and communicative capitalism to explore the ways in which Libera Terra uses social networking on their Facebook site to extend the memories of an agrarian history of antimafia protest to contemporary antimafia activism. Tracing what I will describe as Libera Terra's "public pedagogy" to theories of the commons that resonate with the work of Hardt and Negri (2001), I argue that Libera Terra presents a compelling challenge to claims made by skeptics of social media that new media practices such as blogging, posting, texting, and Facebook are built to neglect organization and revolt. Taking into account the historic background of the formation of Libera Terra and its contemporary focus on both memories of non-violent agrarian protest and the work of non-violent protest, I extend the scholarship on social networking elaborated by Dean (2005, 2010), and Cayli (2013a, 2013b) by situating their work within the context of discussions about societies transitioning from repressive to more democratic political conditions. The intergenerational call throughout Italy as well as in countries such as Egypt, South Africa, the United States, and Turkey for racial and gender justice, access to education and health care, economic opportunity, and dignity in response to repressive political conditions is evidence of a global trend in social movements that is best described as a process of "transitional justice."[4]

My analysis defines transitional justice as a set of judicial and nonjudicial measures that are implemented to redress legacies of conflict and state repression. On a conceptual level, transitional justice emphasizes inclusive and non-adversarial frameworks that seek to prevent a violent past from being repeated. In the context of the antimafia movement in Italy, transitional justice refers to the projects – legislative, economic, educational, cultural, and aesthetic – taken up to redress victims, recognize the rights of victims, promote civic trust, and strengthen the democratic rule of the law. Given the mafia's infiltration of the state, eradicating the mafia from Italy indeed requires similar transformations to those that occurred in countries such as South Africa and Argentina. My intention here is not to compare the human rights abuses in Italy to those in other countries in transition, but to place in relief the human rights abuses in Italy that might easily be overlooked if one fails to recognize the impact that large-scale corruption has on human rights. As Chris Cunneen argues in "Exploring the Relationship between Reparations, the Gross Violation of Human Rights, and Restorative Justice" (2006), state crime is not restricted solely to genocide, mass murder, or torture. It can include petty corruption as well as large-scale corruption of political elites (357). In partnerships with the state and manufacturers in Italy and beyond, the mafia has executed to this day massive human rights abuses and environmental violations (357). To offer just one set of examples, collaboration among the diverse mafia organizations, the state, and manufacturers produce illegal waste cycles in Italy near Naples and in the surrounding region of Campania that have resulted in clusters of liver, kidney, pancreatic, and other cancer cases. The case of illegal waste cycles is one example of the extent to which the law has played a constitutive role in crimes against humanity. The law, in partnership with the mafia, too often legitimates unchecked environmental devastation and unchecked extortion, and facilitates the take over of land for exploitation, as made evident in the building of the Falcone-Borsellino Airport near Cinisi and Palermo, Sicily.

In this chapter, I argue that the process of transitional justice calls for radical approaches to narrative and to teaching that are exemplified by the public pedagogy of Libera Terra. I pay specific attention to Libera Terra's approach to coupling social networking with on-site activism in the midst of persistent social breakdown due to the expansion of the mafia into political and global markets. In this chapter, public pedagogy refers to teaching that takes place outside of formal school settings and focuses on progressive social transformation. Public pedagogy directs its attention to breaking through, disrupting, displacing, and inverting inherited concepts and practices that undermine liberatory solidarities. "In this sense," argues feminist scholar M. Jacqui Alexander (2005), public pedagogies "summon subordinated knowledges that are produced in the context of the practices of marginalization in order that we might destabilize existing practices of knowing and thus cross the fictive boundaries of exclusion and marginalization" (7). Libera Terra's commitment to the commons and their active physical and political engagement in agricultural renewal casts their use of social media in public pedagogical terms that have significant educational import when understood alongside an intellectual and political history tied to agrarian activism and transitional justice. This legacy combines cultural production and spatial justice with participatory politics, in turn complicating critiques of the effectiveness digital media has on the work of cultural renewal.

A Brief History of Libera Terra and the Project of Transitional Justice

In 2012, during a series of interviews with antimafia activists and educators working in Palermo, I asked if they believed that Italy was indeed a society in transition as it recovers from the economic, emotional, and environmental devastation created by the mafia. Vito Lo Monaco, former director of the Italian Communist Party and current president of the Pio La Torre Center (Centro Pio La Torre), reported that the Italian Republic continues to be in crisis and that the lives of people in Italy continue to be affected by organized crime. Yet he asserts that Italy is not isolated in this struggle. "Organized crime," noted Lo Monaco, "is an international enterprise, rooted in exploitation" (interview with the author, 27 July 2014). Lo Monaco maintains that making tangible reparation for mafia-related crimes as the country works on its transition to more democratic practices cannot happen in the courtroom alone. Reparations must happen on the legislative, educative, social, and cultural levels as well. He offered Italy's Rognoni-La Torre Law as one example of a legislative process created in the name of addressing the fiscal and emotional losses accumulated due to Italy's neglect of the violence imposed by organized crime on residents and citizens. Dubbed the "Antimafia Law," this legislation is named after its two authors Virginio Rognoni and Pio La Torre, the Italian Chamber Deputy who was killed by the mafia in 1982. The law was passed by Parliament later the same year. The new law defined mafia conspiracy as a crime in the Italian legal system and made it possible for the courts to seize and to confiscate the assets taken by the mafia and return them to public use for the public good.

Libera Terra was, in large part, made possible by the Rognoni-La Torre legislation. However, this legislation took years to apply fully in practice. It required the efforts of Associazione Libera, a collective of citizens and residents who, in response to the murders of beloved antimafia judges Giovanni Falcone and Paolo Borsellino, petitioned the Italian Parliament to strengthen the Rognoni-La Torre Law in 1996, and implement the provision for redistributing confiscated mafia assets to community groups working to improve social and economic conditions. After the murders of Falcone and Borsellino, communities throughout Italy recognized that they could no longer rely on the government officials to combat the brutality of mafia violence (see Picciotto 2015, 38–48). Associazione Libera brought together educators, artists, journalists, and Italian residents in an effort to cultivate a culture of legality. The campaign slogan, "La mafia restituisce il maltolto" (The mafia returns the stolen goods), emphasized the importance of returning to communities what the mafia had taken illegally and with impunity. Over one million people signed the petition, and the expanded version of the Rognoni-La Torre Law was approved by Parliament in 1996. The 1996 legislation represented what is often called a Copernican Revolution in the Italian legal system. Expanding upon the original 1982 Law n. 646, which established association with the mafia as a crime, the new Rognoni-La Torre Law introduced a reparative commitment to social renewal. "For the first time," notes sociologist Antonio La Spina (2005), "the property confiscated from the mafia became potential flywheels of local economic development and valuable opportunities for the employment of disadvantaged people" (150).

The 1996 Rognoni-La Torre legislation provides for the use of goods and estates confiscated from the mafia for the social good (Frigerio 2009). In her article outlining the history of the Rognoni-La Torre Law and its ties to Libera Terra, Loredana Picciotto (2015) explains that until the expanded 1996 legislation was passed, all goods confiscated from the mafia simply accumulated as state assets; there was no legislation that determined how these assets should be used. As a result, some assets even risked becoming unproductive. The 1996 Antimafia Law clearly states that these goods must be used for collective purposes that are tied to "social rehabilitation and the culture of legality." Candidates applying for work on the cooperatives must belong to specific groups such as the unemployed, youth, disadvantaged, and marginalized people. Social cooperatives such as the Placido Rizzotto Cooperative or Cooperativo NOE are organized around farming, eco-tourism, educational projects focused on deliberative democracy, anti-extortion campaigns, and, most recently in 2012, a summer school in Palermo called "Youth, Entrepreneurship and Innovation," created in partnership with the University of Palermo.

In the last fifteen years, particularly in the south of Italy, a number of social entrepreneurial projects have emerged that generate employment and increase social, cultural, and economic stability. Libera Terra is among the first and most notable leaders in the growing trend to create social cooperatives operated on confiscated mafia properties. In fact, in their study of the implementation of the Rognoni-La Torre Law,

Picciotto and her colleagues (2015) found that communities value this law, not solely for taking resources away from the mafia, but for generating economic and social renewal.

Facebook and the "Taste of Justice"

In 2008, one year after forming Libera Informazione, Libera Terra opened a Facebook account featuring a photograph of the Pietra Longa Vineyard in Monreale taken at dawn in May. Four hundred and sixty-four people "liked" this post with comments such as "Stupenda!! Un nuovo giorno sorge su terre sane" (Gorgeous!! A new day rises on healthy land), "In alto i calici" (Raise the glasses!), and "La nostalgia di questa bella terra natia la porto ancora nel mio cuore, anche se son passati più di quattro decenni da quando l'ho lasciata" (I still carry the nostalgia for this beautiful land, even if it has been more than four decades since I left). By 2009, Libera Terra began to post digital news clips that included videotapes of tours of recently confiscated mafia property, which highlighted the hard work involved in restoring the soil and buildings left by the mafia to fallow and decay. The clips also reported discussions with don Luigi Ciotti about combating corruption, "albums" that included a convocation celebrating the confiscation of mafia boss Toto Riina's home, and invitations to attend events sponsored by Libera Terra as well as to purchase their oranges and lemons at one of their cooperatives.

A cursory scan of the types of entries made on Facebook, the comments as well as the number of "likes," suggests that members of Libera Terra use social networking to engage in the kind of "low-risk" political involvement criticized by Morozov (2009) and Dean (2005). The posts extend invitations to antimafia events, celebrate achievements of Libera Terra, and make news available about mafia and antimafia activity that would ordinarily be marginalized in main stream, private news outlets. While there is a strong sense of participation and inclusion, evident in the numbers of "likes" and comments posted, one could argue that there is little evidence of deliberation or struggle over ideas, policies, or legislation.

A closer analysis, however, suggests a more complicated set of engagements with projects of agricultural renewal that includes an ethical orientation to both virtual and offline ethical action, as well as to cultivating memories of non-violent antimafia protest. Every post on Libera Terra corresponds to political action taken up on the cooperatives throughout Italy. And while not every viewer or "friend" of Libera Terra has literally taken part in the work of reclaiming and restoring the landscapes left to fallow by the mafiosi, each "friend" who responds or comments on the post participates in reconfiguring the traditional agrarian protest spaces by extending prior practices of resistance to the present moment. When Libera Terra posted snow-packed images of the vineyards of Portella della Ginestra on 2 January 2015 and eighty-six people "liked this," participants not only represented and responded to the present production of the Sicilian wine Cento passi, but they also participated in referencing the 1947 Portella della Ginestra massacre. Often remembered by Sicilians as the culmination of local struggles for land rights and land reform between mafia backed landowners and left-wing peasant movements in the area of Piana degli Albanesi and San Giuseppe Jato, the massacre of the peasants who protested carries the symbolic weight of memories of non-violent agrarian activism and reform. But it also carries an unsettled story about the protest and massacre. Was the massacre perpetrated by anti-communist political forces, in particular the Christian Democratic Party and the United States intelligence services?

This subtle but powerful act of posting and "liking" the vineyards on Portella della Ginestra generates resonances among the past and the present and hopes for the future, culminating in what Jacqui Alexander (2005) describes as a palimpsestic method for reading and writing. The palimpsest, which is a parchment that has been written upon, scraped, erased, and then written on again and again, is symbolic of the re-emergence of lost traces and how meaning is influenced by past markings even when those markings are not explicitly seen. The palimpsest operates outside the realm of perception and refuses normative, diachronic divisions between the past and the present, consequently calling forth a continual interplay among different moments of resistance. The imperfect erasure and lingering traces of past events interrupts or disrupts the smooth recording of a seamless, normative history, which in this case deletes more complicated narratives of resistance and protest. Such imperfect erasures are made evident in, for example, the astute study on Casamemoria Vittimemafia's calendar of loss that Amy Boylan conducts in her chapter "Democratizing the Memorial Landscape." Boylan argues that Casamemoria Vittimemafia's archive of loss offers a counternarrative to the mainstream antimafia discourses of memory that privilege masculine histories, self-sacrifice, and a heroic individualism. The intention to "give voice to silence" and "prevent the oblivion of forgetting" can also be read, following Alexander, as instances of imperfect erasures that map memories of persons cast as "bare life" by state sanctioned violence (see Boylan, chapter 4, in this volume at 95).

In her book *Pedagogies of Crossing: Meditations on Feminism, Sexual Politics, Memory, and the Sacred* (2005), Alexander uses the image of the palimpsest to illustrate a method of analysis that examines how discourse moves historically, economically, and ideologically, both horizontally (meaning across borders of nation, gender, sexuality, and race) and vertically (meaning that each figure, such as an agricultural cooperative or an antimafia leader, accumulates historically gendered, raced, and sexualized meaning). According to Alexander, this method captures the depth of history and meaning attached to these figures (vertical analysis), as well as the ways in which these figures move across temporal and spatial rhetorical networks, discourses and sites (horizontal analysis) in order to sustain memories of resistance that are too often omitted from narratives tied to transitional justice. Memories are, as Alexander astutely points out, "the antidote to alienation, separation and the amnesia that domination produces" (190). In the following section, I move in closer to Libera Terra's Facebook site and apply Alexander's method of palimpsestic rhetorical analysis to more fully understand Libera Terra's role as public pedagogue working in a society in and of transition. I frame my analysis around two "figures" that are prominent on their Facebook site: Vino Centopassi (Cento passi wine) and the Cooperativo Placido Rizzotto (Placido Rizzotto Cooperative) where Cento passi wine is produced. The following questions guide the penultimate section of this inquiry: What memory work is taken up and sustained through a social networking project that both promotes justice but also exemplifies communicative capitalism? What memories are generated, lost, or sustained through the work of don Ciotti and the agrarian history of dissent he teaches through a project that frames food and wine as instruments of liberation? What lost traces of resistance are restored to public memory and to what extent are these traces compromised by communicative capitalism's proclivity to depoliticize?

The Figures of the Placido Rizzotto Cooperative and Cento Passi Wine

The Placido Rizzotto cooperative operates in the upper Belice Corleonese Region of Sicily and produces Cento passi wine. The social cooperative and the wine commemorate antimafia activists and social reformers Placido Rizzotto and Peppino Impastato, and work according to what the cooperative describes as the "principles of solidarity and legality." Also important to note is the fact that both the Placido Rizzotto cooperative and Cento passi wine are associated with two Italian films released in 2000, *I cento passi* (*The Hundred Steps*) directed by Marco Tullio Giordana, and *Placido Rizzotto*, directed by Pasquale Scimeca. Millicent Marcus (2007) calls attention to the memorialist impulses at play in both films and argues that they "present themselves as epitaphic, as cinematic tomb inscriptions designed to transmit the legacy of moral engagement and social justice for which their protagonists died."[5] This "memorialist impulse," I believe, is at work in Libera Terra's sponsorship of both the cooperative and the wine. The work of memorializing is intended, observes Dana Renga (2013) in her critical analysis of the film *I cento passi*, "as a pedagogical tool to raise consciousness with regard to the antimafia movement. Hence it could be argued that the biopic introduces younger generations to mafia-related trauma and inaugurates a new millennium of awareness of and protest against the mafia in Italy" (22). Migrating across (horizontally) temporal, spatial, and rhetorical networks vis-à-vis social networking sites, such as Libera Terra's Facebook site, are memories of resistance that also resonate with the Rognoni-La Torre Law that supports Libera Terra. Posted throughout the Facebook site are photographs and memorials organized to commemorate antimafia activist and politician Pio La Torre, who was Rizzotto's successor, also assassinated by the mafia.

The posts on Libera Terra's Facebook site that reference Cooperativo Placido Rizzotto and Cento passi wine continually return to the language of, for instance, progress and advancement (*sviluppo*), transformation (*trasformazione*), and redemption (*riscatto*), as illustrated by various posts: "... è stata trasformata in agroturismo ed assegnata alla cooperativa sociale Pio la Torre – Libera Terra" (... it was transformed into agritourism and assigned to the social cooperative Pio La Torre – Libera Terra); "adesso rappresenta il riscatto dello Stato e dei cittadini e l'affermazione dei valori di legalità e sviluppo" (now it represents the redemption of the state and citizens and the affirmation of the values of legality and development, 4 December 2009). In a post on 22 October 2012, Cento passi wine was described as "dedicato a coloro che onorano il ricordo delle vittime della mafia attraverso il proprio impegno quotidiano" (dedicated to those who honour the memory of the victims of the mafia through their daily commitment). "Centopassi è l'anima

vitivinicola delle cooperative che, sotto il segno di Libera Terra, colti-
vano le terre confiscate alla mafia in Sicilia…" (Cento passi wine is the
soul of cooperatives that, under the sign of free land, farm the lands
confiscated from the mafia in Sicily"). One hundred and thirty-one people "liked" this post and it was shared with fifty people.

If, as Dean (2005) argues, "governance by the people is thought in
terms of communicative freedoms of speech, assembly, and the press,
norms of publicity that emphasize transparency, and accountability,
and the deliberative practices of the public sphere," the communicative practices used by Libera Terra, specifically when posting, "liking,"
and visually representing the social cooperative Placido Rizzotto and
Vino Cento Passi, indeed impact official politics (53). The posts on Facebook directly link, as I noted earlier, to legislative, political, and economic achievements that are made manifest in the range of products
produced on the cooperatives – pasta, citrus, melons, honey, and len-
tils, to name a few. Moreover, by circulating memories of victims and
little-known martyrs in the antimafia cause, the Facebook site works
to reclaim narratives that are typically marginalized in contemporary
transitional justice institutions (Leebaw 2011, 55). What is often left as
unproblematic within the context of human rights advocacy and truth
commission committees working in the name of transitional justice is
an implicit assumption, observes Bronwyn Leebaw (2011):

> … that in remembering political violence we have a dichotomous choice
> between avoiding the stories of those who cannot be characterized as pas-
> sive victims in need of healing, or opening the door to vengeful Furies bent
> on poisoning the land with their grief and rage. To structure investigations
> of political violence in accordance with this perceived dichotomy is to con-
> done the forgetting of those who took action in the name of solidarity and
> change. The stories of those who organize various forms of resistance are
> complicated for contemporary transitional justice institutions. (116)

Drawing on Hannah Arendt's concept of political judgment, Leebaw
(2011) calls for a form of public pedagogy that learns from stories of
those who resist systematic atrocities in an effort to evaluate the problem of complicity in the past and to establish new forms of solidarity,
agency, and community in the future (118). The "memorialist impulse"
expressed horizontally throughout Libera Terra's Facebook site not only
foregrounds themes of resistance narratives inherited from the past,
but also documents the material and emotional compensation, restored

sense of security and dignity, and the ongoing work of restoring deliberative democracy. This work continues, not in a "post-traumatic"
state, as Renga has argued in her study of Italian mafia cinema, but,
given the persistent impact the mafia has on national and international
economies, in the very midst of social breakdown.

Imperfect Erasures

What traces of resistance are lost or compromised given the press of
communicative capitalism? Which memories remain half-spoken
within the antimafia imaginary? Following Alexander's (2005) palimpsestic method of analysis, I would now like to direct our attention to
a vertical reading of Libera Terra's representational practices of Cento
passi wine on their Facebook site. I do so in an effort to capture the
depth of loss that is partly visible – the imperfect erasures.

In her critical reading of the figure of Peppino Impastato in the film
I cento passi, Renga (2013) argues that the "antimafia message" is over-
simplified, depoliticized, and desexualized. Not only is Impastato's
activity in the militant Democrazia Proletaria (Proletariat Democracy)
downplayed, but also his homosexuality is eliminated. Renga strongly
believes, and I agree, that "*I cento passi* allows Peppino's martyrdom at
the expense of both his sexual and political identity. Read further, Peppino's violent murder puts an end not only to his antimafia protests,
but also to the feminine and non-violent ethos that he represents" (23).

The analysis presented by Renga offers a way to think about a vertical reading of the representation of Cento passi wine on Libera Terra's
Facebook site, particularly when read against the diary entries written by Peppino before he was murdered. In her 2007 interview with
Umberto Santino, president of the Centro Siciliano di Documentazione
"Giuseppe Impastato" in Palermo, Anna Paparcone (2009) reports that
Santino confirmed the story of Impastato's homosexuality. "We learned
about Peppino's homosexuality quite early," recalled Santino. But in
order to protect Peppino's memory from discrimination and to sustain
the integrity of his political activism, Santino agreed with Peppino's
family to keep the diary confidential in the Centro Siciliano (108). Not
until 2003, when Santino published the third edition of *Lunga è la notte*,
does Santino seek and gain permission from Peppino's brother Giovanni to publish Peppino's complete diary and finally "to present and
respect him for what he was" (farlo conoscere e rispettarlo così come
era) (109).[6]

The erasure of Peppino's homosexuality from the memorial land-scape on Libera Terra's Facebook site raises questions about the extent to which heterosexualization occupies a "civilizing" nexus in the anti-mafia imaginary more generally and within the context of Libera Terra more specifically. The "face" of the antimafia movement is the face of an apparently heterosexual man. A quick scan of Libera Terra's Facebook site commemorates figures such as Gian Carlo Caselli (6 December 2009), images of men with "courage and passion" working on coopera-tives (7 November 2009), and the call not to forget don Puglisi (another "martyr of justice"), "Per non dimenticare Don Puglisi." Absent from Libera's Facebook site is the face, for example, of Rosario Crocetta, Sic-ily's openly gay governor and antimafia activist as well as the activities of antimafia politician, Lea Savona, the female mayor of Corleone.

The stories of resistance that collect around the figure of Cento passi wine consistently refer to "a distance to cover" (referring to the 100 steps between Impastato's home in Cinisi and the home of mafioso Gaetano Badalamenti, a symbol of the close distance between justice and mafia corruption) and "a land to be redeemed." As with the film *I cento passi*, the use of Peppino Impastato as the "face" of Cento passi wine renders his memory in normative, redemptive terms. Moreover, the narratives that circulate around the making of Cento passi wine hold the promise to actively combat the mafia "all the while," argues Renga (2013), that "Cosa Nostra continues to operate effectively" (35).

A vertical reading of Cento passi wine illuminates imperfect eras-ures of an antimafia history that is anxious about homosexuality and a feminine non-violent ethos. The antimafia narratives promoted on the Libera Terra Facebook site establish civility and legality in heter-onormative terms that remain depoliticized. The public pedagogical project associated with Cento passi wine is built on a concept of martyr-dom that privileges a heterosexual, heroic male antimafia identity that takes coherent, linear sequential steps towards progress and liberation against the mafia.[7] What would it mean if Libera Terra practised a more capacious antimafia pedagogy, one that maps out the genealogies of its own disavowals, particularly with respect to the female body, queer and gay legacies, class, race, and sexuality? What dangers might the antimafia imaginary court if it were to cover another kind of "distance" by reclaiming its repressed feminine, gay, and queer histories?

While Libera Terra's public pedagogy creates a political sphere of communication that has emancipatory potential for cultural and social renewal, particularly within the context of a society in transition, it simultaneously remains uncritically identified with a heteronormativity that undermines fully inclusive conditions of belonging. These erasures are not due, I believe, to communicative capitalism's proclivity to depoliticize. Rather, I want to suggest that the heteronormative ethos of the mafia exerts a strange and haunting influence on antimafia public pedagogies. These heteronormative influences, registered on Libera Terra's Facebook site, imperfectly erase moments of resistance that have the capacity to disrupt the normative order of historical memory. That normative order effaces queer, gay, and feminist antimafia protests. The "taste for justice and civility" spoken of by don Luigi Ciotti is limited in so far as it fails to challenge the anxieties about femininity, maternity and, writes Renate Siebert (1996) in her discussion of male bonding among the mafiosi, "the hatred of feminine qualities in men" (24).[8] The view I advocate is one that more fully politicizes the partial and/or lost memories of queer, gay, and feminist antimafia protest through memory work and political deliberation that sustains a critical relationship with existing norms for civility and justice.

NOTES

1 Libera is organized around the following projects: (a) Libera Education; (b) Libera Terra Cooperatives; (c) Libera Bottegas (or shops), where products from confiscated land are sold; (d) Libera Memoria, which is dedicated to remembering and commemorating the victims of the mafia; (e) Libera e g(i)usto di viaggiare, which promotes ethical tourism; and (f) Libera Informazione, a collective of journalists and volunteers who report on the mafia and antimafia as well as exert pressure on local and national media to cover antimafia voices.
2 See also Morozov (2011) and Angela Maiello's chapter 7 in this book for a similar perspective developed in Italian analyses of social networks and antimafia engagement.
3 For a discussion of what is described as "the networked new citizen," see Valenzuela, Park, and Key (2009).
4 I want to thank Vito Lo Monaco, president of the Pio La Torre Center, and Ansa journalist Antonella Lombardi for generously sharing their time and research on the reparative work being done in the context of antimafia public pedagogy and cultural renewal. I also want to thank Lo Monaco for his insights into understanding Italy as a country in and of transition. His analysis of Italy resonates with the definition of transitional justice offered

by the International Center for Transitional Justice. The Center describes transitional justice as "a set of judicial and non-judicial measures that have been implemented by different countries in order to redress the legacies of massive human rights abuses. These measures include criminal prosecutions, truth commissions, reparations programs, and various kinds of institutional reforms." On a conceptual level, transitional justice emphasizes inclusive and non-adversarial frameworks that seek to keep a violent past from being repeated. The emphasis is generally placed on dialogue between victims and their perpetrators rather than solely on allocating blame.

5 For a discussion of the memorialist impulse in the film *Placido Rizzotto*, see Amy Boylan (2011).

6 In one of several interviews with Paparcone, Umberto Santino points out how unlikely it is that Peppino Impastato would walk the famous 100 steps with his brother. He also raises concerns about the way in which the film *I cento passi* represents Peppino as a singular, isolated hero who has few friends. Not only is this representation false, but Santino fears that it unwittingly teaches youth not to follow Peppino's example given his brutal murder. Santino believes the film serves mafia more than antimafia interests.

7 Robin Pickering-Iazzi (2010) offers an analysis of the problems inherent in conceptualizing antimafia consciousness in linear sequential, developmental terms, specifically when remembering female antimafia activists. I draw extensively on the work of Pickering-Iazzi in my studies of the absence of a female antimafia presence on the Facebook site of Francesco Morvillo as well as in my study of the antimafia photography of Letizia Battaglia.

8 The recent establishment of the cooperative Rita Atria (1974–1992), named after the "martyr of justice" Rita Atria, in the province of Trapani, begins to address the gap in Libera Terra's collective remembering of female antimafia activists. The question remains, however, how Atria will be remembered and to what extent the imperfect erasures within her archive are pursued in the name of a more capacious understanding of civility and legality, one that exceeds the heteronormative face of antimafia activism.

4 Democratizing the Memorial Landscape: Casamemoria Vittimemafia's Calendar of Loss

AMY BOYLAN

Introduction: All Victims Are Worthy of Commemoration

On 10 April 2015, the Facebook page Casamemoria Vittimemafia updated its status to read: "10 April 1998 Catania. The corpse of twenty-year-old Annalisa Isaia was discovered. 'Her crime was that she went dancing with people her uncle did not approve of.'"[1] Accompanying the status update was a link to transcripts of two newspaper articles, one from *La Stampa* and another from *Corriere della Sera*, both written soon after law enforcement authorities had discovered that Annalisa Isaia, at age twenty, had been killed by her uncle.[2] The facts indicate that Annalisa's uncle killed her with two shots to the back of her neck because she spent the evening at a disco in Catania with some boys from a rival clan. (The uncle, incidentally, had only been identified as the killer after he had been arrested for a massacre in which his intended target was killed but which also left a five-year-old boy blinded by a bullet to the face.) Annalisa's father had been killed five years earlier in an ambush by a rival clan in Acireale. In the *La Stampa* article, journalist Fabio Albanese makes the following editorial statement about Annalisa:

> It seems that the uncle punished her in this way for a life that was a little too rowdy, for her dangerous associations with people from other clans; young people whom Annalisa met because they were the same age and were part of the same social circles, certainly not because they were *mafiosi*.[3]

Alternatively, the *Corriere della Sera* simply states that "the man seems to have punished her just because she associated with some kids her age who were linked to a rival clan."[4]

Another status update from the same day commemorates "vice brigadiere Rosario Iozia" murdered on 10 April 1987 in Cittanova. This status update includes a paragraph describing the events leading up to Iozia's death taken from the Associazione Nazionale Carabinieri's official website. The update also includes a link to a blog entry where the authors have compiled a number of articles about the circumstances of Iozia's death while he was involved in confronting a fugitive from justice.

Here, then, on the Casamemoria Vittimemafia Facebook page, the daughter of a minor mafia family and a Carabiniere squad commander killed in the line of duty are commemorated using the same unembellished, straightforward journalistic language.[5] Furthermore, this seemingly democratic approach to commemoration repeats itself on a daily basis on the two Facebook pages and the blog affiliated with the Casamemoria Vittimemafia organization. While the blog and Facebook pages mark the anniversaries of well-known mafia assassinations such as those of Judge Giovanni Falcone and Judge Paolo Borsellino, they also incorporate the deaths of non-famous victims, those killed as collateral damage and even those who have no declared role in the anti-mafia struggle, or whose status remains ambiguous, into their calendar of loss.

Anthropologist Deborah Puccio-Den's (2008) work on the religious and hagiographic characteristics of antimafia commemorative narratives is helpful here in understanding why the more inclusive gestures of Casamemoria Vittimemafia are so unusual:

> To understand these texts, one must go back not only to the practices that drive them, but also the context in which they were produced: The transformation of the antimafia struggle into a religious battle. Called upon in the 1980s to reform society, to set it right and amend its morals, the judges [Falcone and Borsellino] became the representatives of a humanist credo that by getting men to turn away from egotism, encouraged them to devote themselves to others and to sacrifice themselves in the name of an ideal of Justice presented as a higher principle. It is useful to compare these unpretentious, apparently disparate writings to the construction of a true literary genre that flourished in the 1990s and that continues to bear fruit: the biography of anti-Mafia protagonists. This literature also focuses on the theme of sacrificing one's private life for the sake of public good, highlighting the exceptional firmness of the anti-Mafia people in the face of the mortal dangers they are exposed to on a daily basis. Their

extraordinary courage sets them apart from ordinary mortals. They lead solitary, if not hermitic, lives. Their conduct surpasses human limits. This effacement of the self, this ability to withstand an unbearable pace of work for whomever, sometimes without even eating, often without sleeping, this capacity to overcome the constraints of their material and corporeal being and their possibility to cut themselves off from the world, once again make the judges heroic figures. When their "sacrifice" is sealed by death, these heroes turn into "martyrs." (62)

Thus, we see that, as typically happens in any given community, in its attempt to shape cultural and collective memory, the historically dominant voices in the antimafia movement have selected certain figures to celebrate and certain ones to ignore.

Scholars from various disciplines reveal the ways in which certain victims of the mafia who are not perceived as conforming to the qualities listed above by Puccio-Den risk being erased or repackaged by agents of collective memory. For example, in her article examining the way in which Rita Atria's struggle with her own identity, between informer (*collaboratrice con la giustizia*) and a young girl whose childhood had been lived under the influence of mafia culture, Robin Pickering-Iazzi (2010) argues that "as these representations put the raw materials of Atria's life into narrative form, they tend to adopt a model of linear development that progresses from her origins as the daughter of a mafioso to an unconditional break from Mafia culture and practice, resulting in a coherent, stable antimafia identity" (22). Yet, Pickering-Iazzi asserts, while "such discursive strategies clarify the ideals that the texts link to Rita Atria, making her name and what it symbolizes more easily remembered" they also elide "the points of inner conflict and ambivalence" and ultimately "hinder an understanding of the complex problems posed by the very changes in subjectivity that are commemorated" (22–3). Pickering-Iazzi's work on Rita Atria highlights the ways in which the more complex, even unruly aspects of Rita's story have been elided so that her image becomes more easily digestible to those invested in the dominant antimafia narrative. Exploring a different line of inquiry, Dana Renga (2013) offers an example of the way in which the many people living lives that register somewhere between innocent victim and mafioso are considered unworthy of commemoration or communal grief. Renga is particularly concerned with women and those who have little choice about their level of involvement in mafia dealings due to life circumstances imposed on them by systemic inequalities.

Commenting on the depiction of the character Maria's death in the film *Gomorrah* (Garrone, 2008), Renga (2013) writes:

I am suggesting that *Gomorrah* represents another case in which the hierarchy of grievability is laid bare: some lives, such as anti-Mafia martyrs Peppino Impastato and Placido Rizzotto, are acceptable to mourn. Others, in particular those who are ambiguously connected with the system, are not and their deaths will not be worked through. (149)

Here, Renga draws on Judith Butler's (2009) concept of "grievability" to make a provocative statement calling for a reassessment of the way blame for an entire system of inequality and corruption is displaced onto certain figures who are inescapably caught up in it. While Casamemoria Vittimemafia does not go quite that far, it does challenge what might be called the canon of antimafia martyrs. Casamemoria Vittimemafia strives to commemorate all victims of mafia violence, especially, according to the site's authors, "the many whose anniversaries pass unobserved each year."

Finally, in her article "'Eccentric Subjects': Female Martyrs and the Antimafia Public Imaginary" (2012), Paula Salvio argues that while Francesca Morvillo (the wife of Giovanni Falcone and a judge herself, also killed in the Capaci bombing) is included in the social network landscape of antimafia commemoration (on Facebook, for example), she becomes "overshadowed" by the movement and her Facebook commemorative page ultimately becomes "a site of struggle that displaces her memory with iconic images of antimafia history that commemorate masculine histories and relegate her to a figure who lacks political significance worthy of remembering" (397).

Pickering-Iazzi, Renga, and Salvio provide specific examples of how memory makers both include and exclude in order to shape the past and therefore the future. In this context, Casamemoria Vittimemafia can be seen as a project that creates a counternarrative, as a corrective to the narrative that seems to have gained the most traction in Italy. One of the tools that Casamemoria Vittimemafia uses to create such a counternarrative is its calendar of loss which, much in the same way as the Catholic liturgical calendar, marks the date and circumstances of death of victims of mafia violence, and dedicates a special commemorative day to each documented victim (although often victims must share their days since it is not unusual that multiple victims are killed on the same day or that victims are killed in different years but their murders fall on the same calendar date). The calendar created by Casamemoria Vittimemafia expands the definition of who is worthy of commemoration, challenges the notion that one victim is more important than any other (thus raising important questions about privilege and state responsibility), and fundamentally alters the rhythm of annually recurring "sacred" days.[6] Yet if, as sociologist Eviatar Zerubavel (2003) argues, "calendars help establish an annual cycle of remembrance and forgetting designed to ensure that several times every year members will recall certain 'sacred' moments from their collective past and create the frame for 'mnemonic socialization'" (318), what does it mean when a community chooses to observe every day as a day of remembrance? In this chapter, I will address this question as well as the particular role that the Internet and social media play in the creation of the Casamemoria Vittimemafia alternative calendar. Because the alternative calendar contributes to the formation of an antimafia imaginary based on the everyday life experiences of non-elite members of society, it exemplifies an alternative, or complementary, method of constructing a culture of legality, one that does not rely entirely on the state or its legal system. Rather, this calendar creates online spaces and artefacts that "produce terms of antimafia subjectivity."[7] But before I address the questions raised here, I first offer a detailed description of the Facebook pages and blog that are the subjects of this essay.

A House of the Dead in Cyberspace

The Facebook group "Una casa della memoria per le vittime della mafia" (founded in 2009), its affiliated Facebook Community page (Casamemoria Vittimemafia), and affiliated blog at Vittimemafia.it (created in 2011) use the words of author and antimafia activist Aldo Penna to describe their mission: "We give voice to silence. We prevent the oblivion of forgetting. The memory of the victims as remembrance is an antidote to the new violence of today."[8] The Facebook group and community provide (a) curated information to those on whose feed the posts appear and (b) a space for group members to contribute to and shape the identity of a continuous feed dedicated to antimafia commemorative practices. The blog serves another of the organization's essential functions: "The decision to start a blog was born from the need to archive in one single place all the data that had been gathered" (vittimemafia.it). The guiding idea of the three "spaces" combined is encapsulated by a sentence in English (the only one of its kind on the blog or Facebook pages): "A place where mafia victims still live in the memory of those who don't want to forget."

In terms of the project's mission, there is a strong emphasis on "making memory" (*fare memoria*), which, like the idea of a "place" itself, has something of a concreteness about it but also demonstrates an awareness of the need to mould memory as opposed to preserving it. While the names of the sites' administrators are not prominently featured, a number of well-known antimafia activists are quoted on the topic of memory and the ideas voiced stand as the sites' mission statements. The words of don Luigi Ciotti, founder of Libera (1995), appears first in a list of inspirational citations:

> Making memory is an obligation, a duty that we feel we owe to all those who have been killed at the hands of mafias, an obligation to the victims' families, to all of society, but, first and foremost, to our consciences as citizens, as lay people and Christians, as men and women who live their lives without resignation ... We cannot limit ourselves to remembering, even though it is our duty to not forget. We must transform memory into obligation, condemnation, testimony, change. In the garden of a school in Hamburg in which the Nazis killed twenty children there is a commemorative plaque bearing the following words: "Stand here in silence, but when you leave, speak."[9]

The idea that these online projects work to turn the ephemeral into the concrete ("We cannot limit ourselves to remembering, even though it is our duty to not forget. We must transform memory into obligation, condemnation, testimony, change") speaks to the deliberate naming of the project as a "House of Memory" (Casa della Memoria), a name that connotes a brick and mortar structure. In Italy, a House of Memory is generally considered to be a type of study centre, an archive, or a public pedagogical centre that promotes the memory of the Partisan Resistance and other related historical and cultural phenomena such as terrorism within Italy. Among such offline sites are the recently inaugurated Casa della Memoria in Milan, the Casa della Memoria e della Storia in Rome, the Casa della Memoria della Resistenza e della Deportazione in the small town of Vinchio in Piedmont, and the Casa Memoria Felicia e Peppino Impastato in Cinisi. Thus, in aligning the Casa della memoria per le vittime della mafia with other such Houses of Memory the founders also align the antimafia struggle with other national struggles, such as the fight against fascism and Nazism that occupy an unassailable moral high ground.

The project itself, as mentioned above, encompasses three specific sites on the web. The first is a Facebook "Community" page titled "Casamemoria Vittimemafia." It is an open community, meaning that anyone can "like" and "follow" it without having to request permission from the page administrators. Facebook itself defines a "Page" as the following: "Unlike your profile, Facebook pages are visible to everyone on the internet by default. You, and every person on Facebook, can connect with these Pages by becoming a fan and then receive their updates in your News Feed and interact with them."[10] As of 10 April 2015 there were 4,154 people who "like" the Casamemoria Vittimemafia page. Likewise, the page itself "likes" a number of other antimafia Facebook pages such as Associazione Antimafie Rita Atria, Comitato Addiopizzo, Stampo Antimafioso, and Libera Terra. Therefore, it participates in the network of antimafia culture active on Facebook. The Facebook page does not offer any information about the administrators responsible for maintaining the page, however there is a link to the corresponding blog at http://www.vittimemafia.it. In terms of activity, the page updates its status most days (there are sometimes anywhere from one to three days between updates), and some days multiple times (e.g., in the last month new status updates have appeared between one and six times on most days). The updates consist almost exclusively of excerpts from newspaper articles about people who have died due to mafia violence. As mentioned above, the victims range from uninvolved bystanders, to *carabinieri*, to targeted assassinations of antimafia politicians and activists. News articles about the circumstances under which the victims were killed are almost always attached.

The second component of the project is a Facebook group entitled "Una casa della memoria per le vittime della mafia" with 3,682 members as of 10 April 2015. Facebook describes Facebook groups as "the place for small group communication and for people to share their common interests and express their opinion. Groups allow people to come together around a common cause, issue or activity to organize, express objectives, discuss issues, post photos and share related content."[11] The creators of a Facebook group can make the group public or private. Public means that anyone with a Facebook account can become a member, post and comment on the group page; private means that even people with Facebook accounts must request to join and be approved before becoming members. Una casa della memoria per le vittime della mafia is a public group. The cycle of posting that occurs in this group echoes, for the most part, what happens on the Facebook Community page. Posts mostly follow the commemorative calendar produced by Casamemoria Vittimemafia with the one significant difference being that they are posted by members, not updated by the page itself. Members also intermittently post general news or opinion articles on topics of possible interest to the group as well as announcements shared from the Vittimemafia blog site. There are seven individuals listed as administrators of the group, meaning that they have the authority to, among other things, edit or remove posts, block people from becoming members (i.e., set privacy limitations), and control the group's profile and background images.

The third and final component of the project is the Vittime Mafia blog (http://www.vittimemafia.it), which is not a Facebook page (although the opportunity to share articles to one's own Facebook profile is provided, as are links to the organization's Facebook page and group). Here, the organization's mission and self-presentation are elaborated upon with extensive citations from prominent antimafia figures such as don Luigi Ciotti, Aldo Penna, and Sonia Alfano. The site also offers a page with suggested links to articles, a page dedicated to news and issues related to primary and secondary education, a page containing a list of videos documenting protests, interviews, songs, and news footage, as well as a page announcing the publication of books on antimafia topics. The majority of the blog's content, however, can be found by clicking on a tab entitled "Vittime" (victims). This page houses a "Scheda" (data sheet) which lists articles/obituaries in chronological order for as many victims of mafia assassinations as the group has documented so far, beginning with 3 March 1861 and up to 31 December 2014.

In the following sections I will look at this three-pronged project, focusing particularly on the Casamemoria Vittimemafia Facebook Community page, from a number of critical perspectives on collective, cultural and popular memory, countermonuments, and web memorials in order to comment on how the project responds to the needs of the community and what the project's contribution to the culture of the antimafia might be.

Casamemoria Vittimemafia as Countermonument

In the 1990s, German artists attempting to commemorate the Holocaust made use of what has been called the countermonument, constructed to

offer an alternative to the static nature and promise of closure and rec-
onciliation inherent to traditional monuments. Since then, a number of
scholars, part of the "memory boom," have been asking what kinds of
commemorative practices can provoke active remembering as opposed
to passivity or indifference, particularly in cases of trauma and when
marginalized groups insert a contested memory into a dominant narrative. Many assert that traditional monumental and memorial forms fail
to meaningfully bridge past, present, and future, and that while traditional monuments can be used to neutralize political opposition or promote an exclusive view of a particular event, popular commemorations
like spontaneous shrines, demonstrations, and participatory online
memorials can better express countermemories.[12] In other words, these
alternative forms given to oppositional memories resist being incorporated by the "hegemonic cultural memory" (Bold, Knowles, and Leach
2002, 126) and, as James E. Young (1993) notes, reject the process of
forgetting that occurs "once we assign monumental form to memory"
(5). Examples of countermonuments in the antimafia context might be
the Falcone Tree in Palermo, Addiopizzo's Palermo city tour itineraries,
the women of "The Bedsheet Collective" and their hunger strikes in
Piazza Politeama, or the recent initiatives to incorporate Lea Garofalo
(a witness for justice killed by her mafioso former husband because of
her collaboration with law enforcement) into official antimafia memory
through hybrid efforts on social media and in non-cyber public spaces
where demonstrations have taken place. Yet, while in the early years
of the antimafia movement any commemoration of an antimafia figure
could have been considered a countermonument because these figures
were not recognized by official culture or through official channels, now
that it has become more acceptable to commemorate victims of mafia
violence, the boundaries of countermemories have shifted. Today it is
figures like Francesca Morvillo, Rita Atria, or the previously unknown
human collateral damage who must be inserted into the accepted
ranks of antimafia martyrs as worthy of commemoration. And this is
precisely what Casamemoria Vittimemafia does through its attempted
democratization of the memorial landscape.

Tamir Sorek (2015), drawing on the Popular Memory Group, has aptly
summarized the tensions inherent in the struggle among groups to stake
their claim to the "contested terrain" of memory work. Sorek writes:

> This terrain is occupied by many actors with various agendas and diverse
> narratives who compete over the construction of the past. There are real

processes of domination in the field of historical remembrance: at any given moment, certain representations achieve centrality, visibility, and prestige; others are marginalized or muted. (8)

Elsewhere, I have used the term "unresolved commemorations" to refer to instances in which dominant and marginalized groups collaborate but maintain their conflicting positions with regard to commemoration (Boylan 2013). I propose that these types of unresolved commemorations can provide an antidote to what Ann Cvetkovich (2002) identifies as "the mechanisms by which certain forms of suffering are deemed worthy of national public attention, while others are left to individuals or minority groups to tend to on their own" (472). In unresolved commemoration, the struggle between opposing groups becomes the memorial and perpetuates its existence. I see Casamemoria Vittimemafia's insistent revising of the antimafia "liturgical" calendar, while simultaneously asserting the organization's mission to "make memory," as a practice that continuously gives life to the project. In other words, it is an example of unresolved commemoration. However, the larger question of unresolved commemoration and "grievability" can be further explored with a discussion about the specifics of online mourning and virtual memorials.

Enfranchising Grief

Perhaps one of the most important aspects of virtual commemoration has to do with "enfranchising grief that has not been socially sanctioned" (Moss 2004, 78) and expanding "boundaries of who is allowed or expected to participate in the mourning process" (De Vries and Rutherford 2004, 8). This enfranchisement has first and foremost to do with who it is a given community deems worthy of mourning and commemoration. In the case of Casamemoria Vittimemafia, the scope of grief is widened significantly with respect to other institutions both on and offline. For example, a quick glance at other antimafia commemorative Facebook pages and blogs reveals a heavy preference for information related to Falcone and Borsellino. The Facebook Community page entitled "Io non dimentico" (I will not forget) exemplifies this tendency. It features a quote by Borsellino as a background image and a photograph of Falcone and Borsellino together as its profile picture. The posts are dominated by videos and articles related to the two judges punctuated with appearances by

other well-known figures from mafia and antimafia history such as
Peppino Impastato, Luciano Leggio, and Tommaso Buscetta. A cursory survey of the pages "Giovanni Falcone, Paolo Borsellino e tutti
gli altri eroi" (Giovanni Falcone, Paolo Borsellino and all the other
heroes) and "Libera Contro le Mafie" (Libera against the mafias),
the latter being the most popular antimafia Facebook page based on
number of "likes" it has garnered, produce much the same effect. Giovanna Summerfield's *"Per non dimenticare"* (chapter 5 in this book)
makes a convincing case for the importance of well-known figures
like Falcone and Borsellino who have become heroes of traditional
antimafia narratives. She demonstrates how a multitude of memories expressed by everyday people in the form of narratives cohere
around such figures and permit members of the larger community
to identify with their history and legacy, since the events surrounding these figures, such as high-profile assassinations, are often memo-
rable to the general public. Summerfield's analysis suggests that a
starting point of "We all remember what we were doing on 23 May
1992" might then spark a large volume of individual memories that
together form a collective. Yet, for the creators of Casamemoria Vittimemafia, actively commemorating lower-profile victims is another
way in which to foster a sense of community.

As a way to address the limited grievability afforded everyday citizens with whose stories other everyday citizens might identify, Casamemoria Vittimemafia asks that symbolic entrepreneurs "engage in
mobilizing activities similar to those undertaken by social movement
activists. They must frame the event ... and deploy resources to per-
suade others to approve, fund, and participate in commemoration,"
in other words, they need to have access to the "mnemonic capacity"
that arises out of a sense of community identity and organizational
resources, and to draw on a repertoire and history of commemorative
forms (Armstrong and Crage 2006, 726).

Jack Santino (2006) uses the term "performative commemoratives"
to describe sites and rituals that "commemorate a loss but which also
draw attention to the social conditions that contributed to the loss"
(10). According to Santino, these sites of commemoration usually arise
spontaneously in the sense that the state is not involved, an artist is
not commissioned, and planning is minimal. The performative aspect
urges participants to personalize public and political issues and activists employ these types of countermonumental modes of commemoration in order to express opposition to social situations they believe to

be unjust. They potentially counteract a tendency towards the cathartic element often found in traditional monuments.

Electronic memorials also offer the possibility of positioning the personal and affective – blogs, personal web pages, photographs taken by sit-in participants – alongside the documents of a dominant culture – mainstream newspaper articles, television interviews with figures like Falcone and Borsellino – while also allowing for constant modification and expansion. In the case of Casamemoria Vittimemafia, we view mainstream newspaper articles alongside personal blog articles and news from alternative sources, all of which are remediated by the administrators and/or members of the groups producing the memories. The contributors to Casamemoria Vittimemafia seek out forgotten stories and post them among stories of more well-known cases, elevating the unknowns to the importance of the famous.

Calendarization and Control

The calendar-based format of Casamemoria Vittimemafia's Internet presence, enhanced by Facebook's date-centric structure, seems to highlight a tension between traditional and postmodern forms of commemoration. (Incidentally, Facebook has very recently added an "On This Day" function that allows users to look back at their activity on a given date organized by year but that has also made it more difficult to view all posts from a certain page in chronological order.) Pierre Nora (1989) has identified calendars as a "lieux des memoire," a site of memory, a product of the modern age that must be consciously generated and that emerges in place of more organic forms of memory (12). However, the calendar's cyclical nature, its reaching towards eternal life, also connects it to ancient religious rituals and recurring commemorative celebrations. The creation of a calendar is a hopeful act in a certain sense.

If Nora (1989) argues that self-consciously created calendars are an essential element of national identity, others have broadened the concept to include discussions of what it means to create alternative calendars. Todor Kuljic (2006), for example, observes that "holidays, as institutionalized dates of memory, draw attention to not only what we need to remember, but when and how to remember. *New holidays symbolized a radical break with the past*" (as cited in Pavlaković 2012, 322, emphasis mine). Likewise Sorek (2015), writing about the Palestinian population in Israel, notes that "the creation of a political calendar is a form of control over time – an especially valuable asset when control over public space is extremely limited" (6). Modifying the calendar, as Casamemoria Vittimemafia has done, constitutes a radical revision of and a strategy to exert control over antimafia commemorative narratives which, according to its foundational statements, did not include every victim of mafia violence. Facebook, in particular, allows the group to do this because it provides a means of wide-spread distribution of information as well as a repetitive, calendar-like structure that conforms to the needs of the project. Facebook also presents certain obstacles such as the inability to search for a specific date or name, and the inability to organize the archived information according to year. But in an inventive use of multiple platforms simultaneously, Casamemoria Vittimemafia has navigated those obstacles by creating a blog that is searchable and that organizes the deaths of mafia victims by year.

While the emphasis on the calendar structure and the anniversaries of victims' deaths work to simultaneously modify the religious practice of assigning saints days, include figures who clearly do not conform to the definition of saints, and interrogate the need for saints in the first place, it also provides another avenue of resistance. In her essay in this volume, Carla Bagnoli notes that online social networks, by their very nature, challenge notions of geographical territoriality and territorial belonging, mainstays of Italian mafias. Similarly, Casamemoria Vittimemafia's calendar, created in cyberspace and disseminated via social networks, reclaims ancient rituals of mourning and the mafia practice of calendarization, but liberates them from territorial specificity while also maintaining a groundlessness in ritual and tradition. Given that mafia assassinations often occur within the structure of carefully planned symbolic dates according to the rules of the vendetta, this "countercalendar" also provides a parallel narrative that remembers not for reasons of a vendetta but in order to eliminate the culture that remembers in order to avenge.

Renate Siebert (1996) has documented the way in which the vendetta becomes a commemorative ritual carried out on symbolic dates and anniversaries:

> The vendetta was a commemoration of death; for instance, feuds in Calabria are tied to dates and anniversaries, a strategy of memory which reconnects the vendetta with the trauma suffered. By killing at this specific time, it is as if the dead man, through his historical substitute, were acting directly, renewing that principle of reciprocity which regulates and inflects

relationships. The mafia too is attentive to dates and anniversaries, with such arrogance and cynicism as to plan to kill a son on the anniversary of the father's murder. (38–9)

For just one example of this practice, we can remember the murder of beloved antimafia activist and priest don Giuseppe Diana, assassinated as he prepared for mass on 19 March 1994. That day was his *onomastico*, or "name day" according to the tradition in which Italians celebrate the Catholic saint's day that corresponds to their given name.

Siebert (1996) also connects this method of the vendetta to folk forms of feuding and mourning, and notes that "by formally imitating an ancient ritual, emptied of its meaning of reciprocity and reparation, the mafia implies a claim on popular roots and affiliations, while at the same time pursuing its own aim of intimidation and domination which has nothing to do with the balance of traditional community" (39). I believe that it is precisely a connection to traditional forms of mourning, despite the fact that they are both reinvented in a secular form and practised in cyberspace, that makes Casamemoria Vittimemafia's project very powerful for those who choose to engage with it.

Questions of Participation and Engagement

While folk forms of feuding and mourning are performed within a physical community and require various levels of participation from community members, whether they choose to become involved or not, membership in online communities tends to be elective, occasional, and not always quantifiable. It is, therefore, difficult to gauge the impact of the Casamemoria Vittimemafia Facebook and blog initiatives. It seems that there is a small core group of active participants – most posts receive anywhere from one to twenty-five "likes," while comments are more rare and usually along the lines of "*Grazie*" (Thank you), "R.I.P." (by far the most repeated of all comments), or a brief statement on the importance of memory. Many of the articles are also "shared" by anywhere from one to twenty people, including other antimafia organization pages such as "Libera Calabria" (Free Calabria), "Dedicato alle vittime delle mafie" (Dedicated to mafia victims), and "Palma di Montechiaro ricorda i suoi morti per la legalità" (Palma di Mentechiaro remembers its fallen in the name of legality). In addition, some followers of the page shared to other organization's pages such as "Se non ora quando? Donne e informazioni" (If not now, when? Women and information) and "Sosteniamo don Luigi Ciotti e le sue attività" (We support don Luigi Ciotti and his activities).

But still, Casamemoria Vittimemafia's numbers are modest compared to the most popular antimafia-themed Facebook pages. For example, Libera Contro le Mafie has 213,937 total page "likes," and the "likes" of status updates are regularly at 500 plus, while "shares" are often in the hundreds as well. Posts on the page range from announcements of protests or conferences, the sharing of news articles about contemporary politics, and celebrations of initiatives undertaken by the organization. These are the updates that receive the most attention. However, Libera Contro le Mafie also posts commemorative updates for well-known murder cases. These receive numerous "likes" as well. In particular, a status update commemorating don Giuseppe Diana on 19 March 2015 received 2,861 "likes," whereas a similar update on Casamemoria Vittimemafia received only six "likes" and four "shares."

On the other hand, a 30 March 2015 status update by Casamemoria Vittimemafia remembering Daniele Polimeni, a nineteen-year-old boy whose corpse was discovered on 30 March 2005, received five "likes" and four "shares." These numbers are similar to the update for don Giuseppe Diana, yet the update commemorates Daniele in the following way:

> Daniele Polimeni was nineteen years old, a rowdy young man. He did not like to study but in Reggio Calabria he did not have many alternatives and delinquency seemed to be the easiest way in which to distinguish oneself and keep a little bit of money in one's pocket.
>
> But Daniele did not have the opportunity to make a different choice. On March 30, 2005, in Favazzina (Reggio Calabria), his charred corpse was found. Someone had lured him into a trap and then killed him. The family is still waiting for the truth and justice.[13]

Daniele was an aspiring mafioso but his death is lamented because he had no other choice. Thus, Casamemoria Vittimemafia's project has a limited audience of some 4,150 followers of the community page and 3,670 members of the Una casa della memoria per le vittime della mafia group, but it is also important to note that the work they do, by its very nature, leaves it on the margins of mainstream antimafia communities and places it in conflict with organizations that have chosen to feature the more easily grievable figures of antimafia history. And, while other organizations (such as Libera) reproduce the same list of victims' names that Casamemoria uses and circulate them at certain times during the year (e.g., on the "Day of memory and duty in memory of innocent mafia victims" celebrated for the past twenty years on 21 March), Casamemoria Vittimemafia does not elide or minimize uncomfortable details of victims' lives. Rather, it posts them for the public to read and fully digest. Furthermore, Casamemoria Vittimemafia's page and update "likes" are similar to most other antimafia pages (aside from the Libera pages, those I have mentioned above are in the 3,000–5,000 "likes" range). And finally, Casamemoria Vittimemafia continues its work despite its modest audience members who likely view Casamemoria's status updates together with updates from other organizations that appear on their Facebook feeds. Multiple daily updates continue to be produced by the makers of memory who administer the page, group, and blog. On the topic of measuring engagement, Paula Salvio (chapter 3 in this volume) offers a hopeful theory about the act of "liking" pages and posts on Facebook. These small acts have been criticized as "low-risk" activism or "slacktivism," implying that they cannot compare to the power of taking to the streets as a method of protest. In contrast, Salvio proposes that each person who likes or comments on a post commemorating a particular historical event, such as the massacre at Portella della Ginestra, "participates in reconfiguring" traditional spaces of protest and through a "subtle but powerful act of posting and 'liking' ... generates resonances among the past, the present and hopes for the future" (94). Thus, while there may be modest engagement on individual posts, each page's "like," "share," or one-word comment takes on profound meaning and has the power to move beyond that single act. On the other hand, it has been well documented that most politically engaged users of social media do not consider their use of Facebook, Twitter, YouTube, and so on to be the only component of their political engagement. What's more, while page "likes" and web traffic is clearly important to any group that wants to communicate its message, Casamemoria Vittimemafia is simultaneously occupied with fundamentally altering the content and form of antimafia memories, a project enabled to a certain extent by Facebook, but which also takes place in the non-virtual world.

Conclusion

Sociologist Amanda Lagerkvist (2013) observes that because "memory work in the digital age is taken up in the face of three challenges, which deal with the temporality of instantaneity, an all-pervasive networked individualism and concomitant technological capacities that subject memory to endless revision, and an accelerated blurring of the private and the public," one might assume that this corroborates "the sense in which there is a vanishing and ephemeral dimension to all digital culture, as it is situated in the absolute present" (12). Yet, on the contrary, Lagerkvist argues that "in the teeming mediated publicness of death, new cultures of memory may also contribute to the paradoxical solidification of these existential terrains. It cannot be denied that from the vantage point of human experience, there appears to be a surprising steadiness, permanence, and unexpected rootedness in these aspects of web memorialisation" (12).

Lagerkvist's (2013) claims about the effects of commemorative practices on the web have particular resonance in an antimafia activist context and can be illustrated by the desire to create a "casa" (home), which implies "concrete place," within cyberspace. While typically the types of commemoration that exist on the web ("cybershrines," Facebook tribute pages, blogs, and sites like YouTube) exist somewhere between the permanent and ephemeral, and self-consciously allow for a portability, fluidity, internationality, and a collaborative element that non-virtual forms of archiving and commemoration preclude, a "Casa della Memoria" also implies a return to the concrete, the tangible, the core structure of a geographical community. This tension between the concrete and all-encompassing, and the ephemeral and fragmented, between the historical and traditional, and the new and resistant characterizes the Casamemoria Vittimemafia project, and reflects an important aspect of communities attempting to commemorate and grieve persistent, ongoing traumas. Life in these types of communities is so fragile, death so ever-present (evidenced by the fact that in the Casamemoria Vittimemafia calendar almost each day of the year can be linked with multiple victims of mafia violence) that the goal is not self-consciously ephemeral ways of memorializing. Rather, they seek to create fluid and ever-expanding memorials, reminding the community that memories are grounded in ancient rituals and concrete places.

What I propose, then, is that the creators of Casamemoria Vittimemafia participate in an antimafia activist network that covers both the mainstream, and the local or esoteric, place and cyberspace. Casamemoria's alternative memory work is becoming part of a larger system of commemorative practices that have so far succeeded, after prolonged struggles, in creating spaces for figures like Lea Garofalo, who, though she became a witness of justice, was left unprotected by the state and met a gruesome death at the hands of her mafioso husband in 1999. Lea is remembered, along with seventy-two other victims, ranging from police to those who refused to pay extortion money to reckless teenagers, on Vittimemafia's archive page for the month of November. Meanwhile, in the non-virtual world, Lea Garofalo has recently been commemorated with place names at the urging of groups like Vittimemafia. For example, the town of Rosate (Milan) dedicated "Via Lea Garofalo," just around the corner from "Via Giovanni Falcone," in November 2014. In the town of Lissone (Lombardy), a small piazza, renamed "Largo Lea Garofalo – Vittime delle mafie" and located adjacent to the Croce-Dante school complex, was inaugurated in March 2015, scheduled to coincide with the "Day of memory and duty in memory of innocent mafia victims." In addition, this attention to Lea's story coincided with director Marco Tullio Giordana's made-for-television film *Lea*, which premiered on Rai1 in November 2015. Cultural products like the websites, place names, and film referenced above are a testament to the value of a multi-pronged approach to creating an inclusive "culture of legality" that redefines the term "hero" and respects and mourns all victims of Italy's mafias.

NOTES

1 Translation of this and all other citations in this essay are my own. Casamemoria Vittimemafia Facebook page: "10 Aprile 1998 Catania. Trovato il corpo di Annalisa Isaia, 20 anni. 'La sua colpa era di andare a ballare con persone non gradite allo zio,'" http://vittimemafia.it/index.php?option=com_content&view=article&id=100%3A10-aprile-1998-catania-trovato-il-corpo-di-annalisa-isaia-20-anni-qla-sua-colpa-era-di-andare-a-ballare-con-persone-non-gradite-allo-zioq&catid=35%3Ascheda&Itemid=67

2 Both articles were transcribed from the original 1998 versions and typed into the blog entry.

3 Casamemoria Vittimemafia, ibid., Fabio Albanese, *La Stampa*, 19 April 1998: "In questo modo avrebbe punito quella sua vita un po' troppo irrequieta, quelle sue frequentazioni pericolose con gente degli altri clan; ragazzi che Annalisa incontrava perchè erano della sua età, perchè facevano parte del suo stesso mondo, non certo perchè mafiosi."

4 Ibid.: "… l'uomo l'avrebbe punita solo perchè frequentava dei coetanei legati a una cosca rivale."

5 While Iozia's blog entry contains more articles and links to other pages, this is more the result of uneven media coverage and initiatives of people who knew Iozia as opposed to the blog or Facebook page privileging his memory over Isaia's.

6 I speak here of "attempts at" or "gestures towards" democratizing the commemorative landscape because Casamemoria Vittimemafia has not documented and recorded the murders of all victims of mafia violence. This is the case because much more research and documentation still needs to be carried out and also because Casamemoria Vittimemafia, like all groups, intentionally or unintentionally, does select who to include, and therefore who to exclude, from its calendar.

7 Robin Pickering-Iazzi uses this phrase in the introduction to this volume, and suggests that the identification with antimafia subjectivity through acts of solidarity in cyberspace can lead to participants feeling "empowerment as moral agents" in the fight against the mafias.

8 Casamemoria Vittimemafia Facebook page, https://www.facebook.com/groups/vittimemafia/. This citation can be found in the "Description" area of the page.

9 Ibid., https://www.facebook.com/groups/vittimemafia/. This citation can be found in the "Description" area of the page.

10 Ibid., https://www.facebook.com/notes/facebook/facebook-tips-whats-the-difference-between-a-facebook-page-and-group/324706977130.

11 Ibid., https://www.facebook.com/notes/facebook/facebook-tips-whats-the-difference-between-a-facebook-page-and-group/324706977130.

12 The idea of unconventional, vernacular, and contested memorial forms owes a great deal to scholarly investigations of Holocaust memorials and to the Vietnam Veterans' Memorial in Washington, DC, during the 1990s. See, for example, works such as Andreas Huyssen (1993), Scott A. Sandage (1993), Marita Sturken (1997, 1999), and James E. Young (1999).

13 Vittime Mafia Facebook page, http://vittimemafia.it/index.php?option=com_content&view=article&id=218:30-marzo-2005-favazzina-rc-ucciso-il-giovane-daniele-polimeni-19-anni-una-morte-ancora-senza-un-qpercheq&catid=35:scheda&Itemid=67

5 *Per non dimenticare*: Antimafia Digital Storytelling and Reflections

GIOVANNA SUMMERFIELD

Storytelling, according to developmental psychologists, is essential to the way children form their identities, adults discover themselves, and social memories are connected. Marshall Ganz (2011), senior lecturer in public policy at the Kennedy School of Government at Harvard University, remarks,

> Storytelling is the discursive form through which we translate our values into the motivation to act ... A story of self communicates the values that move us to lead. A story of us communicates values shared by those whom you hope to motivate to join us. And a story of now communicates the urgent challenge to those values that demand actions now. (280–2)

The power of storytelling is undeniable in the sense that it is essential to self-identification and the commitment to the social world of community and thus, in turn, a formidable tool to defeat apathy, isolation, and resignation. Following this line of thought, for several reasons digital storytelling is doubly powerful for the ways it makes possible connecting and mobilizing digital storytellers and listeners, and thereby enables cultural and social change. It has a universal imprint, which facilitates efforts to exchange stories of all kinds and create opportunities for immediate feedback. The role of social media is paramount in democratizing communications for the way it challenges the top-down hierarchy of power and operative monopolies in mainstream media. As the communications landscape becomes more complex and accessible, the networked population gains substantial opportunities to learn and engage. Social media enable the fostering of collective action that operates outside of the established social, economic, institutional contexts and restrictions, while seizing affordable and creative resources that allow for ongoing transformations. They function, by now, as coordinating tools for nearly all of the world's political movements. Indeed, most of the global authoritarian governments are now forcibly trying to limit Internet access, which confirms the overall awareness of the power of the media tools and digital conversations. Social media are, thus, recognized tools to promote self-governance (Shirky 2011).

This chapter will consider the fertile sociopolitical context that arises from the power of social media while discussing and analysing the You-Tube video "Per non dimenticare 23 maggio" (Not to forget 23 May), conceptualized and directed by Giuseppe Musumeci (2014), who at the time of production was academic senator of the University of Catania. He produced the video in collaboration with university and high school students, the local prison administration, the university president, and the mayor of Catania. By sharing their stories, their engagements, and their reflections about past events and future plans, these Sicilian citizens show that they are committed and inspirational. In twelve minutes, through a personal and educational platform, they endeavour to involve, befriend, and conquer their audiences while many viewers living in mafia territories are engaged in pitched antimafia battles.

In order to understand the social and symbolic functions this video text performs in the hybrid spaces of daily living in its local and cyberspatial dimensions, my discussion draws on critical notions of digital storytelling and also witnessing. For, in fact, as the social actors from Catania give narrative form to their memories, experiences, hopes, and committed social action, this visual product of the culture of legality bears witness to a traumatic past made present as a foundation for rebuilding civil society. For this reason, "Not to Forget 23 May" serves as a sample text for thinking about the thousands of video texts posted on social networks, which bear witness to the lives of Italian antimafia victims. (See Robin Pickering-Iazzi's introduction in this volume.) The significance of these digital stories cannot be taken lightly, especially in the context of Italian neighbourhoods and cities where the mafia employs violence to enforce omertà, the law of silence. Useful here are John Peters's (2001) insights on the primary meanings of becoming witnesses:

We are all ... witnesses ... simply by virtue of finding ourselves in places and times where things happen ... but witnessing is also the discursive act of stating one's experience for the benefit of an audience that was not present at the event and yet must make some kind of judgment about it ... To witness thus has two faces: the passive one of seeing and the active one of saying. (709)

In mafia territories, to witness also bears the literal and symbolic significance of rebelling against the mafia's law of place by claiming the right to speak out and attest to what happened and its meanings for the past and future. Furthermore, such acts of witnessing involve both responsibilities and transformative power. Peters (2001) proposes that as witnesses we not only have the task to proclaim and immortalize events, but also to commit to risk having life change. In this sense, each witness potentially serves as a transformative force for others who could not share the same experiences (713–14).

These testimonial functions, as well as the designs of the conceptualization of the video "Not to Forget 23 May," its production, forms of sharing the witnessing story, and the multiple effects of the video are explored here through an intimate behind-the-scene interview with the author and director of the video. Giuseppe Musumeci's comments on his expectations and the ways the making of the testimonial video story gratifyingly fulfilled them provide a point of departure for understanding this important genre of antimafia cultural production and the meanings the witnesses attach to their acts of digital storytelling. They also bring to light the ramifications of conducting this project and other digital stories that may similarly testify to rebellion against the mafia.

The Power of Storytelling

In recent years a growing body of work by healthcare professionals, cultural critics, and writers has devoted critical attention to storytelling and its multiple roles for the narrator and listeners/viewers, as well as for processes of identity formation, moral development, and interpersonal relations in private and civic life. Such issues directly affect the potential functions performed by the testimonial videos bearing witness to what the speaker experienced and how the story enables others to participate and change. According to Pam Allyn (2010), executive director of Litlife, a national organization promoting innovative literacy education, "storytelling is one of humans' most basic and effective forms of communication ... a key component of our neurological development, and a skill that will ultimately help create a well-adjusted and resilient youth." Lissa Rankin (2012) focuses more on the healing factor of storytelling, a pertinent issue for antimafia witnessing stories that narrate often traumatic violence and loss. She considers storytelling one of the most powerful medicines humans have:

> Every time you tell your story and someone else who cares bears witness to it, you turn off the body's stress responses, flipping off toxic stress hormones like cortisol and epinephrine and flipping on relaxation responses that release healing hormones like oxytocin, dopamine, nitric oxide, and endorphins. Not only does this turn on the body's innate self-repair mechanisms and function as preventative medicine – or treatment if you're sick. It also relaxes your nervous system and helps heal your mind of depression, anxiety, fear, anger, and feelings of disconnection.

Within the healthcare context, stories are mentally richer than simple instructions; they engage and involve the patient; they trigger empathy; are more likely to be remembered and retold; they promote a two-way conversation; and transfer knowledge. Storytelling has been one of the keys to the highly successful book series *Chicken Soup for the Soul*, which encourages people to submit their own stories and compiles them into a single volume to help people cope with specific issues like grief, stress, or spiritual matters. This well-known series has recognized the power of narrative in health and has formed a partnership with *Harvard Health Publications* to take storytelling and health to a new level (Senelick 2012).

Our identities and stories co-construct each other and, in turn, our communities. The stories we tell and the stories we are told also add up to stories we want to leave behind for others to enjoy and to use as they build their identities and values. "We use stories to make sense of our world and to share that understanding with others" (Rose 2011). On the other hand, Jerome Bruner (2010) states, "Cultures rely upon narrative conventions to maintain their coherence and to shape their members to their requirements. Indeed, commonplace stories and narrative genres even provide a powerful means whereby cultures pass on their norms to successive generations" (45). Marshall Ganz (2007), who founded the Leading Change Network, a global community of organizers, educators, and researchers mobilizing for democracy and cultural change, underscores the crucial role narrative plays in social movements. According to Ganz, in fact, stories not only communicate our challenges, choices, and outcomes, they also share our feelings, our obligations, our values; they not only teach but most important, they inspire. For an organizer or leader aiming to provide directions for change, the biggest challenge is how to break through, how to draw the attention of the people involved, regardless of the urgency of the need. Addressing this issue, Ganz (2009) states, "We don't just talk about hope and other values in abstractions. We talk about them in the language of stories because stories are what enable us to communicate these values to one another." All stories have a plot, a protagonist, and a moral. We, as listeners, may identify empathetically with the actor and with the challenges she or he faces. When the outcome occurs, due to the actions of the protagonist and the choices s/he has made, we, as listeners, can understand the moral of the stories because, according to Ganz (2009), we can feel all the emotions the storyteller is sharing; ultimately we become, by inspiration, agents.

To mobilize others under uncertain conditions, Ganz (2011) proposes, leaders have to challenge the hands, the head, and the heart. The challenge of the hands is one of action or a call to action, the ability to learn, and mastering new skills; the challenge of the head is one of strategy, using the resources to attain power and/for the ultimate purpose; and the challenge of the heart is one of motivation, of sharing hope, and hopefully success. These challenges correspond to a story of self, a story of us, and a story of now, where the story of self communicates the values that move the storyteller (or organizer/leader) to lead, a story of us communicates values shared by those whom the storyteller wants to motivate to join, and a story of now communicates the urgent challenge to those values that demand immediate action (273–82).

Since these are personal stories, some might think that they do not matter, that others are not interested. On the contrary, leaders have an obligation, as public figures, to share their origin, the reason for their mission/action, and the final goals. The personal story becomes thus public story to "justify" in a sense the leadership. All self stories encompass other stories, are influenced by other actors and agents; they draw from one's culture, family, and social environments. Individual stories stem out and intersect collective stories. They distinguish the self but also the community in which the self grows and acts. Shared stories, and thus experiences and values, make us feel safer. And yet it is important to underscore that for people to be able to share a story of us, to become "us," it is necessary to have a storyteller, an interpreter of the story of us. The storyteller, whom we have selected, articulates at this point the challenge, reminds others of the resources available, and incites others to make choices, offering a hopeful but credible vision (Ganz 2011,

284–7). Ganz (2011) states, "Through public narrative, leaders – and participants – can move to action by mobilizing sources of motivation, constructing new shared individual and collective identities, and finding the courage to act" (288).

The Current Status of Storytelling

In *The Healing Art of Storytelling: A Sacred Journey of Personal Discovery* (1996), Richard Stone states that our current culture is experiencing "destorification," which is to say there is a growing lack of the need for stories, due to the growing presence of technology that separates people, increasing the impossibility and unwillingness to interact with others in our contemporary society by destroying the spaces for telling stories (as cited in Jackson n.d.). But are these spaces really disappearing or have they just begun to migrate and create new spaces? Leslie Rule, of the Digital Storytelling Association, astutely charts the connection between age-old storytelling and forms of personal digital narration: "Digital storytelling is the modern expression of the ancient art of storytelling. Digital stories derive their power by weaving images, music, narrative and voice together, thereby giving deep dimension and vivid color to characters, situations, experiences, and insights" (as cited on the Digital Storytelling website, http://electronicportfolios.com/digistory/).

There is no doubt that the techniques to collect and recollect stories have changed dramatically. The collector and/or narrator can be identified as a single individual working on her or his computer but also as a collaborative group, which can include different actors and/or narrators, as well as responders to the collection posted, whether the material is shared through blogs, social forums, or video-hosting sites such as YouTube. The wider reach and circulation of the stories is undeniable, now that these are digitally shared rather than restricted to an immediate group of listeners. In her study "Folk Media Meets Digital Technology" (2010), Emily Polk suggests that within this new framework and with the opportunity "to give a voice to the voiceless, to raise awareness, and promote democracy" digital storytelling thus becomes "part of a larger shift in the media industry toward grassroots, citizen-based journalism in a new public sphere" (1–2). Digital storytelling, she asserts, also contributes to a consistent change of the notion of "community," mirroring and connecting individuals and groups that do not have geographical and temporal boundaries (9). Thus, we could suggest that digital stories, insofar as their content can be disseminated and replicated interactively whether asynchronously or not, could be more valuable and far-reaching than the traditional face-to-face narrations (8). The digital phenomenon has also been able to create and record stories that can be embraced universally and serve as documented real-life data (10).

Whereas the resources used to "digitize" a story can embellish it and make it more poignant, the highlight of these resources is that they keep the story to the point, unwrapping the meaning of the story, the moral so to speak, that goes beyond the practical event(s) narrated. Investing the facts with emotions is made easier with digital storytelling; the author/narrator is able, through her or his media, to share with the audience what she or he feels. Even if she or he is not the main protagonist or a character in the story, the audience is still able to capture the attitude and the sentiments through the details, the setting, a quick close-up, or a panoramic still. We are told that "a picture is worth a thousand words" and an effective digital storyteller exemplifies this proposition. The element of verisimilitude is critical in witnessing texts. As Paul Frosh (2009) reminds us,

> Witnessing texts encourage the conjecture that the world to be imaginatively produced is or was an actual world, not just a lifelike one, that it was witnessed or is being witnessed by the agency producing the text, and that our engagement with this world (and hence our engagement with this text) is morally important. (275)

A digital storyteller, within this context, can then be seen as a facilitator that empowers the participants. She or he is both an advocate and an animator, and engages in a dialogue with the viewers/listeners while creating a safe environment for them to create their own stories in their own voices, whether by adopting the same techniques or with a quick written response to the story that will elicit, in turn, other responses through blog entries, comments on a Facebook or YouTube visual or audio shareable file (Polk 2010, 14). She or he owns her or his own creation while giving others the invaluable opportunity to experiment and integrate their own narratives within the frame provided, whether through acting or responding. In brief, we could suggest that digital storytelling places greater power into the hands of more people and, more importantly, is better preserved for the benefit of posterity. Its longer and safer lifespan exponentially augments the stories' impact and inspiration.

"Per non dimenticare 23 maggio"

Giuseppe Musumeci is the digital storyteller of the witnessing video "Per non dimenticare 23 maggio" (Not to forget 23 May), conceived and produced in late May 2014. The project was carried out to stimulate reflections about the values of legality, active citizenship, and the fight against the mafia. In Musumeci's own words, "It is a story that grows out of pain and that becomes direct evidence, civic bravery; a public declaration of ways in which the local youth and local institutions want to responsibly undertake the moral heritage of facing and defeating the mafia phenomenon."[1] Significantly, Musumeci frames the video upon a very famous and important statement by Judge Giovanni Falcone, assassinated by the mafia on 23 May 1992. Falcone stated, "Men pass, ideas remain and will continue to walk on the legs of others."[2] With this notion of projecting ideas into the future in mind, Musumeci also shares his childhood memories, with no inhibitions. He allows us to delve into his own world, not only to understand his motivation for doing this project, but also to capture our attention as viewers, to assist us in identifying with the protagonist, Musumeci as a young child in a Sicily of the 1970s, and to involve us completely in the demystification and loud, proud condemnation of the mafia phenomenon of years past and present.

Departing from the concept of a hero, viewers witness in the twelve minutes and twenty-one seconds of the video footage a crescendo of faces and voices of university students who pass down a baton clearly marked with the word #*Legalità* (#Legality), which ultimately reaches the office of the Magnifico Rettore Giacomo Pignataro, president of the University of Catania. Pignataro underscores the main role of education to instil the values of democracy and justice, the cornerstones of the culture of legality, for which heroes like Judge Falcone and Judge Borsellino sacrificed their lives. The beauty of the island, underscored by some of the students who do not want to give up by abandoning their native land, is then represented in the video, primarily through shots of the heart of the city and its symbol, the "Liotr" (the elephant) that reigns majestic in Piazza Duomo, the main square of Catania, facing City Hall. Here, Mayor Enzo Bianco reminisces with the viewers about a personal episode that took place in Rome, while he was with Giovanni Falcone and his wife, Francesca Morvillo. It is a moving story that records the wisdom of Judge Falcone and his hope to defeat the mafia, by stating that the mafia, like all other human phenomena, has a beginning and an end. More important, the narrating of the encounter conveys the enthusiasm the mayor and the judge shared that evening. Bianco confesses that they were loaded with the same enthusiasm young people boast. The video cuts, at this point, to the younger faces of high school students, who are indeed our future, a future that does not exist "without the defeat of the mafia."[3]

Thanks to this digital project, these young adults and their community are now documented as parading along the main streets of the city, shouting that for them the 23 of May is a matter of life; it is a matter of courage. It is a battle that needs a collaborative effort, as the mayor mentioned, an initiative that calls for the power and willingness to participate actively, on the part of the individual, the community, and the institutions. This battle cannot be fought by the few, but requires the whole of society. This digital story has thus the purpose to not only involve many, but also to be disseminated among many. Its main scope is to incentivize antimafia efforts among the common citizens. This digital narrative proves to be another effective document to immortalize what has been done, to echo Peters's (2001) words, and what needs to be done through the lessons learned, the remembrance of those few who acted for the benefit of the whole. It is another way of preserving history, like the mural in a popular neighbourhood of Catania picturing the effigies and the names of the local antimafia heroes, which in the video becomes the site of a bouquet of flowers placed by a young Sicilian woman who proclaims that the mafia has already been defeated, "Nobody could ever kill you if you remain in our thoughts."[4]

When interviewed, Musumeci shared frank ideas about the original scope of his digital story: "I wanted to transmit a message that could be educational and cultural, moving beyond mere commemoration, beginning with the main protagonists, the young Sicilian citizens; they will be the future of tomorrow. The future of a freer and better Sicily."[5] In his effort, Musumeci has received important ethical and moral support from the institutions, as mentioned above, from the city, and from the University of Catania. To produce and distribute his project, he has wisely used the social media that are highly conducive to reaching a younger audience, as well as face-to-face assemblies in secondary schools and universities, and symposia, as well as radio and television interviews. The direct involvement of the student body of local schools has been instrumental. It is uplifting, indeed, to see that these young Sicilians take full responsibility for their actions and independently decide on their own destiny, unlike the youth of the 1980s interviewed by Giuseppe Fava for his documentary *Da Villalba a Palermo*, as Baris Cayli reminds us in his study in chapter 2 of this volume. Whereas Fava remarked upon the interrelationship between the power of the mafia and the weakness of the society, Musumeci has been able to capitalize on the courage and the initiative of his peers, perhaps because the web offers a sense of safety created through the numbers of members participating in the community. As the saying goes, "Il numero fa la forza" – there's strength in numbers. Carla Bagnoli, in chapter 1 of this volume, underscores this substantial benefit in her analysis of the social network created by online spaces like Libera. Such online spaces offer motivational support but also a sense of community, which is especially important when and where institutions fail.

When Musumeci mentions the local schools, he wants to make sure that we understand that the campuses of Catania and Palermo (in Sicily), Foggia (in Puglia), and Milan (in Lombardy) are to be acknowledged. They have been the promoters of a pilot project carried out in collaboration with the Falcone Foundation and MIUR (Ministero dell'istruzione, dell'università e della ricerca [Ministry of Education, University and Research]), during the anniversary of the massacre of Capaci, 23 May 1992. The objective of this project was to stimulate above all the reflection, the elaboration, and the production of original works through which it would be possible to highlight the values of legality and antimafia initiatives. All four academic institutions completed their projects: the University of Catania presented Musumeci's film "Per non dimenticare 23 maggio"; the University of Palermo named one of the facilities of the department of jurisprudence after the two beloved judges, Falcone and Borsellino, during its third annual Giornata Universitaria dell'Antimafia (University Day of the Antimafia); the University of Foggia invited Maria Falcone, educator and sister of Giovanni Falcone, to hold a seminar titled "Giovanni Falcone: tra passato e attualità" (Giovanni Falcone: Between past and present), open not only to the academic community, but also to the faculty and student body of the secondary schools of Foggia and its province. Finally, the University of Milan, building on the first course in sociology and organized criminality presented by Professor Nando dalla Chiesa, offered a series of seminars and activities and initiated research projects that focus on global organized crime and education about legality.

The impetus of engaging the local young people has not material-
ized by chance, but is an explicit aim of the video's director and of the
institutional and community initiatives against the mafia. Obviously,
as stated earlier, Musumeci, President Pignataro, and Mayor Bianco
are unanimous in understanding and proclaiming that the young generations represent the future. Nevertheless, the local young people
could also represent their enemies as well, an intrinsic negative force
that not only derides any effort designed to eradicate this powerful
criminal phenomenon, but also capitalizes on resignation and fear.
These dangers are highlighted as Musumeci evokes the experience he
had while filming the last segment of the video, which documents
the march in Piazza Università, in the downtown area of the city of
Catania:

> The march was indeed gratifying, the people and above all the tourists
> gave us an incredible level of energy … To be honest, we were insulted by
> some young people particularly with words that praised the mafia. But we
> were not scared. There were many of us together, we were strong in our
> convictions, and very determined about our project. I, like all the young
> people involved in this video, really believe in it.[6]

Musumeci's conviction is inspired by the words of Paolo Borsellino,
which he himself promptly cites:

> The first problem to solve in our beautiful but damned land should not
> be a work of detached repression but a cultural and moral movement that
> would involve everyone and especially the young generations, the ones
> most appropriate to immediately smell the beautiful and the fresh per-
> fume of liberty that makes one refuse the stench of moral compromise, of
> indifference, of contiguity, and thus of complicity.[7]

With his video project, Musumeci has not only targeted the young
generations by approaching them in a manner that is more suitable to
their age and interest – after all, don't we consider our youngest generation digital natives? The making of the testimonial video also creates
opportunities for young people to give voice to their own concerns, to
put them in touch with one another not only physically, while acting
and directing the project, but also with the aid of the hashtag symbol
(#) that facilitates the search of a particular topic, the pertinence and
relevance of words, themes, people, and localities.

Today, the 43 per cent of the world's population that is constituted by our twenty-five-year-old-or-younger community is impatient and ready to change the world. According to a new global survey, "Millennials: The Challenger Generation" conducted by Havas Worldwide, a future-focused global ideas agency, change for young people has to do with people, people who want to make a change and engage to make this change (Kumar 2013). To them, social media is an important force for transforming society. I suggest that digital stories have demarcated a deterritorialization rather than destorification that has been proven to be very beneficial for the overall outcome. Through intentional plots, characters, and messages, one can harness the power of narrative and create a civic impact while connecting and inspiring more stakeholders. In response to the decline or loss of trust in our democratic systems and institutional agents, these digital stories create counterpublics against Italian organized crime, whose participants, according to Robert Cox and Christina Foust (2009), "[do not] share the attributes of a unified, bourgeois public sphere, [exist] alongside this public … [and] invent and circulate counterdiscourses to formulate oppositional interpretations of their identities, interests, and needs" (611–12).

That said, it is imperative to mention here that both the reformative culture of the antimafia social movements and mafiosi culture compete to regain and govern over the public domains of the state and society at large when it comes to their use of social media and communication tools. Recently, in fact, the new mafia generation is using media platforms like Facebook and WhatsApp as tools for connecting, gaining respect, and producing popular consensus. The mafiosi do so, often camouflaged under fictional names and locations and at the risk of being caught by detectives who are poring over social media that can lead to mobsters' arrests. In July 2014, the case of Domenico Palazzolo was made public by many Italian and international newspapers. His boastful personal photos and diary entries were accompanied by his candid responses to video and résumé postings (D'Ospina 2015). Meanwhile TV stations and newspapers do not hesitate to glamorize Cosa Nostra luminaries and their youthful successors by showcasing hyperbolic biographies and interviews that focus more on private relationships and romanticized roles than on the interviewees and their families' criminal records.

One year from its being posted, "Per non dimenticare 23 maggio" has been viewed on YouTube 3,402 times (while its trailer, which was available two weeks prior to its release, has been viewed 1,518 times). The comments for both the video and the trailer are minimal (one comment for the video and two comments for the trailer), considering the frequency of the views. These results are not surprising. Other digital initiatives against the mafia phenomenon have experienced similar outcomes. Libera Informazione, which since 2007 has actively used social media such as Twitter and Facebook to spread news of corruption and national tragedies at the hands of the mafiosi, to post information about antimafia policies and speakers, and to announce antimafia protests, has over 10,000 followers, yet some posts register few comments. In fact, between October 2009 and April 2013, the two sites have registered 177 comments, a very small percentage in comparison to the number of viewers (Cayli 2013a, 65).

"Per non dimenticare 23 maggio" has been hosted by the LiveUniCT and Zammù multimedia within the University of Catania site and by the Per non dimenticare Facebook page that, up to this date, boasts 126 "likes" and promotes related news and activities. On a nondigital platform, the video has been equally successful: Musumeci has been invited by secondary schools, universities, and institutional entities in various parts of Italy to screen his digital creation. Among these visits, one of great importance has been the special commemoration event held in Catania and titled "Per non dimenticare: sulle orme di Giovanni Falcone" (In order not to forget: Following in Giovanni Falcone's footsteps), which was enriched by the dedication of one of the classrooms in the Department of Political Science at the University of Catania: the classroom known as Aula B di Via Vittorio Emanuele II, 49, was renamed Aula 21 Marzo. As Libera's website states, since 1996, every 21st of March, the first day of spring, is observed as the Giornata della Memoria e dell'Impegno (the Day of commemoration and commitment) in remembrance of the innocent victims of the mafia. It symbolizes the hope for renewal and the opportunity for family members and citizens to remember the tragedy and transform the pain into a concrete tool of action and peace.[8] The same morning of the dedication, 25 November 2014, the Department of Political Science hosted a press conference and a question and answer session with Maria Falcone, president of the Falcone Association and sister of Judge Falcone. The aim of this initiative was once again to pause for reflection and engage in discussion with university and secondary school students. The auditorium where the event was held was overflowing: not a single seat was left, and there was a large standing audience of teachers, authorities, and journalists, among others. Students had priority and were all occupying the cushioned seats.

After the opening remarks of the university president, the mayor, and the chair of the political science department, Professor Barone, the audience viewed "Per non dimenticare 23 maggio." Even though the director and some of the actors were there, no comments were shared. They were not needed. The students in attendance knew exactly that the students in the video were passing the baton to them. Maria Falcone was there to stress this vehemently: "It is up to you now to carry on this initiative, in your role as citizens, as parents; I am passing the baton to you today as in the documentary. Essential values of democracy – liberty, justice, equality. You need to remember it always and forever!"[9] Prompted by this stimulating call to action, students proved to be responsible as well as inquisitive, eager to collaborate and to learn; they boldly demanded the same collaboration and eagerness from the institutions and from the attending adults, asking for sustained dialogue and solutions. Their proposals were immediately accepted by District Attorney Giovanni Salvi who offered, in complete agreement with the university, a series of meetings and seminars open to all interested young community members.

It is through education and memory that one can gain enough courage to fight against the mafia, that one can become a "real" hero, can make a real change, as Giuseppe, Luigi, Alessandro, Chiara, Giulio, and Stella stress over and over in"Per non dimenticare 23 maggio." The mafia fears knowledge more than any other weapon. These heroes will never die as long as they are remembered. This is the overarching message to which these young Sicilian adults bear witness and transmit to us passionately through their digital testimonial storytelling, inviting the viewers to join this campaign of reflection and social change. Don Luigi Ciotti vehemently reminds us that making memory is an obligation to the victims of the mafia and their loved ones who survived them, to our own conscience as citizens, and to society. Amy Boylan stresses the importance of non-traditional monuments like online memorials, which appear especially suited to bridging past, present, and future while resisting the confines of "hegemonic cultural memory" and worse still, the relegation of numbers of victims to the margins of oblivion, the *dimenticatoio*, performed by conventional monumental forms (see chapter 4 in this volume).

Ganz (2011) reminds us that organized collective action or social movement depends on "voluntary participation, shared commitments, and ongoing motivation ... The capacity of a social movement for effective action depends largely on the depth, breadth, and quality of leadership able to turn opportunity to purpose" (273). He reminds us that through public narratives, leaders and participants can really move, motivate, construct, find the courage to act, and change the status quo. These narratives are invaluable resources against inertia, resignation, isolation, cynicism, and fatalism; they turn moments of crises into moments of "new beginnings" (288).

Remembering local antimafia heroes, like Giovanni Falcone, Alfredo Agosta, Giuseppe Fava, Beppe Montana, Giovanni Lizzio, and Paolo Borsellino and his bodyguards, and reflecting on the influence they had and continue to have on the lives of the other community members are narrative exercises through which one acknowledges a common identity and deepens their sense of community (Ganz 2011, 288). It is a leadership practice that Musumeci and his peers have wisely used to inspire, engage, motivate, coalesce, and change. Effectively, through a digital medium, they are not identifying the problem and providing a list of things to do to make a difference, to solve the problem (see Ganz 2007); rather, they motivate us by recalling to memory those who came before us and inviting us to join them in action for an enduring legacy.

Following Ganz's (2007) paradigm, Musumeci starts the storytelling with a story of self, a story of his hero and his credo, a story of us, showing us the experiences and values he shares with the young student body of Sicily. In this sense, these Catanian citizens enact the proposition that "in a world of mass media where all is visible, excuses like 'we did not know' will no longer be acceptable … Ignorance can never be used as justification for inaction" (Frosh and Pinchevski 2009, 6). Musumeci decisively concludes with the story of now, giving visible evidence of the challenges, the choices, the strategies, and the actions involved in realizing the recreation of civil society (see Ganz 2009). In unison, actors and viewers ideally bear witness together, assuming the responsibility to never forget. In harmony, actors and viewers can switch their roles, mingle, react, and act together in a sincere and vigorous fight against the mafia.

NOTES

1 Author interview with Giuseppe Musumeci, 16 July 2014. All quotations are taken from this interview.
2 My translation from the Italian: "Gli uomini passano, le idee restano e continueranno a camminare sulle gambe di altri uomini."

3 Enzo Bianco underscores in the video that "non c'è futuro senza la sconfitta della mafia" (there is no future without the defeat of the mafia).

4 My translation from the Italian: "Nessuno potrà mai uccidervi se restate nei nostri pensieri."

5 Musumeci interview. My translation from the Italian: "Ho voluto veicolare un messaggio oltre che commemorativo anche educativo e culturale partendo proprio dalle figure protagoniste dei giovani perché loro saranno il futuro del domani. Il futuro di una Sicilia libera e migliore."

6 My translation from the Italian: "La marcia è stata davvero un qualcosa di gratificante, la gente e soprattutto i turisti ci hanno dato una carica fantastica ... Ad essere sincero siamo stati derisi da alcuni ragazzi ... soprattutto frasi che inneggiavano la mafia. Ma noi non avevamo paura, eravamo davvero in tanti e soprattutto eravamo convinti e determinati del nostro progetto, io come i giovani che hanno partecipato a questo video ci crediamo davvero."

7 My translation from the Italian: "Il primo problema da risolvere nella nostra terra bellissima e disgraziata non doveva essere soltanto una distaccata opera di repressione ma un movimento culturale e morale che coinvolgesse tutti e specialmente le giovani generazioni, le più adatte a sentire subito la bellezza del fresco profumo di libertà che fa rifiutare il puzzo del compromesso morale, della indifferenza, della contiguità e quindi della complicità." These words were pronounced by Paolo Borsellino on 20 June 1992 in remembrance of Giovanni Falcone, Francesca Morvillo, Antonio Montinaro, Rocco Di Cillo, and Vito Schifani. Borsellino himself would die the following month in a mafia massacre.

8 Libera, Associazioni, nomi e numeri contro le mafie, "Cos'è il 21 Marzo." http://www.libera.it/flex/cm/pages/ServeBLOB.php/L/IT/IDPagina/472

9 My translation from the Italian: "Siete voi che dovete portare avanti questa iniziativa, come cittadini, come genitori; io la staffetta la passo a voi oggi, come nel documentario. Valori essenziali della democrazia – libertà, giustizia, uguaglianza. Voi lo dovete ricordare sempre!"

6 Remediating the Banda della Magliana: Debating Sympathetic Perpetrators in the Digital Age

DANA RENGA

As the centenary of the cinema has come and gone, and the Internet arrived on the scene, it is appropriate to ask what has been the impact of the visual and electronic media this past century? What kind of balance sheet of gain and loss can we draw? Of all the many pro's and con's that immediately come to mind, a peculiar uncertainty has struck many observers: not about the future, but the past ... Future generations, looking at the history of the 20th century, will never be able to tell fact from fiction, having the media as material evidence. But then, will this distinction still matter to them?

> Thomas Elsaesser, "'One Train May Be Hiding Another':
> Private History, Memory, and National Identity" (1999)

Everyone makes their own choices! And then pays the consequences! However, who of us has not empathized with one of them? At least for one moment!

[Ognuno fa le sue scelte! E poi ne paga le conseguenze! Però chi di noi non si è immedesimato in uno di loro? Almeno x un momento!]

> "La vera Banda della Magliana vs. Romanzo Criminale la serie"
> (2011a, b; translation by the author)

Introduction: The Banda della Magliana on the Large and Small Screen

In December of 2014 Massimo Carminati was arrested on accusations of, among other charges, belonging to a criminal (mafia) organization, extortion, fraud, usury, corruption, and bid rigging. Carminati was involved with the right-wing terrorist organization NAR (Nuclei Armati

Rivoluzionari) and the Roman "mafia," the Banda della Magliana, during the height of both organization's most violent periods in the 1970s and early 1980s, and he has since allegedly taken part in a variety of illicit activities up until his recent arrest as a member of "Mafia capitale."[1] In the press, Carminati is described in cinematic terms and is called "the last king of Rome" ("Massimo Carminati Arrestato" 2014), whose "legendary" (Abbate 2014) life story is "worthy of a James Bond villain" (Mezzofiore 2014). At the same time, he is characterized as "ruthless" (Squires 2014), called "the black soul of the most ruthless and branched out Capitoline crime organization" (De Risi 2014), and is described by judges as "dangerous and violent" ("Mafia Capitale, Riesame" 2015). Carminati is also the inspiration for the character of "Nero" in the novel, film, and television series *Romanzo criminale* (Crime novel). Played by Riccardo Scamarcio in Michele Placido's 2005 hit film, Nero is the most politically coded of the Banda who, unlike his onscreen counterparts, commits murders without remorse. And yet, as I argue elsewhere, the film works to humanize and create sympathy for him and his criminal counterparts, as do the film by Costantini and the series (Renga, 2016). Shakespeare long ago provided a blueprint for this situation in Macbeth (Crane 1953, 34–5), but contemporary visual storytellers have added their own specs to that blueprint. The Carminati case raises compelling questions about the representation and appeal of criminals, especially when they are subjects of popular fictionalized accounts.

In his work on caring, Gregory Currie (1997), professor of philosophy at the University of York, asks a fundamental question:

> We frequently like and take the part of people in fiction whom we would not like or take the part of in real life. The desires we seem to have concerning fictional things can be very unlike the desires we have concerning real life – so dissimilar, indeed, that it is hard to see how such disparate desires could exist within any reasonably integrated human mental economy. Why the disparity? (65)

Why do we forge deep relationships with onscreen villains when in our day-to-day lives we strive to protect ourselves from their nonfictional counterparts? Why do we engage emotionally with onscreen characters whom we'd regard as not deserving of any positive ethical judgments if we met them in real life? How does narrative transform "villains" into more ethically complex characters while still representing their villainous behaviour? What changes take place in viewer reaction when fiction and non-fiction converge in remediated texts in web-based digital media?

To answer these questions, this chapter investigates the divergences in allegiance with different representations of the perpetrator, specifically depictions on the large and small screen of members of the Banda della Magliana, considered Italy's "fifth" mafia ("La quinta mafia a Roma" 2009). In particular, I look at three groupings of mediated representations of the Banda. First, I focus on fictional representations: the Placido film *Romanzo criminale*, Stefano Sollima's 2008–10 television series, and the film *Fatti della Banda della Magliana* by Daniele Costantini (2004). I then turn my attention to non-fictional and documentary programs: The History Channel's *La Banda della Magliana – La vera storia*, and the episode on the Banda from the Carlo Lucarelli series *Blu notte*. Finally, and principally, I discuss various remediated texts found on sites such as YouTube: the audio of trials "Atti del processo" and several videos showing images of the Banda sharing their life stories, many of which include images of the characters or songs heard in the film and the series. This chapter focuses primarily on this final section that engages with web-based media and pays special attention to blog materials and user comments, as they raise particularly interesting questions posed by the convergence of fiction and non-fiction, and construct quite different "houses of memory" than those addressed in Amy Boylan's chapter "Democratizing the Memorial Landscape," which act to commemorate the mafias' many victims. Further, this chapter questions to what extent these films, documentaries, and remediated videos might stand as counter-examples to the ideals and values of a culture of legality in that, to different degrees, they work to create sympathy for the perpetrator.

Remediation and Transmedia

In their seminal text on remediation, Jay David Bolter and Richard Grusin (2000) put forward that remediation, mediation, and reality are inseparable because mediation "remediates the real" (59) (and by "real" they mean reality and not the Lacanian real). Bolter and Grusin discuss the pleasures and desires of the viewer of refashioned texts. Hypermediated texts are indications of a desire to transcend "the limits of representation and to achieve the real" (53). The real is not to be thought in terms of metaphysics, but instead is in line with the viewer's experience that "would evoke an immediate (and therefore authentic) emotional response" (53) to the material. In discussing the "social dimension" of remediated material, the authors contend that the "remediation of material practice is inseparable from the remediation of social arrangements" (69), and in the case of my discussion on the Banda, these "social arrangements" are those involving criminal organizations and their membership. If, as Bolter and Grusin maintain, the viewer's interaction with hypermediated material is also an interaction with the real, then the viewers of the many remediated texts discussed below experience, comprehend, and are acquainted with the Banda immediately. Responses analysed below in the section focusing on remediated texts on the Banda are emotional and frequently heated, and suggest that the hundreds of online videos that focus on Italy's fifth mafia and that have been watched by millions of viewers are integral in the process of how the criminal organization is perceived today, and how it will continue to be perceived in the future.

The claim that *all* mediation is remediation" (Bolter and Grusin 2000, 55, original italics), is quite significant when thinking of the diverse and manifold platforms that engage with the Banda, tell its story, and contribute to the creation of its mythology. Marta Boni's study *Romanzo criminale: Transmedia and Beyond* (2014) looks principally at the adaptations of Giancarlo de Cataldo's 2002 hit novel (the Placido film and Sollima series) together with several other transmedia venues that engage with these texts: blog sites, discussion boards, and several "paratexts" such as iPhone aps, Facebook pages, marketing campaigns, merchandising such as T-shirts, trailers and recaps, official websites and fan pages, and the game, all of which "reframe the experience of the fictional universe, adapted to the times and contexts in which they appear" (111). In addition to the texts on the Banda addressed in Boni's study, this chapter also looks at another fiction film, two documentaries, and several online videos where fiction and fact converge. In his work on convergence culture, Henry Jenkins (2011) puts forward that "convergence" is a model to consider media transformation currently as "defined though the layering, diversification, and interconnectivity of media." In turn, I consider the corpus of texts focusing on the Banda as an example of "transmedia storytelling" that Jenkins (2007) famously defined as "a process where integral elements of a fiction get dispersed systematically across multiple delivery channels for the purpose of creating a unified and coordinated entertainment experience. Ideally, each medium makes its own unique contribution to the unfolding of the story." As we will see, however, the integration of historical documents (most frequently photos of ex-members of the Banda) in online videos containing footage from the film and series does not result in a "unified and coordinated entertainment experience" for several viewers who find it difficult to reconcile divergent reactions to men who are criminals yet have become legends on the big and small screen, which opens up new ways of thinking about cultures of legality.

"Structures of Sympathy" in *I fatti della Banda della Magliana, Romanzo criminale,* and *Romanzo criminale: la serie*

In order to understand the potential changes and diverse problems related to digitally remediated representations of historical figures and their fiction counterparts, it is first necessary to discuss representations in the fiction films and television series that provide an essential critical context where we see that viewers are frequently positioned to "ally" themselves with "villainous" characters, borrowing from Murray Smith's (1995) work on structures of sympathy in the cinema (86). As I have argued elsewhere, depicting a criminal in a sentimental light in the cinema is nothing new, especially in the Hollywood gangster tradition where members of organized crime syndicates are presented in sympathetic terms (think of *The Godfather, Goodfellas, The Sopranos,* and so on). Such a poignant representation of mafia perpetrators, however, is scarce in the Italian tradition especially in films in which compassion is usually aligned with those fallen in the battle against the mafia (Renga 2013, 131).[2] As Boylan convincingly argues in her chapter in this volume, this "canon of antimafia martyrs," which includes Paolo Borsellino, Giovanni Falcone, Giuseppe Impastato, and Placido Rizzotto, is in flux and commemorative practices are now in place that create spaces to grieve persistent mafia-related traumas. In the numerous mafia movies made in Italy spanning genres over the last sixty-five years, the mafiosi are represented in ambiguous terms or are cast as straightforward villains. In more current movies, however, we find that the mafiosi are constructed to warrant our compassion, and this is indeed a striking turn. Borrowing from Jason Mittell (2014), the recent prevalence of anti-heroes on the Italian screen "raises a key question: why would we want to subject ourselves to lengthy interactions with such hideous men" (74)?

In keeping with studies done on the allure of the fictional bad guy, this section looks at the mechanics of film identification and spectatorship to demonstrate how the viewer is positioned to feel sympathy for members of the Banda in the film and television series. For example, Mittel (2014) notes that fictional bad guys are frequently given some "redeeming qualities" and are juxtaposed with other, more straightforwardly heinous characters. As Mittell puts it, characters such as Dexter or Tony Soprano are "less hideous than the alternatives" while exuding "charisma." As a result, we "want to spend time with them" and their victims are for the most part "more monstrous" then they are (75–7). Margrethe Bruun Vaage (2013) points to the role of representations of these characters beyond their crimes: "If a criminal character is revealed as having a tender love life, we see this character as sympathetic; we never see the truly bad guys being lovingly affectionate" (232). Conversely to non-fiction representations where the viewer is meant to "*believe* its content," with the fiction film the viewer should "*imagine* its content" (219, original italics).

Costantini's *I fatti della Banda della Magliana* is the first feature film to treat the exploits of the Banda (Costantini n.d.). It is shot in Rome's Rebibbia prison and stars twenty prisoners and four professional actors. Like the Taviani Brothers' *Caesar Must Die* (*Cesare deve morire*, 2013) that was also shot in Rebibbia and features prisoners rehearsing and performing *Julius Caesar*, Costantini's film is a male melodrama that centers on a group of inmates who perform their criminal pasts, and focuses primarily on the collaborator with justice "Accatone" who is based on the historical figure Maurizio Abbatino, the inspiration for Freddo in the *Romanzo criminale* novel. In *I fatti della Banda della Magliana*, gang members confess their crimes and list all of their faults proudly, and narrate their history in front of an unnamed "judge" who never speaks nor passes judgment. Also akin to the Taviani film, criminals are unrepentant with respect to their past crimes. Indeed, many deceased members of the Banda speak from the grave as they return to the group so as to tell their story, and to place blame on the people they feel are responsible for their murders. At several points in the film viewers are positioned to mourn the deaths of these men, as is the case with Marcello Jacobis when a montage of several shots of a golden church alter accompanied by sombre choir music proceeds to images of his tombstone in a church, upon which is mounted a photograph of him smiling.

The film is based on a play written by the director called *Chiacchiere e sangue* (Rumors and blood, 2000) and Costantini has said that both play and film were inspired by his intense interest in gangsters, whom he describes as "exceptional" and "exemplary" figures who live in close contact with death. While filming in the prison, Costantini notes that he frequently thought of films such as Howard Hawke's *Scarface*, Martin Scorsese's *Goodfellas*, and Takeshi Kitano's *Sonatine*, whose protagonist, the director explains, is a "tragic gangster, who is comic, melancholic, and profound" (Costantini n.d.). In turn, gangsters in *I fatti della Banda della Magliana* are depicted as melancholics who desire to return to an idealized and impossible past based on, as stated in the film, "exclusivity and solidarity," an ethos also present in, for example, *Goodfellas*, *The Godfather*, and *The Sopranos*.

Criminals are for the most part imagined in the Placido hit film as likable and meriting our forgiveness. As I discuss elsewhere, *Romanzo criminale* is a male melodrama that focuses on the homosocial bonds between Libanese, Freddo, and Dandi, the three key members of the Banda in the film (Renga 2016). These characters are all, borrowing from Brett Martin's work on anti-heroes in American serial television, "difficult men," who are "trying to get by in the modern world, negotiating relationships, rivalries, and the demands of a [elaborate bureaucracy]" (Martin 2013, 107). In the case of Placido's film this bureaucracy is an amalgam of Cosa Nostra, the camorra, Italian terrorist organizations, and the Italian state. The film presents a particular viewpoint on the *anni di piombo*, or years of terrorism in Italy, from the perspective of several sympathetic perpetrators with whom the audience is positioned to identify. Recalling Janet Staiger's (2008) work on male melodrama, in *Romanzo criminale*, we see that "the fascination with fallen men continues unabated" (74), especially when brooding anti-heroes are interpreted by the likes of Riccardo Scamarcio (Nero), Pierfrancesco Favino (Libanese), and Kim Rossi Stuart (Freddo), some of Italy's most successful (and attractive) stars.

The representation of Freddo is particularly interesting when thinking about how the spectator is positioned to respond emotionally to perpetrators in the film. As Smith (1995) explains, allegiance (the term he prefers to identification) instils the most personal and emotional response in viewers:

> Allegiance depends upon the spectator having what she takes to be reliable access to the character's state of mind, on understanding the context of the character's actions, and having morally evaluated the character on the basis of this knowledge … With allegiance we go beyond understanding, by evaluating and responding emotionally to the traits and emotions of the character. (84–5)

The viewer feels allegiance frequently for the unfittingly named Freddo, which means cold in Italian. He falls in love with someone interested in Renaissance painting and untouched by criminality, he is shown to be distressed at the death of his brother, and breaks off from the Banda after witnessing the Bologna bombing. We also feel for him when he dissuades his companion from shooting the wife of Gemito (Libanese's murderer) because she is with her young daughter (were the young girl not there the murder would have taken place). Most problematically we are positioned to feel sympathy for him after he murders his good friend Aldo Buffoni at the beach at Ostia.

At the same time, however, Freddo, who paradoxically abhors dictators, kills more people than any other member of the Banda.[3] His excessive violence, however, is conveyed as justified as it is motivated by his desire to avenge the murders of his friend Libanese and love interest Roberta whose passing the audience is positioned to grieve as well. Most apposite, Freddo becomes a victim in the Bologna train station bombing in August 1980, the bloodiest event in the years of terrorism in Italy that killed eighty-five people and wounded over 200. As Catherine O'Rawe (2014) has argued, Placido's reconstruction of the massacre constructs Freddo as "a stand-in or proxy for Italians themselves,"and he is "aligned with the voice of left-wing outrage" (110). And a similar process of displacement takes place with Nero, whose character is based on the recently incarcerated Massimo Carminati and interpreted by Scamarcio. Introduced as a "Nazi," Nero is the most politically coded of the Banda. And yet his murder towards the end of the film is followed by a montage of footage, to first the 1981 attempted assassination of Pope John Paul II and then to Italy's 1982 World Cup victory accompanied by Puccini's well-known aria "Nessun dorma." Thus, Nero is not associated with Italian cultural trauma but with Italian cultural heritage (Catholicism, soccer, and opera). With these two examples we see that criminals in *Romanzo criminale* are recast in a nostalgic light and as such elicit viewer sympathy, seeming to promote a culture of illegality.

Much more so than the film, Sollima's 2008–10 two-season series met with controversy due to its depiction of criminality in what some perceived as a glamorous light.[4] In 2009, the right-wing mayor of Rome, Gianni Alemanno, blamed the series for an act of youth violence, explaining that it encourages improper behaviour ("Alemanno" 2009). This sentiment was echoed on several online forums where users comment that the series celebrates crime and one user mentions that trailers should be accompanied by the slogan "crime doesn't pay" ("Romanzo criminale" 2008). Boni (2014) has looked in depth at the controversy around the series, and notes that "the phenomenon of negative role models" on television is potentially more fraught due to the medium's wide viewership with respect to the cinema (100). *Romanzo criminale: la serie* is an early example of Italian quality television that is narratively complex and engages the viewer while inviting what Mittell (2015) terms "participatory engagement" in discussions, forums, and blog posts, a point to which I will return when discussing the remediated texts under consideration.

The series is much truer to De Cataldo's (2002) novel and has the space to more fully develop the narratives of several members of the Banda (and not just the key figures which are the focus of the film), expanding upon their friendships and love interests, delving deeper into their psychological makeup, and, most apposite, allowing viewers access to flashbacks and memories that narrativize traumatic experiences, all of which garners them further compassion.[5] As Giancarlo Lombardi (2012) argues, viewer empathy (as in Noël Carroll's "Sympathy for the Devil" [2004]) in the series "did not arise from the star-power of the cast but from the force of longer story-arcs which endowed their 'anti-heroes' with redeeming traits that would facilitate spectatorial alignment and allegiance" (181).

The series fosters a form of plural engagement and identification (Smith 1995, 93) with several characters, primarily Bufalo, Libanese, Dandi, and Freddo. An "omniscient" narrative moves between various plotlines and "gives us access to the subjectivities" of members of the Banda (Smith 1995, 90). As in the film, men in the series are wounded and haunted by past traumatic experiences. This is particularly the case for Libanese, whose scarred arm is frequently foregrounded in early episodes either during moments of intense homosocial bonding or rivalry. We learn through flashbacks that the scar was inflicted by Terribile as punishment for the theft of a car; Libanese was wounded at the same time that two of Terribile's men raped Libanese's girlfriend Sara. Thus, and akin to Freddo in the film, the gang leader's vengeance is conveyed as justified and is also ingrained collectively into the minds of several other Banda members, made clear when Freddo, Bufalo, Ricotta, and Trentadenari murder Terribile during Season 1, Episode 7, and Freddo plunges the knife originally used to maim Libanese into Terribile's chest. The development of the revenge narrative over the arc of seven episodes (Libanese's trauma and guilt for not protecting Sara are frequently on display) assists in constructing members of the gang as defenders of those abused by sadists and rapists despite their frequent recourse to violence and assorted criminal acts. These three texts convey a fascination with perpetrators that is somewhat mitigated in the documentaries discussed below on the Banda where criminality is foregrounded and the viewer is at times reminded of the historical stakes of the representation of gangsters.

Documenting the Banda

I will now turn to two documentaries that attempt to somewhat temper the sympathetic image put forth in the films and television series through focusing on the Banda's illegal activities. Unlike in the fictional treatments discussed above, at various moments and in particular during the conclusions, *La Banda della Magliana – La vera storia* and Lucarelli's *Blu notte* episode work to demythologize the fictional figures comprised in the Banda, and as such may speak to victims' organizations and antimafia activists. Here, I am curious about "what difference it makes for the spectator to engage emotionally with characters in fiction as opposed to characters in nonfiction film" (Vaage 2013, 219). This question is all the more interesting given that the first instalment of the four-part History Channel documentary was broadcast immediately following the premiere of the third and fourth episodes of the second season *Romanzo criminale: la serie*.

Vaage (2013) argues that "nonfiction film directors are confronted with a moral imperative to demarcate clearly between the morally deviant characters and the morally sound, while the fiction film director is freer in her or his choice of protagonists" (229). We see such a distinction clearly at work in several documentaries and docudramas on the mafia that present victims and perpetrators in a Manichean light, as in the cases of *One Girl Against the Mafia* (*Diario di una siciliana ribelle*, Marco Amenta, 1997), *The Mafia Is White* (*La mafia è bianca*, Stefano Maria Bianchi and Alberto Nerazzini, 2005), and *Excellent Cadavers* (*In un altro paese*, Marco Turco, 2005), all of which can be considered, to different extents, cultural productions of legality. The History Channel documentary on the Banda does regularly describe members as "ruthless," "feared," and "without scruples." Similarly, Lucarelli's *Blu notte* reminds the viewer from the outset that "this is a story about murder, drugs, money, vendetta, betrayal, and *pentimenti* (regret, but also turning state's evidence) ... this is an Italian mystery, and like all Italian mysteries it hides something more, something that involves all of us, and that scares us." At the same time, however, both programs are problematic in that they ultimately mythologize the same gangsters that they intend to denounce.

The title sequence of the History Channel documentary immediately attempts to distance the program from fictionalized accounts of the Banda. The voiceover narrator prepares the viewer for a story about "boys from the Roman periphery who the cinema made into heroes and legends." A brief montage of images of Libanese, Dandi, Freddo, and Nero from the publicity poster of the film follows a shot of a person we later learn is imprisoned ex-gang member and *pentito* Antonio Mancini, who is exclaiming "it wasn't like that," and proceeds with footage of Renzo Danesi, an imprisoned ex-member of the Banda, who confidently asserts that they (we are to assume he is speaking about the Banda) were never together as the gang is in the film. "The true story is another," the voiceover narrator recounts and the viewer is thus introduced to the "true faces and the true names" of the Banda's four bosses who are described by gang members Mancini, Danesi, and Fabiola Moretti as "charismatic" (Franco Giuseppucci), "a samurai" (Danilo Abbruciati), "smiling the moment that he would screw you over" (Maurizio Abbatino), and "a prince" (Enrico de Pedis).

This remediated title sequence captures the various pleasures documentary affords. Elizabeth Cowie (1999) maintains that although documentary is "associated with the serious," the mode does allow the viewer to experience a series of desires: the more scientific and rational "desire for reality as knowledge," which conveys "evidence confirmed through observation and logical interpretation" (19), and a desire for image "as spectacle," which she describes as "a sheer pleasure in looking" (26), and a "feast for the eyes" (25). "We were gangsters," Mancini declares proudly during the documentary's incipit, setting the scene for a thrilling mafia narrative grounded in historical truth. Accordingly, the protagonists of the documentary are not the fictionalized gangsters we see in the Placido film and Sollima series, but instead are different, real-life mobsters who are presented as equally if not more fascinating than their fictional counterparts. As such, the documentary contributes to the enthralling public image of the mafia discussed above in Robin Pickering-Iazzi's introduction and its exploration of the mystique of the mobster.

The documentary does at times underline the Banda's wrongdoings, in particular during segments focusing on the 1978 Aldó Moro kidnap and murder, the 1980 Bologna bombing, and the mysterious

and still unresolved 1983 disappearance of fifteen-year-old Emanuela
Orlandi. At the same time, a frequent trope in the film is a mythologiz-
ing comparison of gang members to Roman emperors who eventually
fall when, for the most part, they are murdered by opposing clans or
enemies made inside of the Banda. De Pedis's death is described in
cinematic terms "like on a movie set of a gangster film" and, significantly, period music and stylized montage celebrate the Banda's climb
to power, in particular during the first two episodes of the series.

The documentary concludes by asserting that the Banda is no longer
active and "today is part of Rome's mythology," in most part due to
Abbatino's decision to collaborate with the authorities and turn state's
evidence. Abbatino's collaboration leads to "operation Colosseo,"
which resulted in "numerous" arrests for "associazione a delinquere"
or belonging to a criminal organization. Now Rome is changed and
there is no room for those belonging to the Banda who were feared by
all. In its closing moments, the documentary again attempts a distinction between fiction and fact. The true story of the Banda is not written
by De Cataldo (2002) and does not contain heroes guided by honour,
but instead is comprised of "a long list of homicides, tyrants, and innocent victims." Such a post-mafia mentality is of course problematic
when considering the 2014 arrest of Carminati and others who have
been active in organized crime in the country's capital, yet helps in the
documentaries' project of telling one of the many "true stories" of the
Banda to viewers who can turn off the television and rest assured that
one of Italy's mafias has been defeated.

Lucarelli's *Blu notte* repeatedly (ten times or more) makes mention of
mafia movies such as *Goodfellas* and *The Godfather* or refers to the films
of Quentin Tarantino, comparing members of the Banda with onscreen
mafiosi. The narrative of de Pedis's death is imbued with suspense and
visually reconstructed in detail, as is the description of the torture and
murder of Abbatino's brother Roberto who was not involved with the
Banda; these two moments create sympathy for the Banda's members.
Towards the end of the program, Lucarelli asks about the nature of the
Banda della Magliana. Judge Otello Lupacchini believes that it was
a criminal organization akin to Cosa Nostra and the camorra, while
police commissioner of Rome Nicola Cavaliere states that the Banda
was more a group of gangsters who worked for other criminal organizations. Professor Giuseppe De Lutiis, the ex-advisor to the Parliamen-
tary Commission on Massacres (*stragi*), speaks to the Banda's collusion
with the Italian secret service, the Masonic Lodge Propaganda 2 (P2),

common criminals, various Italian mafias, and other stakeholders inside the country and internationally, thus presenting a much more cryptic history of the organization. Unlike the comforting conclusion of the History Channel documentary, this program is more open-ended and Lucarelli ultimately dubs the Banda an "Italian mystery" that diverges from the suspense thriller where enigmas are ultimately resolved.

Both documentaries, borrowing from John Parris Springer (2006), "are structured by the intersecting goals of realism and melodrama." The first (realism) "convinces us of the authenticity of the events we see on screen" while melodrama in each "instructs us to respond to these events" (31). Hence, the viewer takes away from these programs the knowledge that the Banda did exist, was nefarious, and has been defeated while imagining the organization's members as criminals endowed with charismatic and cinematic qualities. Ultimately, even though both programs make clear their interest in differentiating fiction from fact, the narrative of each is constructed so as to heighten the allure of the organization and its members, and each perpetuates the myth of the glamorous and sympathetic mobster apparent in the fictionalized accounts discussed above.

Remediating the Banda[6]

So as to problematize the ranges of appeal of the perpetrator seen in the previous two sections of this chapter, I now focus on a number of remediated online videos in which fiction and non-fiction merge. In several of these videos, images of characters from the series are presented alongside photos of the "real" historical members of the Banda. Also, many examples of web-based digital media include scenes or stills from the series or the film before or after "historical" evidence is recounted through voiceover or subtitles. In online videos containing solely fictional images and scenes (tributes to a character's death or trailers for the Placido film or the television series, for example), commenters generally express more straightforward reactions to the material; most frequently the fictional texts are lauded and their protagonists revered, although occasionally in comments historical characters and their violent actions are condemned, as I will discuss below.[7]

Conversely, in several user comments to the videos that include both fictional and non-fictional images (in online chat rooms and in comment sections following the videos), we see a process of "splitting" at work whereby many users experience (albeit mild) dissociative reactions (i.e., users praise the film or series while simultaneously denouncing the actions of the characters). These remediated texts present quite interesting "reality checks" when the viewer is made aware of the "moral and political consequences [that] his or her emotional engagement would have, were the fictional events real" (Vaage 2013, 220). As we will see, it becomes clear that the viewer of these hypermediated short films is less willing to identify and sympathize with the members of the Banda as they might in the case of fictionalized portrayals, and reactions are thus more complicated in terms of an ethical stance. Therefore, contrary to the fiction film and documentaries discussed thus far, the hypermediated short films might contribute to a culture of legality. As explained by Jenkins (2006), "Welcome to convergence culture, where old and new media collide, where grassroots and corporate media intersect, where the power of the media producer and the power of the media consumer interact in unpredictable ways" (2).

Online videos are plentiful on the Banda, and several fans of the Placido film and series have posted videos that heighten the appeal of these texts and the charisma of their protagonists. For example, several such videos show a still image from the series, most often a publicity poster, accompanied by the melancholic score by the group Repertorio Machiavelli, who composed assorted instrumental tunes heard in the series. These videos have been watched several hundred thousand times (some sites show between one and two hundred thousand views) and in the hundreds of accompanying comments, numerous users draw a clear line between fiction and reality, maintaining that historical figures are criminals deserving of punishment whereas fictional characters are fascinating. This is the case of Aless003, who writes in response to a user who takes issue with the series' glamorization of crime (a rare comment on this site):

> I am speaking of the series and not about reality. of course the real men were not saints and their victims were innocent. But that story "romanzo" is not a historical document. Do you understand? it is a semi-fictional film. [Libanese's] decline in the series, the light in the scene, the soundtrack, the symbolic rain that washes away sins ... all of this gives us goosebumps. ("Romanzo criminale la serie" 2009)

For the most part, however, commenters praise the series and, in the case of the Repertorio Machiavelli song that accompanies the credits of the finale of Season 1, which concludes with Libanese's murder, commentators express feeling moved by the music and Libanese's death. Comments such as "stupendous," "beautiful," "libanese was the king of Rome," "splendid … sincere," and "goodbye Libanese" demonstrate that viewers are keen to feel compassion for fictional characters, which is not the case with their historical counterparts ("Romanzo criminale la serie" 2009). As Vaage (2013) explains in her discussion of identification in *The Sopranos*: "If we as our normal, non-*mafiosi* selves, really inhabited th[e] fictional world [of *The Sopranos*], we would … ultimately have to say no to [the mobster's] way of life, although as spectators of a fiction we sympathize with and enjoy it" (224).

Other examples of web-based digital media focus solely on the actual members of the Banda, for instance in "La Banda della Magliana – I Personaggi realmente esistiti" (2011) and the two-part recording of the audio of the trials of members of the Banda. Like the texts discussed above and in line with Vaage (2013), comments here are more straightforward, and tend broadly to indict the actual gang members and their criminal activities. Many users express satisfaction that these men have received, in their opinion, what is due to them (incarceration or death). Interestingly, several women who were involved in the Banda are absent from these texts. The first example is a five-minute video comprised of script containing the name and frequently nickname of twenty-nine members of the Banda (Nicolino Selis "Er Sardo," Franco Giuseppucci "Er Negro," Enrico De Pedis "Renatino," and so on), which precedes a black-and-white photo of the member. The video is divided into four sections based upon the member's "group" (Acilia-Ostia, Tufello, Trullo-Magliana, Testaccio) and is accompanied by Lando Fiorini's melancholic love song "Er canto dei carcerati" (The song of the prisoners), which is about a prisoner who implores his lover to communicate with him – "Manname un saluto" – as he has been abandoned by family and friends. Yet, simultaneously, the song implies that he will not forsake his ties to criminality. Comments on the video, which has close to half a million views, frequently point out that gang affiliates are "criminals" and "murderers" who are deserving of punishment and who "chose to die." One user writes, "it seems that they are idols worthy of respect! when they shouldn't even be remembered!! damn you and your dead!!" Another discussant notes that if it were up to him, he "would face them all up against a wall and burn them with a fire thrower, especially abbatino and mancini and the other villains who didn't even have the balls to take responsibility for what they did." Other users on the site also express hostility towards those like

Abbatino and Mancini who became *pentiti* when they turned state's evidence: "mancini IS a VILLAIN," we read in one post ("La Banda della Magliana – I Personaggi realmente esistiti" 2011). In these comments, we see that the narrative of the video, borrowing from Ward E. Jones's (2011) work on ethical responses to film, "leads its spectators to respond with certain emotions - and the desires and evaluations that go along with them – toward its characters and events." Jones continues to explain that, in encouraging viewers to experience certain feelings towards fictional personages and events, "the narrative reveals *its own* attitude toward that person or event" (6). The images in the video place all ex-members of the Banda on equal footing. The sorrowful lyrics of the song from the perspective of a hardened and unrepentant criminal with a heart, however, encourages viewers such as those noted above to judge *pentiti* like Mancini quite harshly, as they are to blame for the incarceration of those who upheld the code of honour so central to the ethos of organized crime networks.

The nature of the comments posted in response to the videos of the trials of Banda members is similar. The images in the videos are a montage of stills. The first part includes faces of several of the men in the video discussed above, a compilation of fifteen or five mugshots, various interiors of a courtroom, the exterior of a cell with an anonymous prisoner's hands hanging outside of the bars, a gun pointed at the camera with the shooter blurred, and, most common, a script reading "Banda della Magliana 1975–1985." The second part is much more visually rich, and also incorporates aerial shots of Rome and stills of the Vatican, the Roman periphery, and several Roman monuments and statues, images of the missing Emanuela Orlandi, judges, and newscasters, reenactments of crimes, remediated footage from Costantini's film, and photographs of cadavers on the city streets. Together, the two-part series has been watched just under one million times and includes just under 500 user comments, many of which decry the actions of the men under trial. Commenters note that they "talk about their crimes as if it is nothing. it's scary," and are "imbeciles" who are "depraved" ("Documentario il processo alla Banda della Magliana – I confronti parti 1 di 2" 2010). Although a few users condemn Mancini and Abbatino for turning state's evidence, such comments are much less frequent than in the video considered just earlier. Three equations of *pentiti* as villains are present in the first part of the audio trial. Overall users discuss and debate aspects of testimony or quite often malign the men on trial. Unlike in "La Banda della Magliana – I Personaggi realmente esistiti" (2011), here there exists little dissonance between image and audio, save the one very short publicity shot from the Costantini film. As such, viewers are less likely to experience a complicated reaction to the material, which is not the case for a selection of videos in which fiction and non-fiction meet.

I now want to consider the ethical ramifications of these videos that present ambivalent or positive depictions of criminality, yet engage the viewer's ethical consciousness. Several videos can readily be found that show photographs of Banda members and share their life stories but also include either images of characters or short scenes from the film and the series. In one of a series of videos, which have all since been taken off YouTube due to copyright violations, a user remarks: "An undoubtedly fascinating story. However I think that identifying with certain characters is reckless. I also feel admiration for these lives if necessary but they are stories about homicides, money and power ... bad stories."[8] (Another states, "These are fascinating men, but we should not identify with them." Comments such as these in which authors express conflicting emotions with regards to video content constitute a trope where fiction and fact converge.[9]

Unlike with the other videos discussed thus far, the three videos analysed here include content that does not make a clear distinction between reality and fiction, and as such places viewers in much less straightforward positions in terms of allegiance with the images shown onscreen. As Jones (2011) explains, "The attitudes we adopt as spectators of fictional characters and events are of ethical significance" (11). He makes the distinction that viewers can imagine unethical acts without much trouble, but a difficulty arises when a fiction invites spectators to take a certain "moral attitude" towards what is shown onscreen, which might prove challenging when a fiction asks viewers to "celebrate or enjoy" an action that the viewer finds immoral (11). It is clear in the users' comments in the above paragraph that the viewers find the story of the Banda fascinating but they are at odds about identifying with the characters of the series whose deeds are considered unscrupulous.

While the title of the video "Da ROMANZO CRIMINALE (serie) alla BANDA DELLA MAGLIANA (realtà)" (From crime novel [series] to the Banda of the Magliana [reality]) (2009) announces a separation between the series and reality, its content equates historical figures and dramatic personae. After the title appears in the bright red that characterizes the marketing for film and series, we see a still of the popular lettering "Romanzo criminale la serie"

(Crime novel the series), which is followed by a montage of nine stills, each containing a photograph of a Banda member on the left, an image of a character from the series on the right, with an "equals" sign separating the two representations. Stills are headed by the gang member's neighbourhood (Testaccio-Trastevere, Magliana, Acilia-Ostia), and beneath each image we read the name and nickname of the historical figure followed by the name of the fictional counterpart, all in vivid red script. The first four collages focus on the most popular and fully developed characters in film and series, simultaneously some of the most notorious members of the actual Banda: Franco Giuseppucci/Libanese; Enrico De Pedis/Dandi; Maurizio Abbattino/Freddo; Marcello Colafigli/Bufalo.[10]

In the video, fiction and fact converge and viewers are encouraged to equate (=) seasoned offenders with engaging characters, and the Banda associates are further mythologized throughout the video, first when we see the tomb of Enrico De Pedis with the accompanying script: "Tomb of Enrico De Pedis (Dandi) in the basilica of St. Apollinare in Rome: 'Well, maybe he wasn't' a benefactor for everyone, but for St. Apollinare he was' (Giulio Andreotti on Enrico De Pedis)." Hence, De Pedis is remembered by one of Italy's most problematic political leaders as a man who, according to the ex-rector of the basilica, was "generous in helping the poor who frequented the basilica, and also the priests and the seminarists, and in whose intercession the family will continue to practice charitable works, overall contributing to the realization of diocesan projects" (Ceccarelli 2008). We then see a script containing the words of the Roman saying, "'In via de la Lungara there is a step, who does not climb it is not Roman, and who is not roman is not from Trastevere' (The Prison of Regina Coeli)." This is the motto for the newspaper *Lo scalino* of the Regina Coeli prison in the heart of Trastevere that was temporary home to many members of the Banda. One is not Roman, the saying makes plain, if one has not spent time behind bars. The video concludes with the opening footage of the first episode of the series when a man, who we learn at the season's finale is an aging Bufalo, is beaten up by those who now control the Magliana neighbourhood. Bufalo then exacts revenge on his attackers, shooting the leader dead before screaming, "I was in Libanese's gang." Catherine O'Rawe (2014) notes that this ending foregrounds a trope common in the series: "a nostalgia for a lost past, and for lost, beloved men" (102).

These components of the video (that has been watched more that 1.1 million times) fashion gangsters as charitable men and true Roman citizens who are bound by friendship. Those who remark on the video (there are more than 400 comments) are mostly interested in details from the gang members' lives or discuss accuracies in representation in the series. Several commenters do express contradictory reactions to the material, however. One user writes that the series "really mirrors reality. I think that amongst the members of the real banda there was a real and fraternal friendship. they were delinquents, but with a sense of extraordinary friendship. that, combined with the life and traditions of the mid 70s and early 80s must have created a mixture of thrilling sensations." Another user who exclaims "I would marry Giuseppucci right now!" is condemned by another commenter who tells her, "Go fuck yourself … he killed dozens of people." The user then explains herself, noting that she did not mean to praise Giuseppucci's actions, and that she admired his character, "his cold blood, period. It might be strange that I am fascinated by him, but even I do not support those who kill 'to settle scores':)" ("Da ROMANZO CRIMINALE (serie) alla BANDA DELLA MAGLIANA (realtà)" 2009).   The allure of the mobster here parallels that of Milanese criminal Renato Vallanzasca who, as O'Rawe (2014) discusses, received "thousands of marriage proposals from women while in prison" (148). At the same time, however, we see in these comments the double-pull of the stories: the ethical consciousness of users is engaged as they lambaste these men as "delinquents" and do not champion their actions, yet they still remain fascinated by them. Consequently, and dissimilar to several other onscreen treatments of the Banda, these new media texts might push viewers to engage with ethical elements of a culture of legality.

These users experience a splitting of the ego, a process that is described as

> the coexistence at the heart of the ego of two psychical attitudes towards external reality in so far as this stands in the way of an instinctual demand. The first of these attitudes takes reality into consideration, while the second disavows it and replaces it by another product of desire. The two attitudes persist side by side without influencing each other. (Laplanche and Pontalis 2006, 427)

Thus, users understand that the Banda is a violent criminal organization with a bloody past while at the same time disavowing this knowledge and substituting it with a much more pleasurable narrative (the centrality of friendship and sexual desire). This phenomenon is quite common in a video called "La vera Banda della Magliana vs. Romanzo Criminale la serie" (The true Banda of the Magliana vs. crime novel the series) (2011a, b), which has been uploaded to YouTube by two different people and watched a half a million times. The video is composed of a series of sixteen stills, each containing likenesses of the historical and fictional gang members that are positioned below the name of their Roman district. As in "ROMANZO CRIMINALE (serie) alla BANDA DELLA MAGLIANA (realtà)" just discussed, the first four images are of the most popular characters of the film and series (Libanese, Dandi, Freddo, and Bufalo), although "La vera Banda della Magliana vs. Romanzo Criminale la serie" omits the actual names of ex-Banda members and only includes their nicknames, a move that aids to further distance fact from fiction. It also incorporates depictions of twelve "other characters," including Franchino il criminale/Terribile "Terrible," Sabrina Minardi/Patrizia, and Er Pantera/Puma "Cougar," and concludes with first a publicity still from the series that contains almost all of its principle characters and then a compilation of fifteen mug shots below a script that reads "This is the real Banda della Magliana!" in vivid red. The video is accompanied by Vasco Rossi's "Liberi liberi," the song that also accompanies the final minutes of the series finale. In the end of the series, which continues the opening sequence discussed earlier, Bufalo is shot down by police after he imagines the defunct members of the Banda playing pool, their youthful bodies intact. The song adds a melancholic tone to the video and bookends the "ROMANZO CRIMINALE (serie) alla BANDA DELLA MAGLIANA (realtà)," which was uploaded in 2009, and "La vera Banda della Magliana vs. Romanzo Criminale la serie" uploaded in 2011, and complements the conclusion of the series' two seasons. Viewers familiar with the series will call to mind its finale, in which is underlined "the narrative of loss and nostalgia that underpins the entire series" (O'Rawe 2014, 102), an ethos present in "Da ROMANZO CRIMINALE (serie) alla BANDA DELLA MAGLIANA (realtà)," a point to which I return shortly. Jenkins (2007) writes that transmedia texts are quite ambitious, and frequently result in "gaps or excesses in the unfolding of the story" that readers often elaborate and work over "with their speculations, until they take a life of their own," which is the case with this video. Below, we see how several user comments exhibit the double conscience in line with the mechanism of splitting, which was discussed earlier:

Everyone makes their own choices! And then pays the consequences! However, who of us has not empathized with one of them? At least for one moment!

I got really into the series and I even bought the box set. But I am also happy that the state finally won and those not in jail had to pay, even with the worst bill. it is undeniable that we are all under the spell of the criminal it is the cornerstone of the series but people who live that life don't have a have a happy life.

I am not a fan of mafiosi, however I have to say that the guys from the series romanzo criminale best represented the characters from the real banda.

It succeeds at making you take the side of criminals, assassins, drug dealers, etc. Congratulations to all who contributed to the creation of this series: to whoever brought croissants to Libanese on the set! ("La vera Banda della Magliana vs. Romanzo Criminale la serie," 11 September 2011a, b)

Mentions of empathy, being under the spell and on the side of criminals, and claims at verisimilitude in representation suggest that the commenters above experience a thwarted version of Noël Carroll's "Sympathy for the Devil" (2004), which he describes as the paradox whereby a viewer "can be sympathetic (care for, or have a pro-attitude) toward a fictional character whose real-world counterpart she would totally abhor" (122). Different, of course, in my study is that the object of sympathy is a historical criminal and not a fictional one. Carroll explains the above-mentioned discrepancy (why we invite criminals into our homes regularly on small screens, but would not request their company at our dinner table), by stating, "in terms of every pertinent moral property, the fictional Tony Soprano [is not] identical to a real-life Tony Soprano" as the latter is much less "morally palatable" for a variety of reasons (122). The videos discussed in this section, however, work to eclipse the distinction between the two groupings, and thus viewers are free to relate emotionally with real and fictional devils. The comments here invite speculation that the hybridized videos may prompt modes of reflection that fiction films and documentaries generally deny spectators, due to their respective spectatorial systems and generic conventions. Such a proposition clearly deserves further attention, especially with regard to the possibilities it opens for the creation of different kinds of hybridized texts contributing to the culture of legality.

Conclusion: Mafia Capitale

The issues concerning how the Internet figures in making distinctions between fact and fiction, posed by Thomas Elsaesser (1999) in the epigraph opening this chapter, are critical when considering the conflict between the antimafia and mafia, which is made particularly apparent in the web-based digital media discussed here. The mafia in Italy, as I have argued elsewhere, is an ongoing and apparently unending wound to the nation that has none of the cultural cachet that typically delineates cultural traumas (Renga 2013, 3–20). As we have seen in this chapter, the Banda is considered by many as a defeated mafia, yet recent arrests and the revelation of "Mafia capitale" in Rome in late 2014 speak to the presence of a new mafia that has been active in the capital since at least the year 2000. The films, series, and documentaries discussed in this chapter all work to humanize perpetrators while presenting (in the case of the documentaries) the criminal organization as part of Italy's past. Such a moral code creeps into the web-based texts as well. Furthermore, the videos that include scenes and musical scores from the series map the characteristics of the fictional characters (loyalty, honour, compassion, magnanimity, etc.) onto their historical peers. As such, these characters' "morality" is exported and makes for a much less inimical representation of criminality. Viewers can in a sense "have it all" as they are free to identify with the bad guys while simultaneously decrying their actions.

As clearly illustrated by this exploratory analysis of remediated factual and fictional stories of the Banda and viewers' ideas about them, the new aesthetic experiences that Jenkins (2006) perceives in convergence culture may also produce models of identification and ethical judgment that differ from those operating respectively in documentary and fiction film. Viewers see the characters and the historical figures not only as murderers, psychopaths, and drug dealers but also as individuals with whom they can relate, and such a vision mitigates (without eliminating) our negative judgments. Mittell (2014) argues that we can enjoy the exploits of, for example, Dexter, Tony Soprano, or Walter White while "suspend[ing] moral judgment" (80), and thus we remain free from having to make any sort of choice as to how we would act were we to meet their historical counterparts. Instead, this project considers our ethical judgments as multiple and various, and a key part of our experience with these narratives. This investigation of how the specific narrative treatments of these so-called villainous characters complicates our ethical judgments offers a different critical perspective on the raging debates surrounding the culture of legality about various mediations of the mafiosi on the web, such as fan pages devoted to mafia bosses like Bernardo Provenzano and Salvatore Riina and multi-platform mafia games such as *Mafia Wars*, *Mob Wars: La Cosa Nostra*, and the *Mafia* series.[11] The remediation of the merged fiction and non-fiction texts works in line with Bolter and Grusin's (2000) idea of remediation as reform whereby one medium is seen as "reforming or improving upon another" (59). Such remediations might have a social or a political significance, especially when considering digital media where individuals can actively participate in online debates (60), which is a central query of Paula Salvio's chapter in this volume, "'A Taste of Justice,'" where she interrogates the potential for social networks to contribute to "cultural and social renewal" in the era of neoliberalism. Through the resultant dialogic relations they develop with the texts discussed in this chapter, viewers deploy their ethical judgment. Such interventions contribute to the process by which the reality of Banda della Magliana continues to be reformed.

NOTES

Many thanks to Catherine O'Rawe for helpful suggestions on earlier versions of this chapter.

1 For more on the history of the Banda della Magliana, see Bianconi (2013), Camuso (2014), and Lupacchini (2014).
2 The figure of the romanticized criminal has a long-standing, rich tradition in Italian literature and film. The most pertinent antecedents related to the subject of the mafia are Leonardo Sciascia's *Il giorno della civetta* (1966), in translation as *The Day of the Owl* (2003) in literature, and Francesco Rosi's *Lucky Luciano* (1973) in film.
3 Anecdotally, I teach *Romanzo criminale* to approximately 225 students a year at Ohio State University. I regularly ask the class which of the three main gang members is responsible for killing the most people, and well over half of the class responds "Libanese." Freddo kills many more men than Libanese in the film, yet he is remembered as less violent.
4 For more on the "morality" of the film, book, and series and a discussion of the controversy surrounding "negative role models" many felt that *Romanzo criminale* promoted, see Boni (2014, 31–5).

5 For a discussion of how the series differs in this effect from the film, see Boni (2014, 90–104) and O'Rawe (2014, chap. 4, "The Last Real Men"). *Romanzo criminale: la serie* is currently being adapted for the American television network Starz. Set in Philadelphia during the late 1960s and early 1970s, the series will "chronicle the rise of working class criminals who attempt to seize the American Dream by any means necessary" (Andreeva 2013).

6 The research on the hybrid texts was conducted through searches on Google, YouTube, and Dailymotion. The respective numbers of views and comments for the texts are as follows: "Romanzo criminale la serie," 287,789 views, 53 comments; "La Banda della Magliana – I Personaggi realmente esistiti," 600,790 views, 148 comments; "Documentario il processo alla Banda della Magliana – I confronti parti 1 di 2," 722,108 views, 344 comments; "Documentario il processo alla Banda della Magliana – I confronti parti 2 di 2," 385,000 views, 161 comments; "Da ROMANZO CRIMINALE (serie) alla BANDA DELLA MAGLIANA (realtà)," 1,100,455 views, 430 comments; "La vera Banda della Magliana vs. Romanzo Criminale la serie," 380,000 views, 189 comments; "La vera Banda della Magliana vs. Romanzo Criminale la serie," 298,362 views, 83 comments; "ROMANZO CRIMINALE La Serie 2 – Trailer esteso," 270,521 views, 74 comments; "Romanzo Criminale la serie Trailer HD," 140,607 views, 20 comments; "Banda della Magliana la vera storia," 347 views, 9 comments. For my analysis I looked for patterns and trends in comments relating to how viewers either judged, sympathized, or aligned with the Banda members (or a combination of all three).

7 For example, in the comment section for the trailer to the second season of *Romanzo criminale: la serie* that has been watched over 127,000 times, users write, "AWESOME SERIE," "Very nice serie!!!!!!! true cinema italiano !!! congratulations," "semplicemente stupenda ...." ("Romanzo Criminale la serie Trailer HD" 2010, original spelling). This trend is also apparent in the comments to the trailer for the second season, which has been watched by more than 250,000 people ("Romanzo criminale: la serie 2 – Trailer esteso" 2010).

8 This site no longer exists: https://www.youtube.com/playlist?list=PL6350520D64D71EFB

9 The eight-part "Banda della Magliana la vera storia" (2014) hosted on Dailymotion is quite interesting visually, and includes images and scenes from the film and series, photographs of ex-Banda members, reenactments of crimes, and a voiceover chronicling the Banda's activities. It has very few comments, however (nine in total on the eight videos).

10 Other figures included in the montage are Antonio Mancini/Ricotta; Nicolino Selis/Sardo; Fulvio Lucioli/ Sorcio; Giovanni Girlando/Satana; Libero Mancone/ Fierolocchio.

11 For more on debates around fan pages for the mafiosi, such as Bernardo Provenzano and Totò Riina, see Donadio (2009) and the section "Social Media" in Pine (2011). See Remondini (2010) for controversies surrounding the release of *Mafia II*.

7 #NuJuornBuon: Aesthetics of Viral Antimafia

ANGELA MAIELLO

In February 2014, the twenty-year-old rapper Rocco Pagliarulo, aka Rocco Hunt, won the "New Talents" award at the 64th edition of the *Festival della canzone italiana di Sanremo*, the most popular competition of Italian pop music. The song performed by Rocco Hunt was entitled "Nu Juorn Buon," which in Neapolitan dialect means "a good day." What distinguishes the song is the way it imagines a "good day" for Southern Italy, and specifically for the so-called Land of Fires,[1] the farmlands situated in Campania. Once well known for their fertility,[2] the farmlands have been ravaged by thousands of tons of toxic wastes that were illegally dumped by the camorra clans of the Neapolitan mafia. As a result of the Sanremo prize, "Nu Juorn Buon" and its author rapidly gained popularity, becoming a symbol of the antimafia fight against the camorra.

In the following study I analyse the song "Nu Juorn Buon" as a significant case in which the diffusion of an antimafia[3] message is made possible by the utilization of practices and procedures rendered available by digital technologies, and in particular, by social networks. Besides being a song shrewdly written to obtain its goal of winning the competition, "Nu Juorn Buon" is a viral web phenomenon. As such, it represents a good example for initiating reflection on the relation between the antimafia and new media. It is necessary to understand what possibilities are created by new media for promoting the active fight against the different mafias, but also what risks or limits are inherent to the contemporary media landscape with regard to transforming online participation into strong antimafia activism.

My analysis works through the methodological approach provided by the field of aesthetics, drawing upon Emilio Garroni's (1986) theory of sense in its multiple signification of sense, sensation, and meaning, and investigating the conditions of possibility of experience in general. Following this line of thought, aesthetics, as conceived in philosophy, regards not only artistic forms, genres, and works, but also reflection on sensibility as the grounding condition of our experience. Sensibility is not just the faculty of physically feeling or the perception of space and time, but also the faculty of judging, making sense, and comprehending. Today sensibility is greatly influenced and oriented by technologies (Montani 2014), and the pivotal aspect of our current times is the fact that we increasingly delegate the performances of our sensibility to something technological, for several reasons. For instance, to optimize our capacity to guide ourselves in space, we may employ online maps or augmented reality. To form a collective memory based upon the sharing of emotions and affects, as in the case of online websites dedicated to victims of the mafia such as Casamemoria Vittimemafia, we may make use of elective social networks (see Amy Boylan's chapter "Democratizing the Memorial Landscape" in this volume). It is on the backdrop of this specific conception of aesthetics that new media theory encounters aesthetics. This encounter has the potential for developing what I propose as an aesthetics of viral antimafia.

At the outset of my discussion, I examine the complex cultural and medial environment in which to situate the case of "Nu Juorn Buon." On the one hand, the symbolic collective imagination linked to the camorra is traditionally an essential element of Neapolitan culture. Yet, on the other hand, this same symbolic collective imagination is now rapidly evolving, largely due to the new ironic modalities of communication spread by social networks. I then turn to the specific case of "Nu Juorn Buon," analysing the elements that led to it becoming a viral phenomenon. "Nu Juorn Buon" offers a good example of the dynamics that regulate the contemporary participatory media flow, based on the principles of convergence and remediation and on a new form of ludicity, or playfulness. The examination ultimately aims to illustrate the necessity of a techno-aesthetics education, which I propose as a means for transforming online participation into effective antimafia practice.

The Camorra and Popular Culture

Among Italian regional cultures, Neapolitan culture, which is generally associated with the region of Campania, undoubtedly remains among the most popular and recognizable within Italy and beyond its national borders. One of the elements that led to the worldwide recognizability of Neapolitan culture and folklore was the rapid development of Neapolitan music at the beginning of the twentieth century. Marcello Ravveduto (2007) writes:[4]

> From the origins of Neapolitan music, the songs have had two parallel courses, a popular one linked to the daily life of the people that lived in the city's alleys and slums and a refined one influenced by chamber and operatic music. In the middle of the nineteenth century, thanks to the "founding fathers" of classic Neapolitan song, the two trends were unified and thus an interclass orientation became its driving force. Between 1880 and 1945 Naples experienced a musical earthquake creating favourable and unrepeatable conditions. Thus a group of authors and musicians formed, and spread Neapolitan songs throughout the entire world. (7)

As Ravveduto aptly underlines, one of the peculiarities of classic Neapolitan music is precisely that it combines the bourgeois musical taste of the beginning of the century with themes and emotional dispositions prevailing among the Neapolitan subaltern classes. Since the seventeenth century, these poor strata of society were associated with forms of plebeian parasitism best incarnated by the *lazzari*, the bands of unemployed men who day and night roamed and slept in the city's streets. These classes, however, displayed not only unruly behaviour, but also, as Johann Goethe (1982) wrote, "the most ingenious resource, not in getting rich, but in living free from care" (200). It was exactly this "industrious" (Gramsci 1999, 566) character of the Neapolitan people that came to determine the distinctive nature of the city, in which there are deep and profound socio-economic differences that, however, do not lead to the prevailing of a hegemonic class (Masullo 2008).

It is this peculiar condition that facilitated the development of the new hybrid musical genre, animated by recurring musical and literary topoi, which soon became well recognized in the entire world. These topoi, which are often intertwined, are love and the beauties of the city of Naples. Classic Neapolitan music often describes the pains of unfulfilled love, and especially the lover's suffering and agony. This anguish is further amplified through the fashioning of Naples, represented by the sparkle and beauty of its sea, as the stage for the unfolding events. This rhetorical portrayal of the city, untarnished by any references to the squalid, overcrowded slums, was thus elevated to a defining theme of the musical genre. As noted by Daniele Sanzone (2014), Naples, like few cities in the world, lives intensely on a self-narrative that becomes a powerful agent in the constitution of a collective identity as well as the instrument to legitimate an imagery on the border of legality (21).

Although it goes beyond my scope to reconstruct in detail the different phases and modalities of the evolution of Neapolitan music, I want to underscore that the popular element characterizing Neapolitan song since its origins has been interpreted and inflected in various ways, highlighting diversified spirits of the polyhedric Neapolitan culture. In some cases the spirit coincided or intersected with the representation of behaviours and values that are explicitly associated with the camorra as it developed after the Second World War.[5] In other cases, the spirit corresponded to an active and decisive condemnation of the camorra. It is apropos here to chart a few examples, in order to be able to locate "Nu Juorn Buon" in relation to these two currents in Neapolitan culture. The first well-known case representing a celebration of camorra values is the *sceneggiata*, a form of musical drama that was developed at the beginning of the nineteenth century, but was then popularized in the 1970s by Mario Merola, dubbed the "king of the *sceneggiata*." The *sceneggiata* narrates and glorifies the deeds of the popular hero, whose ambiguous morality is justified by his unstable social and economical conditions. This genre gives birth to the figure of the good *guappo* (*il guappo buono*). The term *guappo* indicates an arrogant and boldly impudent man who endeavours to address the shortcomings of the state's legal system and skewed social system with a personal understanding of morality, which can lead to justifying bloody murders in the name of the family, broadly understood. It can be said, as Marino Niola (2003, 25) does, that these theatrical performances fulfil anthropological needs similar to those animating classic Greek tragedies. Indeed, the drama's action revolves around a dual conflict: the conflict between the protagonist with his community, but above all the conflict between the illegality of the common life of the slum and the legality merely proclaimed by the state. Ravveduto (2007) writes:

> The protagonist portrays a hero affected by many troubles that are linked to his belonging to society's more unfortunate classes. He is forced to live with the arrogance and insolence of people in the family, the back alleys, the neighborhood and at times the city, who want to determine his life and destiny. His rebellion is a moral act against abuses experienced by his dear ones, members of his own class. It is a violent rebellion that recreates those ties of solidarity broken by the advent of state law. (20–1)

The *sceneggiata* certainly has not been the only cultural and musical genre able to interpret this popular sentiment, diffused among low-income people who live in a system parallel to that of the Italian state's legality. In more recent times, defined by different social and political conditions, neo-melodic music has assumed this same role (see Pine 2012). Neo-melodic music developed in the 1980s, and in the 1990s became a real national phenomenon that was particularly popular in Southern Italy. The genre has distinct characteristics, signalled immediately by its name, which represents a clear attempt to differentiate this new musical scene from classic Neapolitan music. From a strictly musical point of view, the neo-melodic songs realize a break with the tradition not only by importing sound from the most famous international music forms, such as pop and dance music, but also drawing upon the imagery linked to the figure of the pop star. Neo-melodic music doesn't aim to dignify the figure of the outcast by invoking shared ancestral values, like the family in the case of *sceneggiata*. Rather, it describes in graphic realism the life of the slums made of love, betrayal, pain, suffering, prison, and death. Neo-melodic music primarily addresses people who live in the poorer areas of the city, and in particular young people who perceive the camorra as a natural element of their lives. In this way, this form of music decisively contributes to what can be considered a "sentimental education" (Saviano 2012) of new generations. Both in cases that invite an explicit identification with the figure of the camorra boss, as in the songs "O killer," "Il mio amico camorrista" (My friend the camorrista), and "Nu latitante" (A fugitive), and in cases where such references are indirect, the stories describe the everyday life of people living in collusion with the criminal worlds. They thus contribute to fashioning a new camorra culture, characterized by drugs, television success, and impudent behaviour. The language employed in such songs tends to be a hybridized admixture of dialect and Italian. According to Ravveduto (2007), neo-melodic music is the "expression of postmodern culture" (12), which insinuates itself in the alleys of the city through television, and which homogenizes culture and diffuses the desire for easy success.

The *sceneggiata* and neo-melodic music are probably the most impressive examples of this sort of acceptance of camorra values through successful, diffused forms of popular culture. Significantly, other interpretations of the same popular sentiment lead to contrasting outcomes that represent an instrument of opposition and social condemnation of the camorra. At the end of the 1970s, as an answer to the *sceneggiata*, the so-called Neapolitan Power, inspired by the Black Power Movement, took shape. This new musical trend brought about a veritable revolution of Neapolitan music, and Italian songwriting as well, by assimilating sounds from blues and black music, the Mediterranean tradition, and classic Neapolitan sound (Sanzone 2014, 50). While often claiming to derive from popular culture and express social marginalization as a source of pride, the songs are enriched by evocative lyrics written in authentic dialect, which conjure the city of Naples from a disenchanted and bitter gaze. The positive stereotypes used in classic Neapolitan music are thus overturned in order to describe a situation of poverty and immorality that obliquely crosses the different levels of the community, as exemplified by Pino Daniele's "Terra mia" (My land) and "Na tazzulell è caffè" (A small cup of coffee).

Although the songwriters of Neapolitan Power have viewed the camorra with a certain aloofness, denouncing and keeping a distance from such diffused immorality, for which the Italian state is generically deemed the most responsible, a more explicit engagement characterizes the new wave of musicians who became well known on the regional scene at the beginning of the new millennium. The emerging of this new musical scene, actively involved in the transmission of an anti-camorra message, is first of all due to a transformation of the camorra phenomenon itself. In contrast to perceptions of the camorra prevailing in the 1970s, identified with the contraband of cigarettes, which was a source of income for many families, the image of the crime organization in the 1980s turned deadly. With the rise to power of the boss Raffaele Cutolo, the camorra became a much broader, diffused criminal system that caused thousands of deaths (Sanzone 2014, 79). The outskirts of Naples were absorbed by the camorra system, becoming the outpost for drug dealing and wars between clans. The new musicians come from these very outskirts, from neighbourhoods like Scampia or Secondigliano, and their songs have the explicit goal of breaking omertà, the law of silence that prevails in those areas. The new bands, Co'sang and A'67 among others, though still writing in dialect, are inspired by the American rap tradition. For the first time in the history of Neapolitan popular music, there is a clear and unequivocal condemnation of the camorra system and most of all, of obeying the law of silence that many of us living in mafia territories face every day.[6]

In the cartography of conflicting strains that respectively glorify and condemn the camorra, the innovative rap operates as a force of musical and moral renewal in Neapolitan popular culture, augmented by

Roberto Saviano's non-fiction novel *Gomorrah* (2006)· and its multiple remediations, which constitute the medial flow and the frame in which Rocco Hunt's case must be located. Published in Italian in 2006, the bestselling novel sold over two million copies in Italy by 2009. The author's particular inside story of the camorra incorporates non-fiction materials represented through strategies of narration typical of fiction. Remarkably, the novel accomplishes what all of the news stories on the camorra reported in the press and on television could not. The imaginary narration worked to authenticate (Montani 2010, 8) factual camorra stories and images consumed by the medial flow, becoming testimony to the reality and not its mere medial representation. Saviano's novel inspired both Matteo Garrone's acclaimed film *Gomorra* (2008) and the highly successful television series *Gomorra. La serie* (2014). The television series, which narrates the story of a camorra family, represents a significant evolution in the Italian medial landscape, where narrative formats for TV are still much below the standards of those in other countries, such as the United States. *Gomorra. La serie* aspires to be a strong fictional story, but at the same time its representations of figures and situations tend to operate in the realist mode. The narration doesn't provide explicit judgments, but under the direction of Stefano Sollima, the series gives dramatic form to characters and circumstances in their more banal and ordinary aspects, in their misery and cruelty, free of any epic overtones, but profoundly human. The detailed attention to gestures, situations, and behaviours, as well as the use of Neapolitan dialect (the actors speak in dialect and the episodes are broadcast with Italian subtitles) underscore the characters' humanity, and may strike spectators so deeply that the detailed features become part of her or his daily imagery, thus posing issues that receive close scrutiny in Dana Renga's discussion of *Romanzo Criminale: la serie* ("Remediating La Banda della Magliana" elsewhere in this volume), also directed by Sollima.

The innovative form of characterization crafted in *Gomorra. La serie* inspired a group of young Neapolitan videomakers, The Jackal, to produce video-parodies of the series, titled "The Effects of Gomorra on People," which was diffused online. The videos immediately became viral content, reaching five million views on YouTube in just a few days. In the last video, Roberto Saviano himself plays a role. The dominant approach of the videos is to decontextualize the code of behaviour of the camorra by applying it to ordinary situations. For example, the short videos narrate how a man influenced by the TV series goes to a bar acting like a boss, using the expressions and the rituals portrayed in the series. The parodies effectively transform camorra codes, values, and way of speaking, which some films represent in almost sacral terms, into objects of mockery and ridicule, by virtue of online viral participation.

The case of "Nu Juorn Buon" has to be interpreted in relation to the two elements highlighted thus far. First, there is an implicit dialectic in popular Neapolitan culture between glorification and condemnation of camorra values as articulated by music. Second, the diffusion of new medial forms and formats, ranging from Saviano's (2008) novel to the viral videos of The Jackal, constitutes a significant element in these cultural dynamics, and the web appears to be the place where this dialectic will play out in the future.

#NuJuornBuon: A Viral Song

In January 2011, Rocco Hunt, who at the time was only seventeen years old, recorded his first album, entitled *Spiraglio di Periferia* (A glimpse of the periphery), for a web label. The album immediately attracted the attention of critics, some of whom recognized a real talent in the young rapper from Salerno (see the publications *Piazza*, *Rockit*).[7] Projecting maturity and a strong presence, Rocco Hunt performs a rap that is characterized by his regional cultural background. He sings in dialect and narrates the condition of many people like him who live on the outskirts of the city. In the album, Hunt describes the feelings of frustration experienced by those people living in an area where "everything has a price," but at the same time he frees himself from any stereotypes or trappings linked to the rap worlds. As he states in one song, "This is my rap, serious stuff, no invented stuff" ("Nun ce sta paragone"). All of these elements and the widespread online diffusion of his videos brought him stellar success, especially among young people.

The main themes of Rocco Hunt's songs are relatively consistent, focusing on the difficulties afflicting his land, but also the desire and the determination to obtain a sort of redemption. "Nu Juorn Buon," included in the album *A' verità* (The truth), engages with these arguments, with the important distinction that it imaginatively envisions a new day, a good day, for his land and young people. In fact, the very first words of the song announce the beginning of the new day, conjuring the "different atmosphere" through specific signs for which the Italian south is famous – the "sun's rays" coming through the window, and the land's powerful beauty, prompting nostalgia in its absence. In simple language, the song then raises the two possibilities of life and death faced by the land and its people alike, but casts them in a positive manner by declaring that the land "does not have to die" or the people be forced to leave. Calling upon others to listen to his voice, the singer's spare words focus on the "massacre of garbage" and the proliferating "tumours," in other words, the toxic wastes illegally dumped by the camorra. The last two lines redefine Campania as the "land of the sun" and not the "land of fires." The song's positive message was decisive for its success because, as generally noted, it was in tune with the tastes of the national popular audience that followed the competition and also determined the song's transformation into a viral web phenomenon.

Since his debut, just like other young people his age, Rocco Hunt has always heavily used the web, especially social networks such as Facebook and Instagram, to spread his songs, and moreover, to share fragments of his everyday life. In order to mobilize the public and capture their votes for the Sanremo Music Festival, the rapper found specific hashtags producing real web-trending topics, such as #cemagnamm, which in Neapolitan means "we will eat them up," or #senecadeiltelevoto, meaning "the televoting will crash." Hunt used these hashtags to share photos and videos, but also thoughts and private emotions connected to what he defined as the realization of a dream. Such strategies proved effective. Rocco Hunt's Facebook page attracted more online participation than the one dedicated to the Sanremo Music Festival, registering 860,000 "likes" versus 200,000. The online viral participation helped Rocco Hunt win the competition and transformed a simple rap song into an effective antimafia anthem, which has since been broadcast by national television stations, sung at antimafia demonstrations, and used as a source of inspiration for essay competitions at schools. Understanding how "Nu Juorn Buon" became a viral phenomenon could furnish the basic instruments with which to identify the opportunities that new media offer for the diffusion of anticamorra values as well as the limits they evidence in transforming those values into efficacious antimafia weapons.

Key to examining how viral phenomena operate is the term "participatory culture," which is used to denote the totality of practices and procedures that can be activated within the so-called Web 2.0. The expression Web 2.0 indicates the current configuration of the web (or the immediately previous one),[8] which is characterized by an unprecedented, high degree of user participation and interaction. All rhetoric aside, the Web 2.0 has transformed the Internet into the privileged place for participatory culture, already prefigured by Henry Jenkins (1992) with reference to television. Social networks, along with other forms of organization and sharing of contents, like participatory knowledge websites such as Wikipedia, or blogs, are the main agents of this configuration. They have determined a deep change in the modalities of production and fruition of medial content, fostering the erosion of the consolidated distinction between producers and consumers.

The peculiarity of Web 2.0 is the creation of an interrupted medial flow, continuously updated and updatable, which is fed by the contributions of single users. This flow is regulated by processes of convergence (Jenkins 2006) and remediation (Bolter and Grusin 2000). These are two well-known concepts in the field of media theory that indicate similar medial processes which, however, are not completely overlapping. The concept of convergence designates the fact that with digital technologies, old and new media (for instance a social network profile and a television network) tend to interact at levels of both structure and contents. Convergence is a medial strategy that exploits the functions of more recent devices and proceeds to establish the rules for a new aesthetic experience, understood as a perceptual experience tout court and as fruition of particular content. As a rule, it is now fully used in major and minor productions of medial contents. Convergence denotes the strategy adopted by both big corporations and small companies that results in a flow from top to bottom, and also denotes the everyday utilization of media made by users, which could be defined as a techno-aesthetic[9] practice. As Jenkins (2006) notes, "Convergence is taking place within the same appliances, within the same franchise, within the same company, within the brain of the consumer" (16). The mechanism of convergence is notably evident in the case of "Nu Juorn Buon." The rapper used social networks in order to promote his song and to invite fans to televote him. Without the mobilization of followers the song probably would not have gained the victory that led it and its antimafia message to be diffused through traditional media, which have then themselves been remediated thorough social networks in the form of links, videos, and photos.

While the concept of convergence indicates the interaction between old and new media, the concept of remediation, instead, denotes the process of media redefinition. In the case of "Nu Juorn Buon," for instance, the same video of the final performance of Rocco Hunt at the Sanremo Music Festival acquired a new medial structure and a new modality of fruition once it was posted as a link on his Facebook page, and the television experience was remediated in the form of online participation. Remediation has to be taken in its double acceptation. In other words, the television video is reproposed by new media, but it has also been reformed, amended, acquiring something that it lacked before, which is the active participation of the public that is thus transformed into a community. Indeed, through social networks, the performance video could be commented on, shared, and, above all, potentially manipulated. On YouTube, for example, one can find many mashed-up videos based on the song, ranging from karaoke video to tutorials to learn how to play the song, to many parodies of the song itself.

Remediation answers a double logic (Bolter and Grusin 2000, 5), that is the complementarity between immediacy and hypermediacy: the highest form of immediacy depends on the highest degree of hypermediacy. Immediacy cannot be achieved without hypermediacy. On the one hand there is the attempt to satisfy the need of immediacy in both its acceptations – that of immediate real-time representation and of access to a reality without filters. Remediation then works by projecting different "as if" assumptions: as if I were there, as if it were true, as if I could take part. On the other hand, however, "the same old and new media refuse to leave us alone" (Bolter and Grusin 2000, 6); they are constantly increasing, superimposing one another, converging, and recalling each other. Hypermediacy is what determines the simultaneous organic functionality of different medial layers and levels, and makes the user aware of the mediation itself because it does not erase its traces. Web pages are a perfect example of the functioning of hypermediacy.

Although the double logic of remediation, as sustained by Bolter and Grusin (2000), does not concern only the so-called new media, and does not appear to be a phenomenon typifying our era, it can be considered the pivotal element of one of today's most used social networks, which is Instagram. The application for photo sharing, acquired from Facebook in 2012 and now more popular than Twitter, fulfills the desire for immediacy characterizing media users-consumers. Real or ordinary life is captured and immortalized by the click of a mobile device, then made public, shared with friends and followers, and thus with the rest of the connected world, by a simple hashtag. In this case immediacy has that double acceptation that was underlined above. It refers to real time as well as to the availability of a far-off reality. It is for this very reason that Instagram is one of the tools most used by people in show business, and Rocco Hunt is no exception. However, within the Instagram medial environment, the principal trait of immediacy, of this reality free of filters, is that of being constitutively filtered. As it is well known, once the photo is taken, the application allows editing. In fact, using preset filters, it is possible first of all to modify the size so as to give it the format of an old Polaroid, but one can also adjust the light, colour, frame, and then give it traits according to pre-determined visual registers. Such filtering is thus the highly evident and clearly stated residual trace of hypermediation.

The diffusion of "Nu Juorn Buon" on the web has closely followed this double logic of remediation. Rocco Hunt relied primarily on Instagram and Facebook and their rules to share the images related to his Sanremo Music Festival experience. This strategy facilitated the creation of seemingly close ties and immediacy with the fans that followed him. The efficacy of the song's message itself as well as the creation of the public figure were the product of a powerful remediation process. By means of web hypermediation, a normal, yet talented, young man like so many others from the outskirts, became a star whose success is tightly linked to the immediacy of the contents and to the apparent genuineness of his message.

Although the concepts of convergence and remediation help us to understand the modalities of creation and production of medial contents within the Web 2.0, as in the case of "Nu Juorn Buon," they are not sufficient to comprehend the viral feature of that content, that is to say their capacity for diffusion. First of all, let's eliminate a recurring misunderstanding. To affirm that certain content is viral doesn't imply, as Jenkins sustains (2013), that there is a certain passivity of the users in this process of global diffusion. Viral contents function exactly like viruses. They can replicate by themselves, but in order to reproduce and multiply, they need to come into contact with the cells of a living organism, without which they have no life. Likewise medial content needs the participatory interaction of users through which it can reproduce (mash up, hybridization, etc.) and multiply, thus becoming what the web defines as a meme, a viral content. As recent studies show, several features stimulate user participation, enabling a content to become viral, while certain procedures and protocols regulate the participation, which contributes to exponentially increasing the diffusion of the content itself.[10] In order to become viral, medial content must be strongly characterized and charged in its intensity or affect,[11] that is to say, it has to spread or inspire an emotion that is very distinct and recognizable. This rule applies to both emotions often viewed as negative and those perceived as positive. For instance, anger or indignation can become powerful generators of online political participation, as in the case of the Italian party Movimento Cinque Stelle. The power of positive emotions is exemplified by Pharrel William's song and video "Happy." In 2014, the song became one of the contents most shared and diffused through the web. In the case of "Happy" and "Nu Juorn Buon," both music and text reciprocally contribute to the definition and diffusion of positive feelings and hopes, and those emotions activate users' participation.

In addition to the specific affect produced by the medial content, it is possible to trace a positive affectivity intrinsic to participation itself. Grusin (2010) writes:

> Leaving multiple traces of yourself on socially networked media sites is seen as a necessary goal – and interacting with such sites is made pleasurable or desirable in part because they work to produce and maintain positive affective relations with their users, to set up affective feedback loops that make one want to proliferate one's media transactions. Indeed, something as seemingly innocuous as the fact that Facebook offers its users the option to "like" or "unlike" an item but not to "dislike" it epitomizes its bias towards fostering positive individual and collective affect. (3-4)

The ludic dimension of online participation sheds light on the desire to take part in the different forms of social interaction enabled by digital technologies and the pleasures thus derived. It is a peculiar form of ludicity inherent to that process of gamification that Peppino Ortoleva (2012) deems is the dominant trend of our times. Ortoleva affirms that human beings have always played and could not have evolved fully if this had not been the case. They began to play at the dawn of their appearance, before learning to speak and acquiring a full awareness of themselves. Homo ludens, claims Ortoleva, factually and logically precedes Homo faber and the other types of Homos. However, today we are witnesses to an undeniably new perspective that consists of the erosion of the gap between game and not-game. The ancient Homo ludens is becoming a new ambiguous figure, Homo ludicus (18). The sphere of action of this new Homo entails different ludic forms that are relatively new, like video games and mobile aps, proliferating theme parks, where the ludic sphere is provided not only by the attractions, but also by the space that presents itself as different from reality, new sports, online gambling, and last, but not least, participation within the social networks.

The ludic dimension of social networks is inscribed primarily in the proceduralization of the typical activities related to human relations that in the offline sphere are conducted through discursive processes, which can be relatively long or articulated: becoming friends, exchanging opinions, showing feelings and states of mind, sharing situations and circumstances. Social networks translate those relational modalities into semi-automatic procedures, explicable with a simple click of the touchpad (the "add friend" of "ilike" buttons, or the "retweet" one). However the aim of such a game is not to merely duplicate the so-called real life. These procedures activate new forms of sharing. Indeed, the very concept of sharing is the key to understanding the ludicity of social networks. The aim of the game of social networks is sharing itself. Sharing content generates a pleasure that goes far beyond the forms of voyeurism and self-satisfaction, which the ludic procedure also envisages (like the number of "ilikes" or "retweets" we collect with our posts). The pleasure of sharing derives from the fact that through it we form affiliations and become part of a community. Sharing, whether it is politically or socially engaged as in the case of websites about participatory knowledge or the collection of information about countries at war, or when it is activated by mere amusement content as in the case of a meme or lolcat, is able to create a magmatic flow made by plural intentions, experiences, and knowledges, in which everyone could take part. These forms of communities, whose theoretical status is still unclear, can be created on the basis of specific interest or expertise into which we can pour our knowledge and experience (cuisine, video games, or music, for example), or on the basis of a shared past, feelings, or collective affects.

The game of sharing activated by "Nu Juorn Buon" indissolubly follows both of these criteria. It mobilizes the increasing numbers of young people interested specifically in rap music or in the public figure of Rocco Hunt, as happens in the most traditional fandom base. Moreover, the song's simplicity and immediacy were able to spread a strong emotional intensity that succeeded, as remediated by new forms of online viral participation, to reach and unite thousands of people with different experiences and backgrounds, yet share the hope for a better future, a better day for the south, finally freed from the camorra or other criminal organizations. As stated above, the users didn't simply restrict themselves to listen to or induce others to listen to Rocco Hunt's song. Rather, they appropriated it in order to realize other medial and audiovisual contents, each one very different from the other in terms of intent and creative efforts. (These artful products can be viewed on YouTube.) In the process, such new contents reinforce or transform the song's antimafia message, making its wider diffusion possible. But how, if at all, can such participation be transformed into effective forms of activism and struggle against the mafia? And how might we think about this form of participation within the online sphere in relation to the engaged fight against the mafia, while also avoiding the risk of mistaking mere divertissement offered by the web for socially committed action?

For a Techno-aesthetic Education of Viral Antimafia

The pervasiveness of online practices and the diffusion of mobile technologies has eroded the distinction between "reality" and virtuality that marked the dawning of the contemporary digital era. The rapid and capillary development of digital technologies creates what can be defined as a hybrid[12] public space, a new kind of public sphere, in which physical space is augmented and optimized by information collected on the web. The realization of such a space, and the consequent productive relation between online participation and offline political configurations, clearly appeared during the so-called Arab Springs, those movements of protest and revolution that occurred in parts of the Arab world between the end of 2010 and the beginning of 2011. Notwithstanding the fact that the outcomes of these revolutions in many cases didn't coincide with what some hoped, many journalists and cyber-enthusiasts immediately emphasized the important role played in this movement by social networks and particularly Twitter. In such cases, the web becomes the piazza, the square, and the physical square organizes itself through the web. However, as Clay Shirky (2009) sustains, while it is true that social networks contributed to the organization of the protests, permitting the circulation of news and practical information about them, more important was the way they provoked an emotional response. Social networks permitted users from around the world to empathize with the young protesters and their cause, making them emotionally involved.

The emotional response of social networks on the configuration of offline spaces and the practices performed in these spaces has not been seen as a secondary outcome. On the contrary, it is exactly in this capacity to create a sort of globally diffused affect that the specificity of new media has to be located. As Grusin (2015) writes, networked media have the power "to shock established social patterns, public norms, or collective affective formations in anticipation of and response to changing material and medial conditions" (169). Unlike the previous medial system, which was grounded on the principle of representation, the specificity of contemporary mediality is its effectiveness in "mobilizing people or population" by modulating affect. Grusin (2010) explains:

> Thus thinking of mediality in terms of affect is to think of our media practices not only in terms of their structures of signification or symbolic representation but more crucially in terms of the ways in which media function on the one hand to discipline, control, contain, manage, or govern human affectivity and its affiliated things "from above," at the same time that they work to enable particular forms of human action, particular collective expressions or formations of human affect "from below." (79)

The distinguishing feature of "Nu Juorn Buon" is how it attaches the antimafia message to a positive affect, linked to feelings of hope, optimism, and trust in the future, which are amplified by the authenticity and sunny disposition of Rocco Hunt's persona. This unique affective implication constitutes an original element within the sphere of antimafia communication and narrative. As illustrated by the rapid excursus proposed here about the relation between antimafia and popular Neapolitan culture, antimafia values are often associated with feelings and emotions of condemnation and indignation, that evoke heroic figures who make extraordinary sacrifices, sometimes paying with their lives, while fighting the camorra system. Those sacrifices and deeds are elaborated and recirculated by media and popular narratives which, by magnifying such heroic features, risk simplifying very complex figures. As Lorenzo Misuraca (2015) affirms, these figures allude to a "christological model of the solitary hero, who wittingly faces martyrdom, accepting it as an inevitable price that has to be paid in order to redeem the honest people from the yoke of the mafias." Along these lines we might think of Roberto Saviano, whose continued denunciations of the camorra have made him the target of death threats and have forced him to live under twenty-four-hour bodyguard protection seven days a week, isolated from family and community. This heroic model stands in contrast to the idea of family and conviviality that has always characterized the mafia imaginary, and risks producing a medial narration that is counter-productive to raising and promoting awareness about antimafia values among young people. In this context, social networks and more generally online participation present a concrete risk of becoming what Misuraca calls a mere "proxy device" (*dispositivo di delega*). This notion of proxy echoes Malcolm Gladwell's (2010) and Evgeny Morozov's (2009) perception of "slacktivist" online activity, which Paula Salvio puts into question in her study "'A Taste of Justice'" (see especially pages 88–9). Following Misuraca's line of thought, clicking the "ilike" button on the Facebook page dedicated to an antimafia hero or sharing her or his idea and content, in the form of status, links, or videos are equated to an engaged antimafia commitment, and may weaken the action and direct participation in the involved areas and communities. In this particular sense, the fight against the mafia appears to remain within the borders set by standardized web procedures, as opposed to becoming hybridized according to the paradigm I propose here.

However, as clearly illustrated by Rocco Hunt's case, it is the very standardized and mainly ludic procedures that produce new medial forms, such as hashtag and viral video, that are able to determine the affective horizon in which new generations are formed. The sentimental education of young generations that was performed by the music heard along the city alleys is now built by sharing content through the web. Users can appropriate the content and, moreover, creatively interact with it. The interactive possibilities produced by the web generate an enormous and confused plurality of medial forms that requires a techno-aesthetic education, which would operate to transform standardized online participation into effective global activities of opposition to the mafia organizations. The concept of aesthetic education developed by Friedrich Schiller (1954) at the end of the eighteenth century, indicates the necessity of an aesthetic mediation between the rational sphere and the sensible sphere of human beings. Art represented the occasion to recover a lost reciprocity between sensibility and rationality, which is at the basis of the very specific nature of human beings, a condition that originates the capacity of judgment and thinking. In the contemporary era, as I suggested at the beginning of this chapter, human sensibility, broadly understood, is enormously affected and augmented by digital technologies and procedures. The hypothesis of a techno-aesthetic education is thus based on the idea of the contemporary possibility to work on the original relationship between sensibility and rationality, which is to say the possibility of an exchange between the sphere of feelings and emotions and the sphere of reason, by cultivating knowledge and abilities pertaining to the ways we interact with our technical devices. The idea of techno-aesthetics goes back to a line of thought developed by Gilbert Simondon (2013). For Simondon, the encounter between the world and technical objects creates what he defines as a *milieu associé*, which is to say an environment composed by the technical object, the world, and human beings. Human beings, according to Simondon, play on these diverse planes, bringing into existence not only ever-newer technical objects, but also new connected environments. At the base of the ludic, creative work humans perform is a feeling, which Simondon defines as techno-aesthetic.

The act of technical externalization of our sensibility, today amplified by digital technologies, requires the development of skills and expertise that would enable direct, creative, and critical intervention on devices and softwares, fostering the possibility to activate a virtuous relation between technologies, the world, and our aesthetic faculties. Such interventions would ideally permit users to bypass the standardized procedures imposed by the current configuration of the social web, or at least to creatively utilize them, in order to attempt to increasingly elaborate new medial forms and formats that do not create the occasion to merely express our feelings and emotions. Rather, they would operate as the appropriate place to elaborate and diversify them in more complex, reflexive, but above all effective ways, creating new environments, a new hybrid world. As Pietro Montani (2015) suggests, the idea of techno-aesthetic education could work in significant ways to creatively and interactively organize the relation between the online sphere and "real" space.

The concept of a techno-aesthetic education and practices opens possibilities that go beyond the hope that online participation can be translated into physical activism in territories ruled by the camorra and other mafia organizations, thus achieving what some propose is a more concrete effectiveness. The case of #NuJuornBuon is important because it demonstrates the potentialities of online interactivity. With the enactments of creativity and imagination, solicited by technical possibilities, a new medial environment can be fashioned, enabling users to develop and elaborate conscious, deep antimafia feelings, which would impact our capacity for judgment, and thus empower our daily behaviours as users and citizens. The culture of legality and opposition to all mafias is taken largely as the creative, ludic work that distinguishes young web users' interactivity. The hypothesis of a techno-aesthetic education aims to emphasize the idea that such spontaneous operativity, prepared by the devices we commonly use, must be constantly solicited and always creatively reconfigured, so that our online participation does not become merely a standardized procedure by proxy, as Misuraca (2015) asserts. Rather, in the context of this study, such operativity constitutes the instrument for constructing new interconnected environs, new public spaces, and new communities for performative cultural products of legality.

NOTES

1 The expression "Land of Fires" was utilized for the first time in a report about the ecomafias produced by the Italian environmentalist association LegaAmbiente. It was popularized by Roberto Saviano, who used the name for the title of the last chapter of his famous book *Gomorrah* (2008). Saviano writes: "Hardest hit by the cancer of traffic in poisons are the outskirts of Naples – Giugliano, Qualiano, Villaricca, Nola, Acerra, and Marigliano – and the nearly 115 square miles comprising the towns of Grazzanise, Cancello Arnone, Santa Maria La Fossa, Castelvolturno, and Casal di Principe. On no other land in the Western world has a greater amount of toxic and nontoxic waste been illegally dumped" (249).
2 Many historical travel writings describe the exceptional fertility of this land known as "terra del lavoro" (land of work). See John Evelyn ([1901] 2012).
3 I use the term mafia to generically indicate an organized crime system, with no specific reference to the Sicilian criminal organization.
4 All translations from Italian to English are my own unless otherwise indicated.
5 For a history of the camorra, see Gigi Di Fiore (2005).
6 One of the most famous songs of this new Neapolitan rap is entitled "A camorra song'io" (The camorra it's me).
7 See the rock.it website: https://www.rockit.it/recensione/18379/roccohunt-spiraglio-di-periferia
8 Many journalists have tried to propose the definition of Web 3.0 to indicate the different developments and the various extensions of the web. Although the definition of Web 2.0 is generally considered obsolete, I am of the opinion that it is still useful for highlighting the basic functioning of today's web configuration.
9 For the concept of techno-aesthetics, see Gilbert Simondon (2013).

10 It is well known today that a medial content producing many comments or sharing will have a more efficient diffusion through social networks and search engines than a content lacking such interactions.
11 For the concept of affect, see Brian Massumi (2002).
12 For the concept of hybrid in relation to digital technologies, see Lev Manovich (2013).

References

Abbate, Lirio. 2014. "I quattro re di Roma." *L'Espresso*, 12 December. http://espresso.repubblica.it/attualita/cronaca/2012/12/12/news/a-roma-la-mala-si-fa-in-quattro-1.48981

–. 2012. "Anche la mafia è su Facebook." *L'Espresso*, 26 September. http://espresso.repubblica.it/attualita/cronaca/2012/09/26/news/anche-la-mafia-e-su-facebook-1.4697

"Alemanno: 'Le risse coi coltelli colpa anche di Romanzo criminale.'" 2009. *La Repubblica*, 4 May. http://www.repubblica.it/2009/03/sezioni/cronaca/accoltellati-bar/alemanno-serietv/alemanno-serietv.html

Alexander, Jacqui M. 2005. *Pedagogies of Crossing: Meditations on Feminism, Sexual Politics, and the Sacred.* Durham, NC: Duke University Press.

Allyn, Pam. 2010. "Storytelling Connects Us All." *Psychology Today* (blog), 2 March. https://www.psychologytoday.com/blog/litlife/201003/storytelling-connects-us-all

Amenta, Marco. 1997. *Diario di una siciliana ribelle.* Rome: Eurofilm.

Andreeva, Nellie. 2013. "Starz Adapting Italian Gang Series 'Romanzo Criminale.'" *Deadline Hollywood*, 4 December. http://deadline.com/2013/12/starz-adapting-italian-series-romanzo-criminale-steven-s-deknight-steve-mcpherson-scripted-world-lionsgate-646741/

Anello, Francesca. 2013. "La Mafia nella fiction." In *La mafia allo specchio: La trasformazione mediatica del mafioso*, edited by Marina D'Amato, 228–58. Milan: FrancoAngeli.

"Antimafia sociale." 2015. *I Siciliani.* April, 1.

Arlacchi, Pino. 1986. *Mafia Business: The Mafia Ethic and the Spirit of Capitalism.* London: Verso.

Armstrong, Elizabeth, A., and Suzanna M. Crage. 2006. "Movements and Memory: The Making of the Stonewall Myth." *American Sociological Review* 71, no. 5: 724–51.

Augé, Marc. 1995. *Non-places: Introduction to Anthropology of Super-modernity.* London: Verso.

Bagnoli, Carla, ed. 2011. "Emotions and the Categorical Authority of Moral Reasons." In *Morality and the Emotions,* edited by Carla Bagnoli, 62–81. Oxford: Oxford University Press.

–. 2009. "The Mafioso Case: Autonomy and Self-Respect." *Ethical Theory and Moral Practice* 12, no. 5: 477–93.

–. 2007. "Respect and Membership in the Moral Community." *Ethical Theory and Moral Practice* 10, no. 2: 113–28.

"Banda della Magliana la vera storia." 2014. Dailymotion. 2 April. http://www.dailymotion.com/video/x1ldb2p_banda-della-magliana-la-vera-storia-prima-parte_shortfilms

"La Banda della Magliana – I Personaggi realmente esistiti." 2011. YouTube. 10 November. https://www.youtube.com/watch?v=tnQ_95U1Y4I

Bianchi, Stefano Maria, and Alberto Nerazzini. 2005. *La mafia è bianca.* Milan: BURsenzafiltri.

Bianconi, Giovanni. 2013. *Ragazzi di malavita: fatti e misfatti della Banda della Magliana.* Rome: Baldini and Castoldi.

Blu notte – La banda della Magliana. 2011. Rome: RAI.

Bold, Christine, Rick Knowles, and Belinda Leach. 2002. "National Countermemories: Feminist Memorializing and Cultural Countermemory: The Case of Marianne's Park." *Signs* 28, no. 1: 125–48.

Bolter, Jay David, and Richard Grusin. 2000. *Remediation: Understanding New Media.* Cambridge, MA: MIT Press.

Bolzoni, Attilio. 2015. "L'antimafia docile e oscurantista." *La Repubblica,* 4 March. ricerca.repubblica.it/repubblica/archivio/repubblica/2015/03/04/lantimafia-docile-e-oscurantista33.html

Boni, Marta. 2014. *Romanzo Criminale: Transmedia and Beyond.* Venice: Edizioni Ca' Foscari.

Borsellino, Rita. 2015. "Rita Borsellino dietro la lotta alla mafia nascondono i loro interessi." *La Repubblica,* 4 March. http://www.repubblica.it/cronaca/2015/03/04/news/rita_borsellino_dietro_la_lotta_alla_mafia_nascondono_i_loro_interessi-108734124/

–. 2013. "La lotta alla mafia non è solo repressione." RepubblicaTV, 16 March. http://video.repubblica.it/edizione/firenze/rita-borsellino--la-lotta-alla-mafia-non-e-solo-repressione/122404/120889?ref=search

–. 2009. "Borsellino: Restiamo tutti in Facebook per vigilare." ItaliaChiamaItalia, 8 January. http://www.italiachiamaitalia.it

Bouchard, Norma. 2016. "Fighting *Cosa Nostra* with the Camera's Eye: Letizia Battaglia's Evolving Icons of 'Traumatic Realism.'" In *Italian Women at War:*

Sisters in Arms from the Unification to the Twentieth Century, edited by Susan Amatangelo, 167–82. London: Rowman and Littlefield.

Boylan, Amy. 2013. "Unresolved Commemoration: Memorials to Victims of Homophobic Violence in Italy." *The Italianist* 33, no. 1: 138–57.

–. 2011. "Pasquale Scimeca's *Placido Rizzotto*: A Different View of Corleone." In *Mafia Movies: A Reader*, edited by Dana Renga, 312–19. Toronto: University of Toronto Press.

Brancati, Elena, and Carlo Muscetta, eds. 1988. *La letteratura sulla mafia*. Rome: Bonacci.

Brand, Roy. 2009. "Witnessing Trauma on Film." In *Media Witnessing: Testimony in the Age of Mass Communication*, edited by Paul Frosh and Amit Pinchevski, 198–215. London: Palgrave Macmillan.

Bruner, Jerome. 2010. "Narrative, Culture, and Mind." In *Telling Stories: Language, Narrative and Social Life*, edited by Deborah Schiffrin, Anna De Fina, and Anastasia Nylund, 45–50. Washington, DC: Georgetown University Press.

Bucy, Erik, and Kimberly Gregson. 2001. "Media Participation: A Legitimizing Mechanism of Mass Democracy." *New Media and Society* 3, no. 3: 357–80.

Butler, Judith. 2009. *Frames of War: When Is Life Grievable?* London: Verso.

Camuso, Angela. 2014. *Mi ci fu pietà: la Banda della Magliana da 1977 a "Mafia Capitale."* Rome: Castelvecchi.

Carroll, Noël. 2004. "Sympathy for the Devil." In *The Sopranos and Philosophy*, edited by Richard Greene and Peter Vernezze, 121–36. Chicago: Open Court.

Castells, Manuel. 2007. "Communication, Power and Counter-Power in the Network Society." *International Journal of Communication* 1: 238–66.

Cayli, Baris. 2013a. "Creating Counterpublics against the Italian Mafia: Cultural Conquerors of Web-Based Media." *Javnost – The Public* 20, no. 3: 59–76.

–. 2013b. "Italian Civil Society against the Mafia: From Perceptions to Expectations." *International Journal of Law, Crime and Justice* 41: 81–99.

Ceccarelli, Filippo. 2008. "La salma di Renatino nella basilica: l'ultimo colpo del boss benefattore." *La Repubblica*, 25 June. http://www.repubblica.it/2008/06/sezioni/cronaca/emanuela-orlandi/salma-renatino/salma-renatino.html

Chase, David. *The Sopranos*. 1999–2007. New York: HBO.

Cohen, G.A. 1996. "Reason, Humanity, and the Moral Law." In *The sources of normativity*, edited by Thomas Nagel, Christine M. Korsgaard, Raymond Geuss, and G.A. Cohen, 167–88. Cambridge: Cambridge University Press.

"Il colpo di Vallanzasca: Chiede il diritto all'oblio via i link su Google." 2014. Bergamonews, 10 September. http://www.bergamonews.it/2014/08/08/il-colpo-di-vallanzascachiede-il-diritto-allobliovia-i-link-su-google/193660/

Coppola, Francis Ford, dir. 1972. *The Godfather*. Los Angeles: Paramount Pictures.

"Cos'è il, 21 Marzo." N.d. Libera. Associazioni, nomi e numeri contro le mafie. http://www.libera.it/flex/cm/pages/ServeBLOB.php/L/IT/IDPagina/472

Costantini, Daniele. 2004. *Fatti della Banda della Magliana*. Rome: Goodtime Enterprises.

– . N.d. "Note di regia del film *Fatti della Banda della Magliana*." Cinemaitaliano.info. http://www.cinemaitaliano.info/news/00073/note-di-regia-del-film-fatti-della-banda.html

Cowie, Elizabeth. 1999. "The Spectacle of Actuality." In *Collecting Visible Evidence*, edited by Jane M. Gaines and Michael Renov, 19–45. Minneapolis: University of Minnesota Press.

Cox, Robert, and Christina R. Foust. 2009. "Social Movement Rhetoric." In *Sage Handbook of Rhetorical Studies*, edited by A. Lunsford, K. Wilson, and R. Eberly, 605–27. Los Angeles: Sage.

Crane, Ronald S. 1953. *The Languages of Criticism and the Structure of Poetry*. Toronto: University of Toronto Press.

Cunneen, Chris. 2006. "Exploring the Relationship between Reparations, the Gross Violation of Human Rights, and Restorative Justice." In *A Handbook of Restorative Justice: A Global Perspective*, edited by Dennis Sullivan and Larry Tifft, 355–67. New York: Routledge.

Currie, Gregory. 1997. "The Paradox of Caring: Fiction and the Philosophy of Mind." In *Emotion and the Arts*, edited by Mette Hjort and Sue Laver, 63–77. New York: Oxford University Press.

Cvetkovich, Ann. 2002. "Gender and September 11: A Roundtable: 9–11 Every Day." *Signs* 28, no. 1: 471–3.

Dalla Chiesa, Nando. 2007. *Delitto imperfetto: Il generale, la mafia, la società italiana*. Milan: Melampo.

D'Amato, Marina, ed. 2013a. *La mafia allo specchio: La trasformazione mediatica del mafioso*. Milan: FrancoAngeli.

–. 2013b. "Introduzione: Il ruolo dei media nella costruzione dell'immaginario mafioso." In *La mafia allo specchio: La trasformazione mediatica del mafioso*, edited by Marina D'Amato, 15–22. Milan: FrancoAngeli.

D'Amato, Marina, and Attilio Scaglione. 2013. "Da *Scarface* a *Il Padrino*." In *La mafia allo specchio: La trasformazione mediatica del mafioso*, edited by Marina D'Amato, 259–76. Milan: FrancoAngeli

"Da ROMANZO CRIMINALE (serie) alla BANDA DELLA MAGLIANA (realtà)." 2009. YouTube, 14 October. https://www.youtube.com/watch?v=EO-ihg3Hmro

Dean, Jodi. 2010. *Blog Theory: Feedback and Capture in the Circuits of the Drive*. Malden, MA: Polity Press.

–. 2005. "Communicative Capitalism: Circulation and the Foreclosure of Politics." *Cultural Politics* 1, no. 1: 51–74.

De Cataldo, Giancarlo. 2002. *Romanzo criminale*. Turin: Einaudi.

de Certeau, Michel. 1997. *The Capture of Speech and Other Political Writings*. Translated by Tom Conley. Minneapolis: University of Minnesota Press.

De Risi, Marco. 2014. "Mafia, arrestato Massimo Carminati: l'anima nera del crimine capitolino più spietato e ramificato." *Il Messagero*, 2 December. http://www.ilmessaggero.it/ROMA/CRONACA/mafia_arrestato_massimo_carminati/notizie/1044686.shtml

De Vries, Brian, and Judy Rutherford. 2004. "Memorializing Loved Ones on the World Wide Web." *OMEGA* 49, no. 1: 5–26.

Dickie, John. 2004. *Cosa Nostra: A History of the Sicilian Mafia*. New York: Palgrave Macmillan.

Di Fiore, Gigi. 2005. *La camorra e le sue storie. La criminalità organizzata a Napoli dalle origini alle sue ultime guerre*. Turin: Utet.

Di Piazza, Salvatore. 2010. *Mafia Linguaggio Identità*. Palermo: Centro di studi ed iniziative culturali Pio La Torre.

"Documentario il processo alla Banda della Magliana – I confronti parti 2 di 2." 2010. YouTube, 27 December https://www.youtube.com/watch?v=G4NP6Y-rfPA

Donadio, Rachel. 2009. "On Facebook, Sicilian Mafia Is a Hot Topic." *The New York Times*, 19 January.

http://www.nytimes.com/glogin?URI=http%3A%2F%2Fwww.nytimes.com%2F2009%2F01%2F20%2Fworld%2Feurope%2F20italy.html%3Fpagewanted%3Dall%26_r%3

Donato, Donatella. 2009. "Genovese interviene sul caso della mafia su Facebook." *Omniapress*, 7 January. http://omniapress.net/genovese-interviene-sul-caso-della-mafia-su-facebook (site discontinued)

D'Ospina, Elisa. 2015. "Facebook e mafia: I nuovi padrini online ostentano le loro vite." *Il Fatto quotidiano*, 11 July. http://www.ilfattoquotidiano.it/2014/07/11/facebook-e-mafia-i-nuovi-padrini-online-ostentano-le-loro-vite/1056953/

Editorial. 2012. "Il latitante è su Skype." *L'Espresso*, 26 September. http://espresso.repubblica.it/

Elsaesser, Thomas. 1999. "'One Train May Be Hiding Another': Private History, Memory, and National Identity." 16 April. http://tlweb.latrobe.edu.au/humanities/screeningthepast/reruns/rr0499/terr6b.htm

Etzioni, Amitai. 2004. "Are Virtual and Democratic Communities Feasible." In *Democracy and New Media*, edited by Henry Jenkins and David Thorburn, 85–99. Cambridge, MA: MIT Press.

Evelyn, John. [1901] 2012. *The Diary of John Evelyn*. Vol. 1. New York: M.W. Dunne. Project Gutenberg: http://www.gutenberg.org/files/41218/41218-h/41218-h.htm#p001

Fattorini, Marco. 2009. "La mafia arriva sul Facebook: Combattiamola." 8 January. ItaliaChiamaItalia. http://www.italiachiamaitalia.it

Fava, Giuseppe. 1983a. "I mafiosi stanno in Parlamento." Interview with Enzo Biagi. 28 December. http://archivio.antimafiaduemila.com/notizie-20072011/48/13018-parole-di-pippo-fava-i-mafiosi-stanno-in-parlamento-sono-a-volte-misintri-sono-banchieri.html

–. 1983b. "I quattro cavalieri dell'apocalisse mafiosa." I Siciliani, January. http://www.girodivite.it/I-quattro-cavalieri-dell.html

–. 1983c. "Sindrome Catania." I Siciliani, April. http://www.fondazione.it/sito/i-siciliani/sindrome-catania/

–. 1983d. "Mafia e camorra. Chi sono, chi comanda." I Siciliani, March. http://www.fondazionefava.it/sito/i-siciliani/mafia-e-camorra-chi-sono-chi-comanda/

–. 1983e. "I Siciliani, perché?" I Siciliani, January. http://www.fondazionefava.it/sito/i-siciliani/i-siciliani-perche/

–. 1982. Mafia. Da Giuliano a Dalla Chiesa. Catania: Centro Editoriale Radar.

–. 1981. "Lo spirito di un giornale." Il Giornale del Sud, 11 October. http://www.isiciliani.it/lo-spirito-di-un-giornale/#.V9RrT8mGPHo

–. 1980. "Con amore collera e speranza." Il Giornale del Sud, 4 June. http://isicilianidigiuseppefava.blogspot.co.uk/

Fava, Giuseppe, and Vittorio Sindoni. 1980. "Da Villalba a Palermo (Siciliani-Cronache di Mafia)." Rome: RIA and Terza Rete Siciliana.

Fricker, M. 2011. "Rational Authority and Social Power: Towards a Truly Social Epistemology." In Social Epistemology, edited by A.I. Goldman and D. Whitcombe, 54–70. Oxford: Oxford University Press.

Frigerio, L. 2009. "La confisca dei beni alle mafie: Luci e ombre di un percorso civile." Aggiornamenti Sociali 1: 38–48.

Frosh, Paul. 2009. "Telling Presences: Witnessing, Mass Media, and the Imagined Lives of Strangers." In Media Witnessing: Testimony in the Age of Mass Communication, edited by Paul Frosh and Amit Pinchevski, 49–72. London: Palgrave Macmillan.

Frosh, Paul, and Amit Pinchevski. 2009. "Introduction: Why Media Witnessing? Why Now?" In Media Witnessing: Testimony in the Age of Mass Communication, edited by Paul Frosh and Amit Pinchevski, 1–19. London: Palgrave Macmillan.

Gammaitoni, Milena. 2013. "Donne narrate e narranti." In La mafia allo specchio: La trasformazione mediatica del mafioso, edited by Marina D'Amato, 181–97. Milan: FrancoAngeli.

Ganz, Marshall. 2011. "Public Narrative, Collective Action, and Power." In Accountability through Public Opinion: From Inertia to Public Action, edited

by Sina Odugbemi and Taeku Lee, 273–89. New York: World Bank Group.
http://marshallganz.usmblogs.com/files/2012/08/Public-Narrative-
Collective-Action-and-Power.pdf

–. 2009. "Why Stories Matter: The Art and Craft of Social Change." *Sojourners
Magazine*, March. https://sojo.net/magazine/march-2009/why-stories-matter

–. 2007. "Telling Your Public Story. Self, Us, Now." National Gay and Lesbian Task
Force's Institute for Welcoming Resources, Welcoming Toolkit, Appendix 7, 37–9.
http://www.rmnetwork.org/newrmn/wp-content/BIC_Toolkit/Toolkit/
story_content/external_files/Appendix_7_Telling_Your_Public_Story.pdf

Garrone, Matteo, dir. 2008. *Gomorrah*. Rome: Fandango in collaboration with
RAI and Sky.

Garroni, Emilio. 1986. *Senso e paradosso. L'estetica filosofia non speciale*. Roma:
Laterza.

Ghezzi, Alessia, Angela Guimaraes Pereira, and Lucia Vesnic-Alujevic, eds.
2014. *The Ethics of Memory in a Digital Age: Interrogating the Right to Be
Forgotten*. New York: Palgrave Macmillan.

Giordana, Marco Tullio. 2000. *I cento passi*. Rome: Titti Film and RAI Cinema.

Gladwell, Malcolm. 2010. "Small Change: Why the Revolution Will Not Be
Tweeted." *The New Yorker*, 4 October.

"Gli anni dell'Espresso sera." 2010. *I Siciliani*. http://isicilianidigiuseppefava.
blogspot.co.uk/2010/01/gli-anni-dellespresso-sera.html

Goethe, Johann Wolfgang. 1982. *Italian Journey (1786–1788)*. London: Penguin.

Gramsci, Antonio. 1999. *Selections from the Prison Notebooks*. London: ElecBook.

Grusin, Richard. 2015. "Mediashock." In *Atti del Convegno. L'abitare possibile: estetica,
architettura e new media*, edited by Pina De Luca, 167–80. Milan: Mondadori.

–. 2010. *Premediation: Affect and Mediality after 9/11*. London: Palgrave.

Hallin, Daniel C., and Paolo Mancini. 2004. *Comparing Media Systems: Three
Models of Media and Politics*. Cambridge: Cambridge University Press.

Hannerz, Ulf. 1992. "The Global Ecumene as a Network of Networks." In
Conceptualizing Society, edited by A. Kuper, 34–56. London: Routledge.

–. 1989. "Notes on the Global Ecumene." *Public Culture* 1: 66–75.

Hardt, David, and Antonio Negri. 2001. *Empire*. Cambridge, MA: Harvard
University Press.

Harvey, David. 2011. "The Future of the Commons." *Radical History Review*
109: 101–7.

Hawkes, Howard. 1932. *Scarface*. Hollywood: The Caddo Company.

Hoskins, Andrew. 2014. "The Right to Be Forgotten in Post-Scarcity Culture."
In *The Ethics of Memory in a Digital Age: Interrogating the Right to Be Forgotten*,
edited by Alessia Ghezzi, Angela Guimaraes Pereira, and Lucia Vesnic-
Alujevic, 50–64. New York: Palgrave Macmillan,

Huyssen, Andreas. 1993. "Monument and Memory in a Postmodern Age." *Yale Journal of Criticism* 6, no. 2: 249–62.

Internet Users in Europe. 2015. Internet World Stats. http://www. internetworldstats.com/stats4.htm

"Italiani, il 63% è sul web, stiamo evolvendo. Censis: 'Entriamo nell'era biomediatica.'" 2013. *La Repubblica,* 11 October. http://www.repubblica.it/ tecnologia/2013/10/11/news/italiani_il_63_sul_web_stiamo_evolvendo_ censis_entriamo_nell_era_biomediatica-68376669/

Jackson, Sha. N.d. "The Healing Power of Storytelling." Coming to the Table. http://comingtothetable.org/stories/stories-healing-wounds/healing-power-storytelling/

Jamieson, Alison. 2000. *The Antimafia: Italy's Fight against Organized Crime.* London: Palgrave Macmillan.

Jenkins, Henry. 2013. *Spreadable Media: Creating Value and Meaning in a Networked Culture.* New York: New York University Press.

–. 2011. "Transmedia 202: Further Reflections." The Official Webpage of Henry Jenkins. http://henryjenkins.org/2011/08/defining_transmedia_further_ re.html

–. 2007. "Transmedia Storytelling 101." The Official Webpage of Henry Jenkins. http://henryjenkins.org/?s=transmedia+storytelling+101

–. 2006. *Convergence Culture: Where Old and New Media Collide.* New York: New York University Press.

– 1992. *Textual Poachers: Television Fans and Participatory Culture.* New York: Routledge.

Jones, Ward E. 2011. "Philosophy and the Ethical Significance of Spectatorship: An Introduction to *Ethics at the Cinema.*" In *Ethics at the Cinema,* edited by Ward E. Jones and Samantha Vice, 1–19. New York: Oxford University Press.

Kitano, Takeshi. 1993. *Sonatine.* Tokyo: Bandai Visual Company.

Kitchen Sisters. 2014. "The Pizza Connection: Fighting the Mafia through Food." National Public Radio, 6 May. http://www.npr.org/sections/ thesalt/2014/05/06/306874351/the-pizza-connection-fighting-the-mafia-through-food

Korsgaard, Christine. 1996. *The Sources of Normativity,* edited by Thomas Nagel, Christine M. Korsgaard, Raymond Geuss, and G.A. Cohen. Cambridge: Cambridge University Press.

Kuljic, Todor. *Kultura sećanja.* Belgrade: Čigoja Štampa, 2006.

Kumar, Ravi. 2013. "Social Media and Social Change: How Young People Are Tapping into Technology." The World Bank, YouThink! (blog), 14 July. http://blogs.worldbank.org/youthink/social-media-and-social-change-how-young-people-are-tapping-technology

Lagerkvist, Amanda. 2013. "New Memory Cultures and Death: Existential Security in the Digital Memory Ecology." Thanatos 2, no. 2. https://thanatosjournal.files.wordpress.com/2012/12/lagerkvist_newmemorycultures_than2220133.pdf

Laplanche, Jean, and Jean-Bertrand Pontalis. 2006. *The Language of Psychoanalysis*. London: Hogarth Press.

La Spina, Antonio. 2013. "Prefazione." In *La mafia allo specchio: La trasformazione mediatica del mafioso*, edited by Marina D'Amato, 11–13. Milan: FrancoAngeli.

–. 2005. *Mafia, legalità debole e sviluppo del Mezzogiorno*. Bologna: Il Mulino.

Lebar, Mark. 2001. "Korsgaard, Wittgenstein, and the Mafioso." *The Southern Journal of Philosophy* 39: 261–71.

Leebaw, Bronwyn. 2011. *Judging State-Sponsored Violence: Imagining Political Change*. Cambridge: Cambridge University Press.

Levy, Pierre. 1997. *Collective Intelligence: Mankind's Emerging World in Cyberspace*. Cambridge: Perseus.

Lipari, Lucia. 2013. "Diffamazione e diritto all'oblio." Liberainformazione, 18 March. http://www.liberainformazione.org/2013/03/18/diffamazione-e-diritto-alloblio/

Lise, Francesco Pellegrino. 2009. "Mafiosi su Facebook, esplode la polemica sul Web." *Il Tempo*, 7 January. http://www.iltempo.it/cronache/2012/12/12/mafiosi-su-facebook-esplode-la-polemica-sul-web/

Lombardi, Giancarlo. 2012. "Fictions: The Moro Affaire in Primetime Drama." In *Remembering Moro: The Cultural Legacy of the 1978 Kidnapping and Murder*, edited by Ruth Glynn and Giancarlo Lombardi, 171–86. Oxford: Legenda.

Lupacchini, Otello. 2014. *Banda della Magliana: alleanza tra mafiosi, terroristi, spioni, politici, prelati*. Rome: Koinè.

"Mafia Capitale, Riesame: 'Carminati capo di una organizzazione ramificata.'" 2015. *La Repubblica*. 7 January. http://roma.repubblica.it/cronaca/2015/01/07/news/mafia_capitale_riesame_carminati_capo-104463558/

Maiello, Angela. 2015. *L'archivio in rete. Estetica e nuove tecnologie*. Florence: goWare.

Mancini, Paolo, and Gianpietro Mazzoleni, eds. 1995. *I Media Scendono in Campo*. Roma: Eri.

Manovich, Lev. 2013. *Software Takes Command*. New York: Bloomsbury.

Marcus, Millicent. 2007. "In Memoriam: The Neorealist Legacy in the Contemporary Antimafia Film." In *Italian Neorealism and Global Cinema*, edited by Laura E. Rorato and Kristi M. Wilson, 290–306. Detroit, MI: Wayne State University Press.

Martin, Brett. 2013. *Difficult Men: Behind the Scenes of a Creative Revolution: From The Sopranos and The Wire to Mad Men and Breaking Bad*. New York: Penguin Press.

"Massimo Carminati Arrestato. L'ex Nar tra neofascismo e banda della Magliana." 2014. *L'Huffington Post,* 12 December. http://www.huffingtonpost.it/2014/12/02/massimo-carminati-vita-tra-neofascismo-magliana_n_6253186.html

Massumi, Brian. 2002. *Parables for the Virtual: Movement, Affect, Sensation*. Durham, NC: Duke University Press.

Masullo, Aldo. 2008. *Aldo Masullo intervistato da Claudio Scarmardella*. Naples: Guida.

Mazzoleni, Gianpietro. 1995. "Towards a Videocracy? Italian Political Communication at a Turning Point." *European Journal of Communication* 10: 291–319.

Mezzofiore, Gianluca. 2014. "One-eyed Neo-fascist 'Last King of Rome' Mobster Massimo Carminati Arrested in Mafia Probe." *International Business Times,* 2 December. http://www.ibtimes.co.uk/one-eyed-neo-fascist-last-king-rome-mobster-massimo-carminati-arrested-mafia-probe-1477674

Misuraca, Lorenzo. 2015. "L'antimafia felice." *Il lavoro culturale,* 5 February. http://www.lavoroculturale.org/lantimafia-felice-ricostruzione-di-un-immaginario-inerte/

Mittell, Jason. 2015. *Complex TV: The Poetics of Contemporary Television Storytelling*. New York: New York University Press.

–. 2014. "Lengthy Interactions with Hideous Men: Walter White and the Serial Poetics of Television Anti-Heroes." In *Storytelling in the Media Convergence Age: Exploring Screen Narratives*, edited by Roberta Pearson and Anthony N. Smith, 74–92. New York: Palgrave Macmillan.

Montani, Pietro. 2015. "Prolegomeni ad un'educazione tecno-estetica." *Mediascapes Journal* (May): 71–82.

–. 2014. *Tecnologie della sensibilità. Estetica ed immaginazione interattiva*. Milan: Carocci.

–. 2010. *L'immaginazione intermediale. Perlustrare, rifigurare, testimoniare il mondo visibile*. Roma-Bari: Laterza.

–. 2007. *Bioestetica. Senso comune, tecnica e arte nell'età globalizzata*. Rome: Carocci.

Morozov, Evgeny. 2011. *The Net Delusion: How Not to Liberate the World*. London: Allen Lane.

–. 2009. "Foreign Policy: Brave New World of Slacktivism." National Public Radio, 19 May. http://www.npr.org/templates/story/story.php?storyId=104302141

Moss, Miriam. 2004. "Grief on the Web." *OMEGA* 49, no. 1: 77–8.

Musumeci, Giuseppe. 2014. *Per non dimenticare 23 maggio.* https://www. youtube.com/watch?v=NAS98YRGwgc

Niola, Marino. 2003. "La macchina del pianto." In *La sceneggiata*, edited byPasquale Scialò, 25–42. Naples: Guida Editore.

Nora, Pierre. 1989. "Between Memory and History: Les Lieux des Mèmoire." *Representations* 26: 7–24.

Nunes, Mark. 2006. *Cyberspaces of Everyday Life.* Minneapolis: University of Minnesota Press.

O'Neill, Onora. 1996. *Toward Justice and Virtue.* Cambridge: Cambridge University Press.

Onofri, Massimo. 1995. *Tutti a cena da don Mariano: Letteratura e mafia nella Sicilia della nuova Italia.* Milan: Bompiani.

O'Rawe, Catherine. 2014. *Stars and Masculinities in Contemporary Italian Cinema.* New York: Palgrave Macmillan.

Ortoleva, Peppino. 2012. *Dal sesso al gioco.* Turin: Espresso Edizione.

Pantaleone, Michele. 1993. *Omertà di stato.* Naples: Tullio Pironti Editore.

–. 1992. *Mafia e antimafia.* Naples: Tullio Pironti Editore.

–. 1966a. *The Mafia and Politics.* London: Chatto and Windus.

–. 1966b. *Mafia e droga.* Turin: Giulio Einaudi Editore.

Paparcone, Anna. 2009. "Echoes of Pierpaolo Pasolini in Contemporary Italian Cinema: The Cases of Marco Tullio Giordana and Aurelio Grimaldi." PhD diss., Cornell University.

Pavlaković, Vjeran. 2012. "Conflict, Commemorations, and Changing Meanings: The Mestrović Pavilion as Contested Site of Memory." In *Confronting the Past: European Experiences*, edited by Vjeran Pavlakovic et al., 317–51. Zagreb: CPI, Centar za politoloska istrazivanja: Znanstveni Forum.

Peters, John Durham. 2001. "Witnessing." *Media, Culture & Society* 23: 707–23.

Piazza, Enrico. 2012. "Recensione – Spieraglio di periferia." *Rock.it*, 16 January. https://rockit.it/recensione/18379/roccohunt-spiraglio-di-periferia

Picciotto, Loredana. 2015. "Social Entrepreneurship and Confiscated Mafia Properties in Italy." 4th EMES-SOCENT Conference Selected Papers, n. LG!#-73.

Pickering-Iazzi, Robin. 2015. *The Mafia in Italian Lives and Literature: Life Sentences and Their Geographies.* Toronto: University of Toronto Press.

–. 2010. "(En)gendering Testimonial Bodies of Evidence and Italian Antimafia Culture: Rita Atria." *Italian Culture* 28, no. 1: 21–37.

–. 2007. *Mafia and Outlaw Stories in Italian Life and Literature.* Toronto: University of Toronto Press.

Pine, Jason. 2012. *The Art of Making Do in Naples.* Minneapolis: University of Minnesota Press.

–. 2011. "Transnational Organized Crime and Alternative Culture Industry." In *Routledge Handbook of Organized Crime*, edited by Felia Allum and Stan Gilmour, 335–49. Abingdon, Oxon: Routledge.

Pine, Jason, and Francesco Pepe. 2013. "Transnational Neomelodica Music and Alternative Economic Cultures." *California Italian Studies* 4, no. 1: 1–50. https://escholarship.org/uc/item/0rm113j6

Placido, Michele. 2010. *Vallanzasca – Gli angeli del male*. Rome: Twentieth-Century Fox Italia.

–. 2005. *Romanzo criminale*. Rome: Cattleya.

Polk, Emily. 2010. "Folk Media Meets Digital Technology for Sustainable Social Change: A Case Study of the Center for Digital Storytelling." *Global Media Journal* 10, no. 17: 1–30.

Puccio-Den, Deborah. 2008. "The Anti-Mafia Movement as Religion? The Pilgrimage to the Falcone Tree." In *Shrines and Pilgrimages in the Modern World: New Itineraries into the Sacred*, edited by Peter Jan Margry, 49–70. Amsterdam: Amsterdam University Press.

"La quinta mafia a Roma e nel Lazio dalla Banda della Magliana a oggi." 2009. *La Repubblica*, 15 December. http://roma.repubblica.it/dettaglio/la-quinta-mafia-a-roma-e-nel-lazio-dalla-banda-della-magliana-a-oggi/1805078

Rankin, Lissa. 2012. "The Healing Power of Telling Your Story." *Psychology Today* (blog), 27 November. https://www.psychologytoday.com/blog/owning-pink/201211/the-healing-power-telling-your-story

Ravveduto, Marcello. 2007. *Napoli … Serenata calibro 9*. Naples: Liguiri Editore.

Remondini, Chiara. 2010. "Mafia Victim Families Fight Violent Video Games." *Bloomberg Business*, 17 December. http://www.bloomberg.com/news/articles/2010-12-16/mafia-victim-families-complain-as-violent-video-games-increase (online account required)

Renga, Dana. 2016. "Michele Placido's *Romanzo Criminale* as Male Melodrama: 'It is in reality *always* too late.'" In *Nuovo cinema politico: Public Life, Imaginary and Identity in Contemporary Italian Cinema*, edited by Giancarlo Lombardi and Christian Uva, 373–86. Oxford: Peter Lang, Italian Modernities Series. .

–. 2013. *Unfinished Business: Screening the Italian Mafia in the New Millennium*. Toronto: University of Toronto Press..

–, ed. 2011. *Mafia Movies: A Reader*. Toronto: University of Toronto Press.

"Reporter nel mirino. Le testimonianze su Repubblica.it." 2015. *La Repubblica*, 14 May.

Rinaldi, Luca. 2011. *Antimafia senza divisa*. Pavia: Blonk.

Rizzo, Roberto. 2005. "E Facebook non chiude i gruppi a favore del boss Riina." http://www.corriere.it/cronache/09_gennaio_05/facebook_gruppi_mafia_roberto_rizzo_cde8c078-db0a-11dd-b0de-00144f02aabc.shtml

Romanzo criminale: la serie. 2008–10. Rome: Cattleya and Sky Italia.

"ROMANZO CRIMINALE la serie 2 – Trailer esteso." 2010. YouTube, 4 August. https://www.youtube.com/watch?v=zP6cMUFifJM

"Romanzo Criminale la serie Trailer HD." 2010. YouTube, 30 May. https://www.youtube.com/watch?v=Olvcfgan0c4

"Romanzo criminale la serie." 2009. YouTube, 29 September. https://www.youtube.com/watch?v=6Qr8V_IXTCE

"Romanzo criminale." 2008. *Sky*, 18 August. http://forum.sky.it/romanzo-criminale-t90598-10.html

Rose, R. 2011. "The Art of Immersion. Why Do We Tell Stories?" *Wired*, 8 March. https://www.wired.com/2011/03/why-do-we-tell-stories/

Rosi, Francesco. 1973. *Lucky Luciano*. Paris: Les Films La Boetie.

Rossi, Roberto Salvatore. 2006. "Web Man Walking: Giornalisti e informazione antimafia al tempo di internet." *Problemi dell'informazione* 31, no. 2: 183–96.

Salvio, Paula. 2014. "Reconstructing Memory through the Archives: Public Pedagogy, Citizenship and Letizia Battaglia's Photographic Record of Mafia Violence." *Pedagogy, Culture and Society* 22, no. 1: 97–116.

–. 2012. "'Eccentric Subjects': Female Martyrs and the Antimafia Public Imaginary.'" *Italian Studies* 67, no. 3: 397–410.

Sandage, Scott A. 1993. "A Marble House Divided: The Lincoln Memorial, the Civil Rights Movement, and the Politics of Memory, 1939–1963." *Journal of American History* 80, no. 1: 135–67.

Santino, Jack. 2006. "Performative Commemoratives: Spontaneous Shrines and the Public Memorialization of Death." In *Spontaneous Shrines and the Public Memorialization of Death*, edited by Jack Santino, 5–16. New York: Palgrave Macmillan.

–. 2015. *Mafia and Antimafia: A Brief History*. London: I.B. Tauris Publishers.

Santino, Umberto. 2000. *Storia del movimento antimafia: Dalla lotta di classe all'impegno civile*. Rome: Riuniti.

Sanzone, Daniele. 2014. *Camorra Sound*. Milan: Magenes Editoriale.

Satta, Andrea. 2013. "Munizza, il cortometraggio per ricordare Peppino Impastato." 9 May, LaStampa. http://www.lastampa.it/2013/05/09/multimedia/italia/munizza-il-cortometraggio-per-peppino-impastato-IZppIlsZmbmbZkhc2QbNEP/pagina.html

Saviano, Roberto. 2015. "Il giornalista licenziato su ordine del boss. Nella terra della camorra padrona in redazione." *La Repubblica*, 14 May.

–. 2012. "Canzone criminale. La musica di Gomorra." *La Repubblica*, 12 February. http://www.repubblica.it/spettacoli-e-cultura/2012/02/12/news/saviano_neomelodici-29737271/

–. 2008. *Gomorrah: A Personal Journey into the Violent International Empire of Naples' Organized Crime System*. New York: Ferrar, Straus and Giroux.

–. 2006. *Gomorra: Viaggio nell'impero economico e nel sogno di dominio della camorra*. Milan: Mondadori.

Schiller, Friedrich. 1954. *On the Aesthetic Education of Man in a Series of Letters*. New Haven, CT: Yale University Press.

Schudson, Michael. 1998. *The Good Citizen: A History of American Civil Life*. New York: Free Press.

Sciascia, Leonardo. 2003. *The Day of the Owl*. Translated by Archibald Colquhoun and Arthur Oliver. New York: New York Review of Books.

–. 1966. *Il giorno della civetta*. Turin: Einaudi.

Sclaunich, Greta. 2008. "Diritto all'oblio, tra i link oscurati anche quello su Vallanzasca." *Corriere*, 14 August.

Scorsese, Martin. 1990. *Goodfellas*. Burbank: Warner Brothers.

Senelick, Richard. 2012. "The Healing Power of Storytelling." *Huffington Post*, 9 April. http://www.huffingtonpost.com/richard-c-senelick-md/patient-care_b_1410115.html

Shirky, Clay. 2011. "The Political Power of Social Media: Technology, the Public Sphere, and Political Change." *Foreign Affairs*, January/February. https://www.foreignaffairs.com/articles/2010-12-20/political-power-social-media

–. 2009. "Q&A with Clay Shirky on Twitter and Iran." TEDBlog, 16 June. http://blog.ted.com/qa_with_clay_sh/

Siebert, Renate. 1996. *Secrets of Life and Death: Women and the Mafia*. Translated by Liz Heron. London: Verso.

Simondon, Gilbert. 2013. *Sulla tecno-estetica*. Milan: Mimesis.

Smith, Murray. 1995. *Engaging Characters: Fiction, Emotion, and the Cinema*. Oxford: Oxford University Press.

Soja, Edward W. 2010. *Seeking Spatial Justice*. Minneapolis: University of Minnesota Press.

Sorek, Tamir. 2015. *Palestinian Commemoration in Israel: Calendars, Monuments and Martyrs*. Stanford, CA: Stanford University Press.

Springer, John Parris. 2006. "The Newspaper Meets the Dime Novel: Docudrama in Early Cinema." In *Docufictions: Essays on the Intersection of Documentary and Fictional Filmmaking*, edited by Gary D. Rhodes and John Parris Springer, 11–26. Jefferson, MA: MacFarland and Company.

Squires, Nick. 2014. "'Mafia Capital': Rome Hit by Mobster Scandal." *The Telegraph*, 3 December. http://www.telegraph.co.uk/news/worldnews/europe/italy/11271882/Mafia-capital-Rome-hit-by-mobster-scandal.html

Stack, Steven, Liquin Cao, and Amy Adamzyck. 2007. "Crime Volume and Law and Order Culture." *Justice Quarterly* 24, no. 2: 291–308.

Staiger, Janet. 2008. "Film Noir as Male Melodrama: The Politics of Film Genre Labeling." In *The Shifting Definitions of Genre: Essays on Labeling Films, Televisions Shows and Media*, edited by Lincoln Geraghty and Mark Jancovich, 71–91. Jefferson, NC: McFarland and Company.

Stille, Alexander. 1996. *Excellent Cadavers: The Mafia and the Death of the First Italian Republic*. New York: Vintage.

Stone, Richard. 1996. *The Healing Art of Storytelling: A Sacred Journey of Personal Discovery*. New York: Hyperion.

Sturken, Marita. 1999. "Narratives of Recovery: Repressed Memory as Cultural Memory." In *Acts of Memory: Cultural Recall in the Present*, edited by Mieke Bal, Jonathan Crewe, and Leo Spitzer, 231–48. Hanover, NH: University Press of New England.

–. 1997. *Tangled Memories: The Vietnam War, the AIDS Epidemic, and the Politics of Remembering*. Berkeley: University of California Press.

Tambini, Damian. 1999. "New Media and Democracy: The Civic Networking Movement." *New Media & Society* 1, no. 3: 305–29.

Taviani, Paolo, and Vittorio Taviani. 2013. *Cesare deve morire*. Rome: Kaos Cinematografica.

Turco, Marco. 2005. *In un altro paese*. Rome: Doclab S.r.l.

Vaage, Margrethe Bruun. 2013. "Fictional Reliefs and Reality Checks." *Screen* 54, no. 2: 218–37.

Valenzuela, Sebastián, Namsu Park, and Kerk F. Kee. 2009. "Is There Social Capital in a Social Network Site? Facebook Use and College Students' Life Satisfaction, Trust, and Participation." *Journal of Computer Mediated Communication* 14, no. 4: 875–901.

Vallanzasca, Renato, and Carlo Bonini. 2009. *Il fiore del male: Bandito a Milano*. Milan: Marco Tropea Editore.

"La vera Banda della Magliana vs. Romanzo Criminale la serie." 2011a. YouTube. 14 January. https://www.youtube.com/watch?v=7ni4oSv70g8&spfreload=1

"La vera Banda della Magliana vs. Romanzo Criminale la serie." 2011b. YouTube. 11 September https://www.youtube.com/watch?v=P5aIwrFOC7k

Walker, Andrea. 2014. "Italian Journalists Living in Fear from Mafia Threats." *Breitbar*, 9 August.www.breitbar.com/london/2014/08/09/italian-journalists-living-in-fear-from-mafia-threats/

Ward, Brendon. 2007. Preface. *Violence: A Sicilian Drama in Three Acts*. By Giuseppe Fava. Translated by Gaetano Cipolla, 1–7. Ottawa: Legas.

Young, James E. 1999. "Memory and Counter-memory: The End of the Monument in Germany." *Harvard Design Magazine*, no. 9: 1–10.

–. 1993. *The Texture of Memory: Holocaust Memorials and Meaning*. New Haven: Yale University Press.

Zerubavel, Eviatar. 2003. *Time Maps: Collective Memory and the Social Shape of the Past*. Chicago: University of Chicago Press.

Contributors

Carla Bagnoli, Professor of Theoretical Philosophy, University of Modena and Reggio Emilia, Italy

Amy Boylan, Associate Professor of Italian Studies, University of New Hampshire

Baris Cayli, Fellow, Scottish Centre for Crime and Justice Research, University of Stirling, Scotland, UK

Angela Maiello, Doctor of Philosophy, Research Assistant, University of Rome La Sapienza, Rome, Italy

Robin Pickering-Iazzi (Editor), Professor of Italian and Comparative Literature, University of Wisconsin-Milwaukee

Dana Renga, Associate Professor of Italian and Film Studies, The Ohio State University

Paula M. Salvio, Professor of Education, University of New Hampshire

Giovanna Summerfield, Professor of Italian and French, Associate Dean for Educational Affairs, Auburn University

Index